Anthropology and the Study of Religion

Anthropology and the Study of Religion

Edited by

Robert L. Moore and Frank E. Reynolds

C
 S
  S
   R

Center for the Scientific Study of Religion
Chicago, Illinois

Studies in Religion and Society

Center for the Scientific Study of Religion

Center for the Scientific Study of Religion
5757 University Avenue
Chicago, Illinois 60637

ISBN: Cloth: 0-913348-20-1
       Paper: 0-913348-21-X

Library of Congress Catalog Card Number: 83-71781

**In Memory of
Victor Turner
1920-1983**

STUDIES IN RELIGION AND SOCIETY

edited by

Robert L. Moore, W. Alvin Pitcher,
W. Widick Schroeder and Gibson Winter

Other CSSR Publications in the Series:

Bernard O. Brown, *Ideology and Community Action:
The West Side Organization of Chicago, 1964-67* (1978)

John B. Cobb, Jr., and W. Widick Schroeder, eds., *Process
Philosophy and Social Thought* (1981)

Philip Hefner and W. Widick Schroeder, eds., *Belonging and Alienation:
Religious Foundations for the Human Future* (1976)

Paul E. Kraemer, *Awakening from the American Dream: The Human Rights
Movement in the United States Assessed during a
Crucial Decade, 1960-1970* (1973)

William C. Martin, *Christians in Conflict* (1972)

Victor Obenhaus, *And See the People* (1968)

W. Widick Schroeder, Victor Obenhaus, Larry A. Jones, and
Thomas Sweetser, SJ, *Suburban Religion: Churches
and Synagogues in the American Experience* (1974)

W. Widick Schroeder and Gibson Winter, eds., *Belief and
Ethics: Essays in Ethics, the Human Sciences and Ministry
in Honor of W. Alvin Pitcher* (1978)

Walter M. Stuhr, Jr., *The Public Style: A Study
of the Community Participation of Protestant Ministers* (1972)

Thomas P. Sweetser, SJ, *The Catholic Parish: Shifting
Membership in a Changing Church* (1974)

Lawrence Witmer, ed., *Issues in Community Organization* (1972)

Order from your bookstore or the Center for the Scientific Study of Religion

Other Books in the Series:

Thomas C. Campbell and Yoshio Fukuyama, *The Fragmented
Layman* (1970)

John Fish, *Black Power/White Control: The Struggle
of the Woodlawn Organization in Chicago* (1973)

John Fish, Gordon Nelson, Walter M. Stuhr, Jr., and Lawrence Witmer
The Edge of the Ghetto (1968)

W. Widick Schroeder and Victor Obenhaus,
Religion in American Culture (1964)

Gibson Winter, *Religious Identity* (1968)

Order from your bookstore

Table of Contents

Preface

This collection of essays has emerged from a series of panel discussions sponsored by the Religion and Social Sciences Section of the American Academy of Religion. We wish to thank all of those who participated in these discussions, especially Walter Capps, James Foard, James Fernandez, Kees Bolle, William LaFleur, Ronald Grimes, Richard Hecht, and Stephen Tobias.

We are also very grateful to the several individuals and institutions who have contributed to the editorial process. Neil W. Gerdes, Eugene McKay, and Margaret D. Moore have provided sound editorial advice. The Divinity School of the University of Chicago and the Chicago Theological Seminary have made available the necessary office and secretarial assistance.

As editors we are especially indebted to our contributors who have been unusually cooperative in revising their manuscripts and unusually prompt in meeting the inevitable deadlines. Each of them has worked very hard, and the results have—we are convinced—fully justified their efforts.

Robert L. Moore
Frank E. Reynolds

Introduction

Frank E. Reynolds

Religious studies is, or at least purports to be, the primary locus for the study of religion in contemporary academia.[1] Yet certain disciplines that operate quite separately from religious studies continue to produce analyses and interpretations of religion, myth and ritual that are of great interest and importance, both theoretically and substantively. Among these other disciplines, anthropology is perhaps the most important.

Religious studies scholars have reacted to this situation in several different ways. Most have simply ignored the work of their anthropological colleagues. Some have responded by propounding simplistic caricatures of anthropological methods, depicting them as universally reductionistic or non-historical. Others have responded in a manner that is more positive, but equally superficial. They have, for example, appropriated, in piece-meal and unsystematic ways, certain anthropological catch phrases such as "model of, model for," "liminality," and "binary opposition." But fortunately there have been a few individuals who have pursued a more interesting and fruitful course. These individuals, mostly from the younger generation, have made a serious effort to understand anthropological insights, categories and methods; and they have then gone on to explore the potential contributions and limitations of these insights, categories and methods for their own areas of research.

In 1978, when Robert Moore became the Chair of the Religion and Social Sciences section of the American Academy of Religion, he asked that I organize a series of panels that would highlight and encourage the work of religious studies scholars who did, in fact, take a serious interest in the anthropological study of religion. After an introductory session held at the national meeting of the Academy in 1979, it was decided that the project should take as its focus the writings of three particular anthropologists whose studies of religion, myth and ritual were widely known and highly respected. Thus the panelists at the 1980 meeting discussed the work of Victor Turner and its relevance for their own religious studies research. The papers presented at the 1981 meeting dealt both appreciatively and critically with the work of Clifford Geertz. At the 1982 meeting the participants discussed and evaluated the work of Claude Lévi-Strauss and, in one instance, went on to consider another linguistically-oriented approach developed by Michael Silverstein.[2] The present collection of essays, which represents the state of the project as of August, 1983, includes revised versions of eight papers that were presented at the various panels. The collection also includes two papers submitted by interested scholars who were unable to attend the meetings in person.

The project as a whole, as well as the ten papers that have been selected for inclusion in the present volume, clearly demonstrate that at the present time there is a very significant convergence that is taking place between certain kinds of work being done under the rubric of religious studies, and certain parallel kinds of work being done under the rubric of anthropology. Readers should be cognizant of the fact that the project has been conceived and implemented almost exclusively by scholars in the area of religious studies. The only anthropologists who have participated have been James Fernandez, who made an important contribution to the introductory panel, and Stephen Tobias, who provided an excellent critique of the papers presented in the panel devoted to the work of Clifford Geertz. Readers should also keep in mind that the scholars who have participated in the project exhibit a level of interest in the anthropological study of religion that is not shared by most of their religious studies colleagues. And they should also note that the three anthropologists whose works have been the focus of the project display an appreciation for the importance and richness of religion, myth and ritual that is not characteristic of the anthropological community as a whole.[3] But even when all of these mitigating factors are taken into account, it remains the case that the project and the papers have demonstrated that the process that Clifford Geertz has called a "blurring of genres" is, in fact, taking place.[4]

In the context of this short introductory essay, I cannot possibly spell out in any detail the historical developments that have set the stage for this convergence. However, it is possible to identify three crucial differences that have, in the past, established a more or less clear distinction between religious studies on the one hand, and the anthropological study of religion on the other. It will then be possible to highlight some of the more recent work in religious studies and anthropology in which these traditional emphases have been mutually modified and balanced. The essays in the present volume can then be seen as a further extension of an ongoing process of interaction and enrichment.[5]

The first difference that has traditionally distinguished scholarship in religious studies from scholarship in the anthropological study of religion has to do with the kind of religious traditions and expressions that have characteristically been selected for study. Within religious studies there has been a strong tendency to focus attention on "classical," and to a lesser extent "modern," forms of religion as these have been expressed in literate traditions produced and preserved by religious elites. With the emergence and development of the history of religions, an earlier preoccupation with Christianity has been supplemented by studies covering a much broader range of religions and religious expressions.[6] Still, the inherited emphasis on the study of literate and elite modes of expression has remained at least partially intact. Within the anthropology of religion, there has been a strong tendency to select for study "non-literate," "tribal," "folk" or "village" traditions as these have been expressed in the common life of contemporary peoples.

The second difference in emphasis that has traditionally distinguished the two realms of scholarship flows quite naturally from the first. Scholars in religious studies have focused primarily on the study of written texts. In some instances these scholars have studied texts as religious expressions in their own right. In other instances they have studied these same texts in order to reconstruct the beliefs, rituals, and institutional structures to which they refer. But whichever approach they have chosen, the preeminent methodological focus has remained the analysis of written documents. Anthropologists of religion have taken a different tack and have focused their attention on ethnography and the interpretation of enthnographic data. In the early stages in the development of anthropological studies observations of native behavior and reports from native informants were often received second-hand. More recently the situation has changed and personally conducted field work has become a *sine qua non* for professional credibility. Still, the important point to note is that in both cases the gathering and interpretation of ethnographic data have constituted the central methodological issues.

The third difference that has traditionally marked the distinction between religious studies and the anthropological study of religion has to do with basic theoretical orientation. Because of its more theoretical character this third difference is much more subtle, much more problematic and much more controversial than the differences previously noted. On the religious studies side the salient point is the strong emphasis which this tradition of scholarship has placed on the study of religion *qua* religion. This does not mean that religious studies scholars have ignored other aspects of the phenomena they have studied. Quite the contrary, many of those who have been most insistent that their task is the study of religion as such, have taken great pains to understand the cultural, the sociological, the political and other dimensions of their data. But it does mean that the understanding of religion *qua* religion has been the ultimate goal toward which research has been directed. Anthropological students of religion, on the other hand, have worked within a tradition in which religion is generally presumed to be an aspect or expression of culture or society. From the point of view of religious studies, this anthropological mode of understanding religion has had a tendency to generate "reductionist" interpretations. From the anthropologists' own point of view, this emphasis on culture or society has served as a prophylactic against theological mystification and, by so doing, has provided the necessary basis for truly scientific analyses and interpretations.

Over the years these very real, though by no means absolute, differences between the kinds of scholarship pursued in religious studies and the kinds of research carried on by anthropologists involved in the study of religion have been reflected in the existence of separate institutional contexts. Scholars in the two areas have generally worked in different academic departments; they have participated in different professional associations; and they have published in different journals. This institutional separation has, in turn, worked to reinforce and reify the substantive and theoretical differences. But in recent years, despite the continuing existence of these very formidable institutional barriers, changes have begun to take place. As a result of common external influences, and of the internal dynamics that have been operative in each of the areas, the intellectual gap that separates the two traditions of scholarship has been significantly narrowed.

Consider, first of all, the kind of subject-matter chosen for study. Within religious studies, historians of religions have always considered "non-literate," "tribal," "folk" and "village" religions to be within their ken; and they have always taken into account the descriptions and interpretations provided by the anthropologists who have studied them. However, in the last decade or so an increasing number of historians of religions have chosen to specialize in "tribal" or "non-literate" traditions; and an increasing number of specialists in the so-called "great" religions have chosen to study these religions as they appear in villages and other contemporary communal settings. At the same time, anthropologists, while they have retained the traditional anthropological interest in "tribal" and "non-literate" religions, have begun to concentrate much of their research on communities in which religions such as Christianity, Hinduism, and Taoism hold a prominent position. Thus *both* religious studies specialists *and* anthropological specialists are now studying indigenous African religion, Navaho religion, Chinese religion, Buddhism, etc.

At the level of method, two types of convergence between religious studies and anthropology can be identified. The first follows directly from the fact that scholars in both areas are beginning to deal with the kinds of subject matter that had previously been consigned primarily to the other. Thus, religious studies scholars who are becoming involved in the study of religion in contemporary communal settings are finding it necessary to use participant/observation and other field work methods that have been developed in anthropology.[7] Similarly, anthropologists who are becoming involved in the study of "great" religions such as Judaism, Islam and Buddhism are finding it necessary to study texts. As a part of this process they have begun to utilize methods originally developed in religious studies and other humanistic fields.[8]

The second type of convergence that has taken place at the methodological level has occurred as religious studies scholars and anthropologists have borrowed strategies and categories of interpretation from one another in order to understand better the kinds of religious expression they have traditionally studied. For example, religious studies scholars have borrowed particular structuralist techniques from anthropology in order to interpret important aspects of ancient Hindu mythology.[9] Or, to cite a rather different kind of example, they have appropriated insights developed by anthropologists who have studied contemporary millenarian movements in order to analyze more adequately the origins and development of early Christianity.[10] On the anthropological side, this kind of borrowing process has been more subtle and less explicit. However, it is quite clear that anthropologists have become increasingly interested in history, and have increasingly assimilated religio-historical methods and insights in order to illuminate the religious traditions and expressions they study.[11] More recently still, certain very prominent anthropologists have taken up and developed the notion (previously set forth in the religious studies context by Paul Ricoeur) that the kinds of religious discourse and activities that have traditionally been studied through the use of classical anthropological methods can and should be approached from the perspective of hermeneutics. These anthropologists have recognized that the religious discourses they record and the religious activities they observe can and should be "read" as "living texts."[12]

A final and very fundamental kind of convergence has also taken place in regard to the theoretical emphases that have traditionally differentiated religious studies and the anthropology of religion. Scholars in religious studies have become much less defensive in their insistence on the *sui generis* character of religion. Some have even gone so far as to identify the insistence on this point as a case of special pleading, and to reject it entirely. The notion that the study of religion is a distinct and discrete field of study has generally been retained, but without the kind of explicit or implied dismissal of other approaches that was often evident in the past. The closely correlated anthropological counterpoint to this trend in religious studies is that many of the contemporary anthropologists engaged in the study of religion have significantly revised the positivist presuppositions that characterized much of the work of their predecessors. Taking "symbolic," "structuralist" and "semiotic" approaches, they have given a much more generative and determinative role to religion; and they have developed much richer descriptions and analyses of various modes of religious expression. These scholars have generally retained the basic anthropological position that religion, myth and ritual should be understood primarily as cultural or social phenomena; but they have so modified their notions of culture and society that many aspects of what religious studies scholars have considered to be the anthropological "reduction" of religion have been clearly and definitively transcended.

The collection of essays that follows both exemplifies and extends this process of convergence. The contributors are all religious studies scholars whose own research has been influenced by an intensive encounter with the writings of anthropologists—specifically Clifford Geertz, Victor Turner and Claude Lévi-Strauss. Though the approaches taken by the ten authors differ considerably, there are at least three common elements. In each case the author delineates a specific contribution or set of contributions which the work of the chosen anthropologists has made or can make to a particular area of religious studies research. In each case the author identifies certain methodological or substantive limitations in the work of the selected anthropologist that need to be recognized and taken into account. And in each case he or she discusses the issues that are involved in direct relation to personal research in progress.

The collection as a whole illustrates or addresses each of the areas of convergence that we have identified. The trend toward the sharing of subject matter is highlighted by the fact that two of the authors—Lawrence Sullivan and

Joanne Waghorne—are engaged in research on the kinds of religious traditions that are more typically studied by anthropologists. What is more, Sullivan and Waghorne have given careful attention to the work of a particular anthropologist whose subject matter closely coresponds to their own. Thus Sullivan, who is a historian of religions specializing in the indigenous religions of South America, focuses his essay on the work of his fellow South Americanist, Lévi Strauss. And Waghorne, who is a historian of religions presently involved in the study of a contemporary (19th-20th century) Hindu tradition, focuses her essay on the work of Clifford Geertz who has written a major book dealing with a very similar tradition in Indonesia.

All ten of the authors consider problems and possibilities that are involved in the methodological convergence between religious studies and anthropology. This was the specific task they all accepted when they joined the project, and they have all been faithful to their assignment. Viewed from this perspective, the ten essays can be classified very roughly into four distinct groups. The first group is constituted by the papers of Sullivan and Waghorne that consider the character and adequacy of anthropological methods and categories in the anthropologist's own home territory. The second group consists of three papers—the one by Richard Martin on Geertz, and the two by Dario Zadra and Caroline Bynum on Turner. These three papers explore the potential and the limitations of the methods and insights of the selected anthropologists for the study of important historical aspects of "great" religions, specifically Islam and Christianity. The third group is constituted by the three papers on Lévi-Strauss (and Silverstein) in which David Jobling, Elizabeth Struthers Malbon and Naomi Janowitz test the usefulness of methods developed in linguistic anthropology for the study of classical religious texts, specifically Biblical texts and Rabbinic texts. The fourth group consists of two papers—one by Judith Van Herik on Geertz, and one by Robert Moore on Turner. These papers consider the relevance of anthropological methods and insights for developing new ways of exploring the interface between religion and psychology.

Finally, the various authors have taken a range of different stances concerning the convergence between religious studies notions of religion and anthropological notions of religion. Clearly the contributor who presents the most polemic position is Joanne Waghorne. From her point of view, the appropriate religious studies conception of religion is quite different from the conception of religion that is characteristic of anthropology in general, and of the work of Geertz in particular. She goes on to argue that this difference at the theoretical level has a significant impact on the kinds of research questions that are asked, and the kinds of answers that are generated.[13] More conciliating formulations of the traditional distinction between the two ways of viewing religion, myth and ritual are put forward by Dario Zadra, Robert Moore, Lawrence Sullivan and Elizabeth Struthers Malbon in their discussions of the work of Turner and Lévi-Strauss. These scholars, each in their own distinctive way, make it quite clear that from their perspective there is a difference between the religious studies and anthropological ways of viewing religious phenomena, and that these differences have a significant methodological and substantive impact. But what is perhaps most interesting is the fact that for the remaining five contributors (Martin and Van Herik on Geertz, Bynum on Turner, and Jobling and Janowitz on Lévi-Strauss and Silverstein) the traditional distinction between religion as a distinctive subject of study and religion as a purely cultural or social phenomena is rejected. Or perhaps it would be more accurate to say that these authors do not consider the distinction to be sufficiently relevant to require discussion.

The essays in this volume should make it clear to all who read them that a significant number of first-rate religious studies scholars are presently engaged in a very diversified and highly creative interaction with the work of anthropologists who share their interest in the study of religion, myth and ritual. It is the hope of the editors that the publication of these essays, presented together in this kind of format, will encourage some of our more adventurous colleagues to join the conversation.

Notes and References

1. In this paper I use "religious studies" in a broad sense to cover the whole range of non-confessional approaches to the study of religion that are commonly represented in departments of religious studies and in professional associations such as the American Academy of Religion.

2. The response to the project by the constituency of the Academy has been very positive, and as a result the series of panels will be continued. Joanne Waghorne has taken over the leadership role, and has recently announced that the December, 1983 session will be focused on the writings of Mary Douglas.

3. Kees Bolle, in a strongly phrased paper presented at the project's introductory panel held in 1979, highlighted the continuing positivistic orientation of most practicing anthropologists, particularly those who populate the large departments established at most state universities.

4. Clifford Geertz, "Blurred Genres: The Refiguration of Social Thought," *The American Scholar* 49 (Spring, 1980).

5. For some earlier discussion of important issues see the section on the "Religio-Anthropological Approach" in Laurie Honko, ed., *Science of Religion: Studies in Methodology—Proceedings of the Study Conference of the International Association for the History of Religions*, held in Turku, Finland August 27-31, 1973 (*Religion and Reason* 13; The Hague: Mouton, 1973). The section contains articles by Ugo Bianchi and Melford Spiro, as well as commentaries on their papers by other scholars from both religious studies and anthropology.

6. The relationship between "religious studies" and "history of religions" is notoriously complex. In this context, I am accepting as descriptively accurate the notion that religious studies is a broader field within which the history of religions is encompassed. Elsewhere ("Maps, Models and Boundaries," *Criterion* 21, 1 [Winter, 1980]; and "History of Religions: Condition and Prospects" in *Bulletin of the Council for the Study of Religion* 13, 5 [December, 1982]), I have taken a more prescriptive stance, and have suggested that the history of religions is a discipline that could and should provide the basic theoretical and methodological orientation in terms of which the various component elements of religious studies are structured and integrated.

7. For an excellent religious studies interpretation of religious life in a contemporary community based largely on participant/observation and other field work methods, see Winston Davis, *Dojo: Magic and Exorcism in Modern Japan* (Stanford: Stanford University Press, 1980).

8. For an excellent anthropological study that appropriates and utilizes modes of textual interpretation that have traditionally been applied in religous studies, see Alton L. Becker, "Text-Building, Epistemology, and Aesthetics in Japanese Shadow Theatre," in Alton L. Becker and

Aram Yengoyan, eds., *The Imagination of Reality* (Norwood, New Jersey: Ablex, 1979). Note especially Becker's proposal for a "new philology."

9. Wendy Doniger O'Flaherty, *Asceticism and Eroticism in the Mythology of Siva* (London: Oxford University Press, 1973).

10. John Gager, *Kingdom and Community in the Community in the Social World of Early Christianity* (Englewood, New Jersey: Prentice-Hall, 1975).

11. Stanley Tambiah, *World Conqueror and World Renouncer* (Cambridge: Cambridge University Press, 1976). Also Michael T. Taussig, *The Devil and Commodity Fetishism* (Chapel Hill: University of North Carolina, 1980).

12. Many of the key issues involved are insightfully discussed from an anthropological perspective by James Boon in a collection of essays entitled *Other Tribes, Other Scribes* (Cambridge: Cambridge University Press, 1983). See also Charles Keyes, "Ethical Action and Economic Discourse in a Buddhist Community," forthcoming in Donald Swearer and Russell Sizemore, eds., *The Ethics of Wealth and Poverty in Theravada Buddhism.*

13. Ideally Waghorne's contribution should be read in tandem with her earlier article, "A Body for God: An Interpretation of the Nature of Myth Beyond Structuralism," *History of Religions Journal* 21, 1 (August, 1981).

Part One

The Work of Clifford Geertz

CHAPTER I

Clifford Geertz Observed: Understanding Islam As Cultural Symbolism

Richard C. Martin

My purpose is to assess the contributions of Clifford Geertz to the study of cultural symbolism, particularly in reference to two areas in which I maintain academic interests — history of religions and Islamic studies.[1] Historians of religions like to change venue frequently, as indeed they must, for religion gets hauled before courts of scholarly opinion conducted in virtually all of the arts and sciences. In the present case of religionists evaluating the work of anthropologists, I admit to being *amicus curiae*, for some of the writings of Clifford Geertz on cultural symbolism have been particularly illuminating for my work in Quranic Studies. Yet the problematic, as I see it, is not simply to rustle promising theories and methods from other "fields" and put our *HR* brand on them once we get them into our corral, as we might say in Arizona. If, as humanists trained to interpret the textual manifestations of human religiousness, we find that some anthropologists are asking questions pertinent to the data we too are trying to interpret, as Prof. Jacob Neusner has suggested,[2] then it seems to me we must still reflect on and criticize all disciplined studies of religion in relation to history of religions research.

The position I wish to take is that the ethnographers' problematic of "interpreting culture" as defined by Geertz entails a symbolist concept of culture that sheds light on the study of religion and on the study of Islam in local contexts. Less clear than his concept of culture, which includes religion along with other dimensions of human thought and social activitiy, is the sort of interpretation Geertz's notion of culture calls for. In the humanities, theories of interpretation propounded for literary and historical studies have been the concern of hermeneutic philosophy. The question I want to explore is whether or not Geertz's revisions of ethnographic notions of culture can be accommodated by a hermeneutic theory, as he himself has suggested, that would encompass the broad spectrum of textual and social data which the historian of religions proposes to interpret.

THE PROBLEM OF CULTURE AND ITS INTERPRETATION

"Culture" is a gelatinous term that means many things to different people. In the humanities, culture is referred to regularly in discourse about intellectual,

11

literary and religious history, but the real debate as to the concept and theory of what culture comprises has been the province of the social sciences. In 1871, E. B. Tylor formulated the outlines of a general theory: "Culture or civilization, taken in its wide and ethnographic sense, is that complex whole which includes knowledge, belief, art, morals, law, custom, and any other capabilities and habits acquired by man as a member of society."[3] Tylor's concept of culture made a sharp distinction between nature and culture — the latter being essentially man's adaptation to the former and hence the study of the artifacts and learned behaviors that distinguish one human group from another.[4] The Tylorean definition was so broad as to allow eventually ample room for heated debates between those who insisted that the key problematic was the interpretation of "culture" and those who insisted it was the explanation of "society." Following Talcott Parsons and others, Geertz regards "culture" and "social system" as different abstractions from the same phenomena. Thus, he defines "the former as an ordered system of meaning and of symbols, in terms of which social interaction takes place; and . . . the latter as the pattern of social interaction itself."[5] This distinction is useful insofar as it conforms broadly with the views of many American social scientists, and it seems to reflect Geertz's discussion of world view and ethos, to which I shall return later on.

Humanists were also concerned about cultural studies in the late-nineteenth century, although their field of inquiry was constituted by the literary production of past generations and ages and thus their problematic belonged to the realm of textual hermeneutics. An important question for the humanistic disciplines has been to determine *how* to interpret meaning in the literary production of others. Nineteenth-century German philosophy essayed a distinction between the humanistic disciplines (*Geistes-* or *Kulturwissenschaften*) and the natural sciences (*Naturwissenschaften*). It was generally agreed that the natural sciences had as a goal the explanation (*Erklären*) of natural phenomena through inductive discovery of general laws. For humanists, the obvious differences among historical periods and cultures seemed to require special epistemological considerations that would enable the researcher to "understand" the cultural variables of human subjectivity. In "The Understanding of Other Persons and Life-Expressions," Wilhelm Dilthey (viv. 1833-1911) postulated that "Understanding [*Verstehen*] and interpreting are the methods used in human studies [*Geisteswissenschaften*] . . . At every stage the understanding reveals a world. The understanding of other persons and life-expressions [*geistige Lebensäusserungen*] is built on our own experience and on our understanding of it, and on the continuous interplay of experience and understanding."[6]

The theory that categories of universal human subjectivity constitute experience and thus rational and scientific knowledge had been argued by Kant a century earlier. E. D. Hirsch observes: "Dilthey and others postulated that, beyond this universal subjectivity, there exists a cultural subjectivity, structured by further categories which are analogously constitutive of all cultural experience."[7] Whether this quality of intersubjectivity or "empathetic" understanding opens the door to cross-cultural understanding of humanly produced phenomena by "bracketing" out determinates of meaning (Husserl) or locates interpretation within the hermeneutic circle that operates between the text and the world of the interpreting subject (Heidegger) is a problem that has generated much discussion. The philosophical argument between Heidegger and Husserl is still very much alive in the writings of Hans-Georg Gadamer, E. D. Hirsch and Paul Ricoeur, *inter alia.*

Husserl held that "meaning" *(Sinn)* is what the author intended to say, and this can be bracketed out of original historical (and presumably cultural) contexts by the interpreter's explanation of the text. "Significance" *(Bedeutung)* is what the author's original meaning becomes in the context of the interpreter's historico-cultural world. Thus Hirsch, following Husserl, suggests that interpretation involves "binocular" vision that brings original meaning and contemporary significance into focus. Heidegger took the position that understanding is necessarily rooted in the interpreter's historical situation. Heidegger's hermeneutic circle pressed the part-whole paradox in explaining the necessary grounding of interpretation in the interpreter's particular historico-cultural circumstances that differ from those of the author. An individual's experience is part of a totality of experiences that a personal view of the world comprises; in order to know a part (meaning) of a text, or text as part of a world, the interpreter must preconceive the whole to which the particular experience is related. Since the life-world within which one experiences the whole changes through historical time and differs among cultures, meanings of texts constantly change in relation to the changing wholes or views of the world. Thus, instead of "bracketing out" from a text an absolute meaning which is constant between author (or text) and interpreter, Heidegger and pursuers of the New Criticism and the New Hermeneutic focus on texts in relation to the interpreter's activity of construing a world of meaning, which is necessarily the one construed by the interpreter, not the actual historical circumstances of the author.

Later in this paper, I will pursue further the relevance of hermeneutic philosophy to Geertz's concept of culture. Before moving to consider the concept of culture of a well-known Islamicist, Gustav von Grunebaum, I would like to suggest that phenomenological studies in history of religions and textual studies among Islamicists seem to echo more the approach of Husserl than that of Heidegger. The possibility of discovering absolute transcultural meanings and intentions of authors in the Islamic textual corpus has been fundamental to orientalist scholarship since the nineteenth century, and phenomenologists of religion have employed the metaphor of "bracketing out" the interpreter's subjectivity in order to achieve an objective grasp or vision of the meaning of religious phenomena. In addition to their goal of objectively describing the essence of the human experience of the "sacred," phenomenologists have construed the object of their studies (the sacred, holy) as a class of *unusual* objects, rather than an unusual class of objects (to paraphrase a remark made by Geertz).

The question I want to pose is whether the hermeneutic circle of Heidegger and Gadamer, which conceives of interpretation as the fusion of the horizon of the interpreter with that of the text[8] is applicable to the social aspects of culture. I contend with hermeneutic philosopher Paul Ricoeur (and echoed in the later writings of Clifford Geertz) that it is, though with some qualifications, and that cultural meanings are not only intra- and intertextual — as between scripture and exegesis — but also inter*textured* among the literary and nonliterary kinds of evidence that evince human religiousness. I think that this can be demonstrated in talking about Quranic studies, for example, where both literary and oral, textual and contextual, constituents of meaning require coordinated and interrelated analyses. I will return to this topic later.

ORIENTALISM AND CULTURAL ANTHROPOLOGY: THE CASE OF VON GRUNEBAUM

The several works of Gustav E. von Grunebaum about cultural anthropology and the study of Islam are better known to Islamicists than social scientists, for reasons that are not hard to find. Fieldwork, which is a characteristic of ethnography and the backbone of social science research generally, is noticeably lacking in von Grunebaum's analysis of Islamic culture, nor does he refer much to data collected by ethnographers working in local Islamic contexts. Von Grunebaum's training in classical philology in Vienna, his competence and command of Middle Eastern Languages and texts, and his association with the University of Chicago, where German social theory, civilization studies and *Religionswissenschaft* had come to be concentrated on this continent, contributed to his subsequent reputation and achievement as director of the Near Eastern Center at the University of California, Los Angeles. It was his stated conviction that Near Eastern studies were likely to be more creative and effective if integrated with other historical and social science research. To this end he sought to construct a theory of culture that would provide a framework for a cross-disciplinary understanding of Islam in history.

Von Grunebaum defined culture as "a 'closed' system of questions and answers concerning the universe and man's behavior in it which has been accepted as authoritative by a human society."[9] This implies a scale of values which indicates, von Grunebaum argued, a fundamental "aspiration" of the culture in question. Hence, "as the experience of the community changes, the power to formulate and answer new questions in terms of the traditional values and the decisions previously arrived at will indicate a culture's ability to continue."[10] Once historical and political changes place sufficient stress upon the hypotheses and insights of the closed system (i.e., culture), unquestioning adherence to its basic values may diminish, transformation might then occur and a new aspiration with a new scale of values could result, or the closed system might attempt to resist all such changes. Thus, with a theory of culture as part of his scholarly apparatus, von Grunebaum sought to establish a means of explaining the predicament in which he perceived Islam to be in the modern period. He contrasted the cultural transformations of seventh-century Arabia, which he offered as an example of "orthogenetic transformation" with the "Westernization of Islamic civilization in the last 150 years"—an example of "heterogenetic transformation."[11] He argued that in the latter case, the traditional cultural system of Islam could be seen not to have borne the intrinsic capability to formulate and answer the new questions posed by Westernization and modernization. One important result in the view of von Grunebaum and others was that Islam seemed to have lost its ability to achieve a self-understanding consistent with the classical models and paradigms of the productive periods of the caliphate from the seventh to the eleventh centuries.[12]

The linkage between self-understanding and cultural studies meant for von Grunebaum that cultural anthropology in the contemporary world of scholarship could be a program of "human self analysis by means of a *Kulturlehre*" and thus could hold "the key position in the organization of the sciences." Along with Vico and Dilthey, von Grunebaum believed that in the human sciences, as distinct from the natural sciences, *understanding* "other" human phenomena rested upon self-knowledge and subjectivity, which all human beings in all times and places share; hence, the paradox that we know others by knowing ourselves, and we know ourselves better by knowing others. Cultural anthropology is not the "capstone" of the sciences, as theology and philosophy once had been, but rather the "hub of such scientific endeavor as serves our overriding existential urge to understand ourselves through an understanding of our cultural place," and from this perspective it helps us "to understand that place through an understanding of all the cultural answers to the problems of living which have been devised by man."[13]

Von Grunebaum's concept of gaining cultural understanding of the "other" through Dilthey's method of self-understanding led him to conclude that "it is essential to realize that Muslim civilization is a cultural entity that does not share our primary aspirations. It is not vitally interested in analytical self-understanding, and it is even less interested in the study of other cultures, either as an end in itself or as a means toward clearer understanding of its own character and history."[14] In fact, however, von Grunebaum confused cultural comparison with the gratuitous contrast between Islamic culture and cultural anthropology—the thing studied with the study of it. The pursuit of *Religionswissenschaft* along the same phenomenological lines of *Verstehen*, despite the goal of bracketing out the subjectivity of the investigator, falls into the same trap. Indeed, the categories of phenomenological analysis of religion have often had Western theological overtones that suggest more than a modicum of bias in the "descriptions" of "sacred" objects and phenomena.[15]

The point I wish to make here is that with a massive array of textual evidence at his disposal, and with a solid education in German social thought, von Grunebaum was able to say a great deal about an entity he called Islamic culture without getting down to specific cases of time and place except to provide an occasional illustration of the logic of his scheme. Abdallah Laroui comments that with this kind of analysis, "everything comes to us in a framework of culture and ideology; we have a theory of religion and few evidences of the actual lived religion . . . a theory of social structure and few indications of lived behavior . . . . We are in constant danger of confusing theory with fact: the one is readily available, while the other demands research and elaboration."[16] The confusion of the study of an object with the object of study—physics with the physical world, to use Geertz's example[17]—turns out to be a real danger, especially, I think, in cultural studies.

The fact that von Grunebaum was able to make a number of negative assessments about Islamic culture is too well known for me to belabor here. Like the typical analyses of Islamic religion which note that Islam has no *ecclesia, sacramenta* or concept of *politēs*, and which then try to explain why these important Western institutions are missing in Islam, von Grunebaum's theory of culture has seemed suspiciously loaded in the scale of comparison, even before the data has been consulted. And the data he consulted were symptoms and patterns of culture extracted from the normative textual tradition. Historians of religions reading von Grunebaum's influential writings on Islam [and many of us do] can find a theory of religion and provocative comparisons with Christendom, but little evidence of actual lived religion.

I have reviewed what I consider to be some faults of von Grunebaum's argument, despite my persisting admiration for the erudition and conceptual powers he brought to his writing, because I believe he was quite right to emphasize that a proper concept of culture is propaedeutic to understanding any civilization, such as Islam. Understanding culture as a closed system, however, is problematic. Given the historical realities of human civilizations, is any cultural system ever really closed? As Northrup Frye has put it, every culture is adjacent to other cultures in time and space.[18] This is not simply to observe that Islam and Byzantium were contiguous or that religion in Arabia after the Prophet was preceded by a pagan symbolism whose meanings it used and transformed. More significantly, various degrees [or forms] of Islamization often exist simultaneously among social and ethnic groups that are bound together within the same cultural region.[19] To place the emphasis upon "Islam"—an abstract entity—as an ideal system rather than upon its living exemplars in various times and places, working out what Islam is under the conditions of their existence, comes dangerously close to confusing the roles of scholar and shaykh.

Finally, I agree with Clifford Geertz's warning about the dangers of moving from "ethnographic miniatures" to "wall-sized culturescapes"—what he refers to as the Jonesville-is-America fallacy. Yet this is the thrust of what Geertz tried to accomplish in *Islam Observed*—to reconstruct Islam from the similarities evinced in separated local environments rather than starting from a unified normative notion.[20] The orientalist's and historian's of religions version of this fallacy focuses on intellectual history and argues that a central literary figure such as al-Ghazali is the best window into Islam, or that the passion of al-Hallaj epitomizes the ethos of Islam. It would not be difficult to demonstrate that a few Islamicists [and most Muslims] assume that the Qur'ān and Sunna of the Prophet are the best and most proper sources for interpreting Islamic culture. Even the noted work by Rueben Levy, *The Social Structure of Islam*, attempted what the title promised by consulting the normative texts of scripture, prophetic logia and early Muslim juristic philosophy.[21] It might be argued that in past periods for which social evidence is not available, social ethos must be inferred from such documents.[22] The hermeneutic problem both of literary texts and social textures, however, is that they present to the interpreter cultural symbols that reflect at best and often conceal local meanings.

To be fair to von Grunebaum, he was not a cultural anthropologist, but a Middle Eastern historian – an orientalist, some would say – who reasoned that the specialists in his field should enlarge the vision of what they were doing by looking at the data of Islam through different theoretical lenses. Consonant with his earlier training he came to the conclusion that the concept of culture implied in nineteenth-century *Verstehen* methodology could shed light on his own field of historical studies, and the direction he gave to the Middle East Center at UCLA was reflected in his commitment to cross-disciplinary airings of specialist understandings. Both his achievements and his failures in this direction are worthy of reflection.

The problem for von Grunebaum, and I think for many Islamicists and historians of religions, was that his theory of culture as a closed system ran headlong into the cross-disciplinary findings he so vigorously sought. Where he found Islam to differ from what he conceived to be its original and classical forms, his notion of symbols required him to think of them as losing content or power, not as changing and working differently under new social and historical circumstances. Islam is, *inter alia*, how a people perceive the wonder of a *sūra* of the Qur'ān, a mufti's legal opinion, an Ayatollah's political authority, missing the Friday prayer, the tragedy of death, or the benefits [or miscreance] of a mystical *tarīqa*. The theory of culture von Grunebaum retailed so articulately, and others have presumed nearly as strongly if less clearly, was not so constructed as to account for all these aspects as important constituents of a variable Islam in history; unable ultimately to accommodate the *variety*, he was forced to locate Islam's *unity* in classical ideal stages and types.

CULTURE, SYMBOLISM, AND THE STUDY OF ISLAM IN THE WORK OF CLIFFORD GEERTZ

The work of Clifford Geertz has been primarily associated with three prestigious American institutions of social science research – Harvard, Chicago, and the Institute for Advanced Study – and two major, though quite different, areas of field observation – Indonesia and Morocco. Behaviorism and the sociological theories of Talcott Parsons dominated the atmosphere of Harvard's Department of Social Relations when Geertz trained there as a graduate student in the 1950s. Geertz's dissertation and postdoctoral research on the religion of Java resulted in an enormously influential ethnographic study, which in title and concept bears the stamp of Max Weber's classic works on religion in China and in India. *Religion in Java*[23] analyzed the extreme case of Islam in cultural symbiosis with other social systems—native Javanese and Hindu-Buddhist. His approach helped to establish an important alternative to the tendencies of Islamicists and historians of religions to describe and categorize their subject matter in social and cultural isolation from the realities of local context.

At Chicago in the 1960s Geertz, as von Grunebaum before him, was associated with that institution's broad commitment to comparative studies of civilizations and religions, and in that context he emerged as a major exponent of symbolist approaches to cultural anthropology. To the generic social science question of the relation between *Kultur* and *Natur*, meaning and environment, Geertz brought a discussion of symbolism and symbolic acts—a concept he candidly imported from Susanne Langer, Kenneth Burke, and other neo-Kantians in the humanities. Convinced that the human sciences had not contributed much of significance to the study of religion since the pioneering works of Durkheim, Weber, Freud, and Malinowski, through symbolist anthropology Geertz sought an interpretive strategy that would avoid the functionalist limitations of these masters while at the same time preserve their more enduring conceptual achievements. In one passage he described these as "Durkheim's discussion of the nature of the sacred, Weber's *Verstehenden* methodology, Freud's parallel between personal rituals and collective ones, and Malinowski's distinction between religion and common sense."[24]

During his years of teaching at Chicago, Geertz's field experience shifted to include Morocco. Thus, with original ethnographic fieldwork in Southeast Asia and northwest Africa, the geographical and cultural extremes of *dār al-islām*, he undertook to chart his own approach to comparative and civilization studies. This approach was brilliantly set forth in the Terry Lectures at Yale in 1967, published as *Islam Observed: Religious Development in Morocco and Indonesia* the following year.[25] Among the themes he stressed were the focus on symbolism and the need to project ethnography beyond its village base into the larger discourse about civilizations and religious traditions. The years at Princeton's Institute for Advanced Study have included additional trips to the field, but the major thrust of Geertz's work since the beginning of the 1970s has been to refine his notions of culture, symbolism and interpretation, which he has reapplied in frequest articles and monographs on Java, Bali and Morocco, as well as in more general essays on the role of ethnography in the interpretation of culture.

Although Geertz, by virtue of his appointment at the Institute, has not been required to teach, and he seldom attends the paper-reading sessions of professional associations, his published work does not convey a sense of intellectual solitude, cloistered from the contemporary issues dividing academe. With culture as the pivotal concept, he has attempted to orient his work as anthropologist toward the interests and concerns of other disciplines—perhaps more so than toward other points of view in anthropology. Hence, his

essays on interpreting religion, art, ideology, cock fights, bazaars, and so on, as
"cultural systems" go beyond the parochialisms of village anthropology, by attempting to balance his own perspective with those of others on the fulcrum of
native conceptions of things. His programmatic essay, "Thick Descriptions:
Toward an Interpretive Theory of Culture,"[26] sought to provide theoretical
justification for the ethnographer's role in such discourse. In *Peddlers and
Princes*[27] and "Suq: The Bazaar Economy in Sefrou,"[28] for example, Geertz
tested contemporary models of explanation in economics against local patterns
of exchange. In *Negara* he addressed problems in political and historical
analysis. In "Deep Play: Notes on the Balinese Cockfight," he showed how in
the supercharged atmosphere of village matches, the betting—which Bentham
would have called "deep play" that is inimical to the common weal—brings
villagers into curiously patterned mob behavior where the themes of "death,
masculinity, rage, pride, loss, beneficence" get ordered into an encompassing
structure and thus reveal the essential nature of these themes in Balinese
culture.[29]

In *Islam Observed*, he stepped beyond the bounds of village anthropology to
consider the more expansive notions of Islam held by orientalists and
historians of religions, offering constructive criticism of venerable theories and
categories in Islamic studies.

Thus, although Geertz borrows from and cites freely the historical and normative studies of Islamicists, in theory and interpretation he prefers to chart his
own course. Like Redfield, von Grunebaum and Hodgson (fellow observers in
Islam from the "Chicago" perspective).[30] Geertz is dissatisfied with disciplinary
boundaries that confine the task of explaining and interpreting culture to
discipline in the narrow sense of "a discipline," which implies for none of them
that scholarship can do without a disciplinary base. What it does imply for
Geertz is that the study of civilization must adapt notions of ideal types,
Verstehen, normative structures, and other analytical categories to local, and in
any given moment changing, but in the long run ongoing, traditions of con-
ceiving and ordering reality. Geertz firmly believes that symbolist ethnography
has an important function to perform in getting at those native constructions
of reality—both normative-textual and everyday-social—which are explored by
the various branches of the human sciences.

In "Ethos, World-View, and the Analysis of Sacred Symbols,"[31] Geertz's
analysis of cultural symbolism reflected strongly the views of Ernst Cassirer and
Susanne Langer.[32] Man is a symbolizing animal, and symbols, like Kant's
categories and concepts, "do not mirror an objective world, but are constitutive
of it."[33] Cassirer distinguished three kinds of symbolic constructions of reality—
the objective world of science, the mythical world of religion and the ordinary
language world of common sense. Cassirer held that the conservative tendency
of science, religion and language to preserve or "store" meanings in symbols is
constantly in tension with the historico-social evolution of conceptual, experiential and semantic change; tradition makes communication possible

and change evokes human creativity. In "Religion As a Cultural System" (first presented in 1963),[34] Geertz pursued this line of thought further, giving considerable play to the categories of religious phenomenology (the sacred, cosmic order and chaos, theodicy, etc.). Indeed, the expository commentary he gives to his five-part definition of religion as "a system of symbols . . . ." has enjoyed enormous popularity among historians of religions, though noticeably less so among anthropologists and social historians. The problem, quite simply, has been to devise a way to test such a notion of culture, given the great number of variables and the elasticity of each set.

In a somewhat different formulation Geertz holds that symbols or symbolic action mediate between world view and ethos. In a typical formulation of the general shape he gives to this process, he tells us that "in anthropology, it has become customary to refer to the collective notions a people has of how reality is at base put together as their world view. Their general style of life, the way they do things and like to see things done, we usually call their ethos. It is the office of religious symbols, then, to link these in such a way that they mutually confirm one another."[35] The world view—symbolism—ethos construction has held more interest for the social study of religion, although the implication that symbols "store" meanings remains too static and problematic to account for how symbols act as vehicles of meaning that connect variable psychological, social and physical phenomena over historical time and change. It was not until Geertz began to explore semiotic and, later still, speech act theories of meaning that the world view/ethos construction courted disciplines with methodologies that could test culture as a dynamic process that accommodates psychological, social and historical variables of meaning for the same symbol[s].

An aspect of semiological analysis in which Geertz has made an important contribution is in the discussion of semantic fields. His discussion of the terminology of the sūq [bazaar] in Sefrou, bringing the economic and social activities of a Moroccan village into the range of Islamic religious and cultural concepts, is extremely useful to the research interests of Islamicists and historians of religions.[36] It constitutes an ethnographic exegesis of orientalist philology, a clear demonstration of scholarly binocular focus on the social textures and normative texts of Islam's little and great traditions.[37] What I am suggesting is that an important shift rather than a wholly new direction can be seen in Geertz's more recent discussions of cultural symbolism. The problem of the scholarly *Verstehen* of other cultures, of the human drive to order and rationalize perceptions of reality, and of the symbolism of social interaction were all to be found in Weber's *Religion in India*, *inter alia*, and in Geertz's *Religion in Java*. In the course of his career Geertz has refined his discussion of cultural symbolism by consulting recent developments in linguistics and semiology. It is in this vein that his work parallels recent trends in history of religions, and these trends—taken as a whole—may be construed as problems that bear upon hermeneutic theory.

THE HERMENEUTICAL PROBLEM

The concept of culture Geertz has come to espouse is essentially, then, a semiotic one. "Believing, with Max Weber," Geertz tells us, "that man is an animal suspended in webs of significance that he himself has spun," Geertz understands "culture to be those webs, and the analysis of it therefore to be not an experimental science in search of law but an interpretive one in search of meaning."[38] Given the "thickness" of such webs of significance as are found in even the small, restricted village environments where Geertz often prefers to observe, the problem is how to project a coherent notion of culture on the scale of Weber's more embracing notion of "religion in India" or von Grunebaum's "Islamic civilization." Wherever it spread, Islam brought such key symbols as the Qur'an, prophetic *hadīth*, the normative prescriptions of sacred law, the authority of the *'ulamā'*, etc., which as symbols provide similar, but not identical, patterns of signification within the varying linguistic, ethnic, socio-political and historical circumstances of Muslim peoples.

Social scientists would like, and have long sought (often in futility) to have their work recognized as science. Geertz does not abandon his discipline's view that science is the activity in which the anthropologist is ultimately engaged.[39] Nonetheless, Geertz tilts toward the humanities for metaphors, examples and analytical models for interpreting society in cultural terms. Indeed, what the ethnographer observes, in Geertz's view, are texts in the broadest sense of the term: textures of socially shared meanings interwoven among those aspects of social expression which, for analytical reasons, the observer often chooses to isolate as religion, politics, economics, art, play, etc. Geertz's general approach implies the need for a hermeneutic, a theory of interpretation, that would enable the observer to construe within his own horizon of understanding the meanings displayed within and among a culture's verbal and nonverbal texts and social textures.

In this regard, Paul Ricoeur's essay, "The Model of the Text: Meaningful Action Considered As a Text,"[40] exemplifies a metaphor he has invoked to describe his intentions: a mountain divides the work of ethnographers from other disciplinarians in the human sciences; in digging a tunnel to meet the other, though starting from opposite sides, the ethnographer and other scholars must orient themselves toward each other's work. Ricoeur directed the theory and methods of textual hermeneutics toward the problems of social analysis, and Geertz introduced the data of socio-cultural symbolism into the universe of discourse about hermeneutics. The results of such ecumenical gestures across the rigid boundaries that divide academe can be of enormous significance to Islamicists and historians of religions, in my opinion.

The case in hand, the Ricoeur/Geertz "model of the text," provides a useful point of departure for assessing the application of hermeneutics to socio-cultural studies. Ricoeur asked in what sense "the human sciences may be said to be hermeneutical [1] inasmuch as their *object* displays some of the features constitutive of a text as text, and [2] inasmuch as their *methodology* develops the same kind of procedure as those of *Auslegung* or text-interpretation."[42] In the first half of the essay he proposed four ways in which the literary notion of "text" presented a paradigm for the object of social science research. His formulations are interesting and controversial, but it is in the second half of the essay, the paradigm of text interpretation, that practical and methodological implications are drawn for social science research.

Addressing himself to the perplexities raised by Dilthey as to the relation between *Verstehen* and *Erklären*, understanding and explanation, Ricoeur argues that the hermeneutical circle may be broken into two procedural arcs. In the case of the first, the interpreter proceeds from intelligent preconception of a text's meaning—a hypothesis or "guess"—to test the validity of that particular meaning by means of historical, linguistic, and other available canons of judgment. If interpretive circularity remains characteristic of the hermeneutical dialectic between text and interpretation, it need not be vicious. Ricoeur maintains that the validation of interpretation in this manner "is an argumentative discipline comparable to the judicial procedures of legal interpretation."[43] In this conception of the hermeneutic arc, one attempts to "make a case" for a particular interpretation of a text or pattern of social action.

Ricoeur's analysis of the *Verstehen→Erklären* hermeneutic arc is implicit, I think, in many of Geertz's later writings, and it surfaces explicitly in "Thick Descriptions" and "From the Native's Point of View."[44] In the latter, Geertz sought to expound upon the concepts of "person" in the cultures of Java, Bali and Morocco. He enlarged Ricoeur's presentation of Heidegger's notion of *Horizontverschmelzung*, incorporating the ethnographer's "continuous dialectical tacking between the most local of local detail and the most global of global structure in such a way as to bring them into simultaneous view."[45] (Thus, in this manner, Redfield's little tradition/great tradition distinction, the insider versus outsider dilemma, and von Grunebaum's attempt to bring unity and variety in Islam into focus, might become aspects of the case-making activities of hermeneutic analysis.) "All this is, of course, but the now familiar trajectory of what [Heidegger, reflecting on the writings of] Dilthey .[had] called the hermeneutic circle, and my argument here is merely that it is as central to ethnographic interpretation . . . as it is to literary, historical, philological, psychoanalytical, biblical . . . ."

Geertz's more recent discussion of symbolism relies, as I have tried to show, more on linguists' theories of semiotics and somewhat less, it seems to me, on Cassirer's theory that symbols store meanings although he still maintains with Cassirer that symbols constitute reality. Whereas the symbolist view is often regarded by historians of religions as being more amenable to phenomenological, synchronic analyses of the experience of the "sacred," the semiological revision defines symbols as complexes of signs or vehicles of meaning that display webs of socially shared significance in what human beings say and do. The semiological "turn" in Geertz's writing also implies that symbols are not opposed to the real "as fanciful to sober, figurative to real, obscure to plain . . . ." That, Geertz points out, was a nineteenth-century prejudice. Rather, in accounting for native world views (and in the broadest sense of the term "native," Geertz follows Cassirer in including Western science among symbolizing world views) "the real is as imagined as the imaginary."[47] As David Schneider has put it, "culture is man's adaptation to nature, too, but it is more. Nature, as a wholly independent 'thing' does not exist, except as man formulates it."[48]

Despite its conceptual appeal, the Thick Description/Model-of-the-Text analysis of culture warrants some criticism. There is a tendency in Geertz's writing, and in the conceptions of symbolists generally, to invest analysis too heavily in the symbolism of native interpretations, and to neglect or plead the ineffability of the actual historical and social circumstances we presume they are about. Semiotics get limited to noetics, causes to blueprints of effects, observation of empirical fields of activity to deciphering the views others have of the world and of their activities in it. The ethnographer has come dangerously close to inhabiting a Berkeleyan world that can only be known in the mental realm of ideas and symbols.[49] The hermeneutic distinction between the *Welt* created by textual symbolism and the *Umwelt* of the interpreter leads to less critical attention paid to the empirical *Umwelt* of the native which, despite cultural differences, must be presumed to be in some important epistemological senses the same as that of the interpreter. Texts, whether considered as sacred laws, social rituals or scripturalist reform movements are products not only of separate "worlds" in the symbolist sense but also of world history in Marshall Hodgson's conception of *The Venture of Islam*. The ethnographer and the historian of religion must attempt to grasp both in their interpretations of evidential materials. Most of us who study religious phenomena share with Geertz the danger of opting for a form of Platonic Idealism in our interpretive writing. In other words, I think we need to distinguish critically between our notions of meaning and behavior, even though as Geertz correctly contends, the two are merged in what we observe of culture. Otherwise the tension between world view and ethos, map and territory, cannot be accounted for and factored into the interpretation of culture.

Ricoeur argues for a second arc of the hermeneutic circle, a discussion that is noticeably lacking in Geertz's analyses. Taking the structuralists' position that texts—including narrative myths, rituals, and social dramas—may be "read" with respect to surface and deep semantic codes or messages, Ricoeur proposes a second hermeneutic arc of moving from *Erklären* to *Verstehen*, from semantic, structural analysis to discovery of more deeply embedded meanings. Levi-Strauss has argued that myths mediate between fundamental oppositions in life, such as birth and death, blindness and lucidity. "Meaning" in this interpretive arc is discovered within the nonostensive *Welt* or world view of the text, which at base is about the *aporias* of life in the *Umwelt* of human existence. That is to say, although for the purposes of analysis a text may be regarded at one level as an internally bounded system of meanings, as a human expression its meaning stands in relief against the background of nonmeaning, chaos, and anomoly in the confrontation of world view with the realities of life.[50]

A good example of this dimension of meaning in culture in the case of Islam is demonstrated in M. Piamenta, *Islam in Everyday Arabic Speech*.[51] Piamenta analyzes the socio-emotional contexts in which speakers of Arabic (primarily, but not exclusively, Muslim) utter pious formulae from the Qur'ān, prophetic sayings, and the idioms of local dialects. His study illustrates how stereotyped phrases indicate vehicles "of affective communication, of feelings and emotions stimulated by situation, and of attitudes and emotions communicated in response. These formulae are largely inspired by religion, and in most instances include the name of Allah explicitly or implicitly. They are habits established and performed as a result of learning and training in socio-emotional situations."[52] Most of the contexts studied by Piamenta—such as fearing, warning, alienating, helplessness, and offending—may be construed as boundary situations within Muslim world views; they seem to be structured by the awe-full greatness of God, the precariousness of human existence, and the danger of forgetting (to mention) God in certain kinds of situations.

Another example of this dimension of textual meaning is recognized by Geertz himself in his definition of religion as a cultural system:

> There are at least three points where chaos—a tumult of events which lack not just inter-pretations but *interpretability*—threatens to break in upon man: at the limits of his analytical capacities, at the limits of his powers of endurance, and at the limits of his moral insight. Baffle-ment, suffering, and a sense of intractable ethical paradox are all, if they become intense enough . . . radical challenges to the proposition that life is comprehensible and that we can . . . orient ourselves effectively in it . . . ."[53]

Although Geertz finds justifiable fault with the overly schematized pro-cedures of structuralists, especially when they seem to lock analysis away from the realities of everyday life, it nonetheless seems that structural analysis holds theories of meaning that are consonant, in principle, with Geertz's notion of cultural symbolism. Moreover, the locative arrangements and semantic opera-tions of bazaar activities in Sefrou would seem to me to be just as amenable to structural analysis as sacred texts, rites of passage, and other fields of structured meanings.[54]

An issue which lacks adequate discussion in the writings of Geertz (and Ricoeur) is the interrelationship between analyses of literary and nonliterary texts. How are the ethnographer and historian and literary critic to consider literary *and* social textures of meaning in more holistic, integrated programs of analysis?[55] The highly symbolic presence of the Qur'ān in Muslim society, in both written and oral forms—in both literary and performative modes—is an important case in point for the historian of religions. In the next section

I shall conclude my evaluation of Geertz's contribution to the study of religion with a brief discussion of the applicability of some of his concepts to Quranic studies. Despite my reservations on a few matters of concept and method, the ground Clifford Geertz has traversed and charted so well is the same general territory that I, in my study of the Qur'ān, must also cover, albeit from another direction. I find it useful and productive to focus and build upon his approach to understanding Islam as cultural system(s).

QURANIC STUDIES IN LIGHT OF GEERTZ'S CONCEPT OF CULTURE

Clifford Geertz has written briefly about the speech-act nature of Quranic symbolism in Moroccan society.[56] The root of the Arabic term for Muslim scripture, qur'ān, suggests the meaning of "recitation" rather than "writing"–an etymology that virtually all Islamicists have accepted. Not until recently, however, have historians of religions showed much interest in the liturgical and oral aspects of Quranic studies, which I should like to regard as the ritual dimension of sacred speech (lingua sacra).[57] The historian of religions, perhaps more than the ethnographer, must consult the normative texts of Islam as such, and not simply local conceptions of them. Unlike most Islamicists, however, it is relevant for the historian of religions to study scripture also in the contextual spaces of Muslim culture where Qur'ān-school pedagogy, memorization, ritual performance and verbal reference take place. In short, the Qur'ān is not only a revelation in the monotheistic theological sense, nor yet simply a literary text in the philological sense, but a cluster of symbols–written, oral, and performed–which infuse Muslim world views and social ethos.

I have written elsewhere about the theoretical and methodological problems of a speech-act approach to Quranic studies,[58] and admittedly, considerable room remains for criticism and testing of this general approach before we can claim to be able to understand how Quranic meanings arise within the contextual spaces of Muslim culture. In the course of my research, however, I have found that Geertz's concept of culture, especially in his later writings, provides helpful insight into how Quranic symbols become vehicles of meaning in Islamic contexts. It is not unreasonable to anticipate that this discussion might also contribute to the study of scripture generally in the history of religions.

The highly formulaic nature of Quranic speech has been noted by specialists.[59] In his study of pre-Islamic poetry, Michael Zwettler argued that Quranic, like poetic, diction may have developed as the specific oral mode of enunciating a special message, in this case the sacred symbols of the divine revelation. The formulaic nature of Quranic speech enhances its effect as performance in ritual and liturgical contexts.[60] Again, at the surface level of semantics, the constituent analyses of prayer texts by Gill (Navajo) and Sebeok (Chemeris) suggest that patterns of meaning recur throughout the larger body of texts, and that these patterns take on significance in relation to different mythological, ritual and motivational contexts in which the text is recited or performed.[61]

Speech-act theorists, such as Mary Louise Pratt, contend that to make an utterance, oral or literary, "is to perform an act. A person who performs a speech act does at least two and possibly three things. First, he performs a *locutionary act*, the act of producing a recognizable utterance in the given language. Second, he performs an *illocutionary act* of a certain type. "Promising," "warning," "reminding," "informing," or "commanding" are all kinds of illocutionary acts . . . . . Finally, a speaker who performs an illocutionary act may also be performing a *perlocutionary act*; that is, by saying what he says, he may be achieving certain intended results in his hearer in addition to those achieved by the illocutionary act. By warning, a person may frighten him, by arguing one may convince, and so on."[62] It is striking to note that many of the main classes and subclasses of illocutionary acts (discussed at length by philosopher John R. Searle) are obvious functions of Quranic speech. The socio-emotional contexts of Islam in everyday Arabic speech, discussed by Piamenta,[63] also seem relevant. The chief structural ingredient of speech-act contexts is the speaker/audience or text/addresses relationship. An interesting problem for the historian of religions who chooses to work with sacred speech *(lingua sacra)*, especially the Qur'ān, is that in the mythological context of sacred speech, God is the speaker and humankind the addressee. Thus one of the contextual features of authentic Qur'ān recitation is the paradigmatic symbolic context of revelation, to which the Muslim commonwealth *(umma)* refers its consitution. The Prophet's recitation of *sūras* and *āyas*—themselves communicated by Allah through the angel Gabriel to Muhammad—is presented as having taken place on specific occasions during Muhammad's messengership in Mecca and Medina. These specific moments or contexts of revelation (recitations) are adumbrated in various exegetical genres, such as in the "occasions of revelation" *(asbāb al-nuzūl)* literature. It is highly significant that the special moments that continue to give the Muslim community its special Islamic character—corporate and individual prayer, rites of passage, calendrical festivals, and socio-political events—are the kinds of occasions during which the Qur'ān is recited in the Islamic world today; I see these as symbolic reflexes on the sacred time of the Prophet.

Geertz's discussion of world view and ethos, and as well, his essay on thick descriptions, illuminate part of the hermeneutical task of understanding the Qur'ān in text and context. At the level of local cultural context, the ethnographer must uncover perceptions of the normative understandings of the Qur'ān through the uses to which it is put and the elicited pronouncements about its meaning—world view in Geertz's terminology. The historian of religions must go beyond the problematic at the local level by considering the symbol system or "cosmology" of the Qur'ān itself, for as the sacred paradigm of the divine human speech act, it is an important source of world view as this is expressed within specific cultural contexts.

In an attempt to adjust Geertz's use of these terms to a history of religions analysis of Quranic meanings in text *and* context, I take cosmology to constitute a symbolic vision of a supramundane ordering of and relation to mundane reality—a *cosmos* in the classic monotheistic sense of the term. World view refers to the implications this has for normative socio-cultural forms, relationships and institutions. Cosmology is narrated in sacred texts and requires, as Erich Auerbach has so cogently argued for biblical narrative, interpretation.

> The world of Scripture stories is not satisfied with claiming to be a historically true reality—it insists that it is the only real world, is destined for autocracy. All other senses, issues, and ordinances have no right to appear independently of it, and it is promised that all of them, the history of all mankind, will be given their due place within its frame, will be subordinated to it. The Scripture stories do not, like Homer's, court our favor, they do not flatter us that they may please us and enchant us—they seek to subject us, and if we refuse to be subjected we are rebels.[64]

As a species of "ritual language," scriptures also need contextual interpretation, as Wade T. Wheelock has pointed out, because at the level of surface semantics enunciation is choppy, editorial divisions are frequent (chapters, verses, and recitational indicators), and content is largely pronominal and symbolic, not substantive and expository, as in most other kinds of religious writings.[65] Thus, the liturgical or ritual language of the Qur'ān seems to reach out for meaning in the various exegetical and performative contexts that have evolved in Islamic culture.

In light of these observations, I locate cosmology in the sacred text of scripture; it comprises a system of symbolic speaker/addressee events which Muslims learn, recite and perform through repetitive and repeatable oral formulae. By world view I take to mean the normative conceptions of reality which each generation and cultural group of Muslims understands in relation to its own historical situation, through cognitive fusion of sacred symbols with socially shared ranges of semantic and empirical knowledge. Ethos concerns the actual forms people's lives take—the resulting attitudes and ways of doing things that characterize their personal and social existence. Discerning and interpreting the relationships of Quranic cosmology, world view and ethos— symbolization between text and context—is a task that invites history of religions research. To this task I propose to bring speech-act and structuralist analyses, for I think it can be shown that the text of the Qur'ān in its traditional literary and oral forms is an intelligible speech act; it does not require philological exposition and reconstruction to make sense or illumine life's meanings for Muslims, even for—and especially for—those who are functionally illiterate. Moreover, at the deep level of the *langue* of the text, restricted but powerful sets of divine-human interactions appear to have structural relationships: these involve binary oppositions between God and man, obedience and disobedience, angels and satans, faithful and unfaithful humans, reward and punishment, and so on. The *actants*, their doings, and the implicit message of this in the cosmology of the text frames, as Auerbach has said in different words, believers' perceptions of their *Lebenswelt*. The dialectical tacking of this kind of hermeneutic involves bringing into focus the semantic and structural properties of the oral and written text with the literary and socio-cultural contexts of exegesis, pedagogy and performance. Working within the text, the researcher must ultimately find and account for local Muslim significance(s) of its message and meanings; yet in the field the observer must also focus back on the texts that frame such meanings. Writing about the Qur'ān in the history of religions implies both procedures, ultimately perhaps in unending and unendable tension with one another, for meaning, like history, is a social process.

The role of the historian of religions should be neither one of quietly poaching anthropological data (cast in phenomenological terms), nor one of testy rejection of all hearsay evidence gathered by participant observers. We are now in the process of learning, as Clifford Geertz has, that "we look not for a universal property—'sacredness' or 'belief in the supernatural', for example—that divides religious phenomena off from nonreligious ones with Cartesian sharpness, but for a system of concepts that can sum up a set of inexact similarities, we sense to inhere in a given body of material."[66] There is no range or class of data that belongs exclusively to religion, much less to the historian of religions. If a field ethnographer and a hermeneutic philosopher have attempted to grope toward each other in the interpretation of culture, it may be that the historian of religions can play a significant role in the discussion—working as he or she must in both directions from which they, by disciplinary preference, choose to orient themselves.

Notes and References

1. Several colleagues offered valuable comments and criticisms of earlier versions of this paper. They will recognize the significance of their contributions by contrast with the paper in its present form. I am particularly indebted to Dale F. Eickelman of New York University and Robert Hefner of the Institute for Advanced Study for helpful conversations about anthropology and the study of religion.
2. Jacob Neusner, "The Talmud As Anthropology," Annual Samuel Friedland Lecture, The Jewish Theological Seminary, 1978 (pamphlet).
3. Edward Burnett Tylor, The Origins of Culture (New York: Harper and Row, 1958), p. 1.
4. See David Schneider, "Notes Toward a Theory of Culture," in Meaning in Anthropology, ed. Keith H. Basso and Henry A. Selby (Albuquerque, N.M.: University of New Mexico Press, 1976), p. 203.
5. Clifford Geertz, "Ritual and Social Change: A Javanese Example," American Anthropologist 61 (1959); here cited in idem, The Interpretation of Cultures (New York: Basic Books, 1973), pp. 144-45.
6. Wilhalm Dilthey, Gesammelte Schriften VIII, quoted in Theories of History, ed. Patrick Gardiner (New York: The Free Press, 1959), p. 213.
7. E. D. Hirsch, Jr., The Aims of Interpretation (Chicago: University of Chicago Press, 1976), p. 46.
8. Heidegger's term is Horizontverschmelzung; see David Couzens Hou, The Critical Circle: Literature and History in Contemporary Hermeneutics (Berkeley: University of California Press, 1978), pp. 95-98, and E. D. Hirsch, Jr., Validity in Interpretation (New Haven, Conn.: Yale University Press, 1967), pp. 252-54.
9. Gustav E. von Grunebaum, Modern Islam: The Search for Cultural Identity (Berkeley: University of California Press, 1962), p. 13.
10. Ibid.
11. Ibid., pp. 14-15.

12. Cf. Wilfred Cantwell Smith, *Islam in Modern History* (Princeton, NJ: Princeton University Press, 1957), pp. 28-29.
13. Von Grunebaum, *Modern Islam*, p. 37.
14. *Ibid.*, p. 40.
15. See, for example, the discussion of theological perspectives implicit in Friedrich Heiler, *Prayer: A Study in the History and Psychology of Religion* trans, and ed. Samuel McComb (London: Oxford University Press, 1932) by Wade T. Wheelock, "Ritual Language: From Information to Situation," *Journal of the American Academy of Religion* 50/1 (1982): 49-71.
16. Abdallah Laroui, *The Crisis of the Arab Intellectual: Traditionalism or Historicism?*, trans. Diarmid Cammell (Berkeley: University of California Press, 1976), p. 72. Edward W. Said, *Orientalism* (New York: Pantheon Books, 1978), pp. 297-98, cites Laroui's critique of von Grunebaum with approval, although he seems to me to have misunderstood Laroui's point.
17. Clifford Geertz, "Thick Descriptions: Toward an Interpretive Theory of Culture," in *Interpretation of Cultures* (see note 5), p. 15.
18. Northrup Frye, "Criticism and Environment," paper delivered to the International Federation of Modern Languages and Literatures, Scottsdale, Ariz., 1981.
19. See, for example, the approach of Clifford Geertz to this problematic in *The Religion of Java* (Chicago: University of Chicago Press, 1976).
20. See also Geertz, "Thick Descriptions," pp. 20-30.
21. This point was made by Laroui; see note 16 above.
22. Geertz addresses this problem in interesting fashion in the opening essay of *Negara: The Theatre State in Nineteenth-Century Bali* titled "Bali and Historical Method," (Princeton: Princeton University Press, 1980), pp. 3-10.
23. See note 19 above.
24. Clifford Geertz, "Religion As a Cultural System," in *Anthropological Approaches to the Study of Religion*, ed. Michael Banton (London: Tavistock Publications, 1966), (pp. 1-46); republished in Geertz, *Interpretation of Cultures*, p. 88.
25. Clifford Geertz, *Islam Observed: Religious Development in Morocco and Indonesia* (Chicago: University of Chicago Press, 1971).
26. See notes 17 and 5 above.
27. Clifford Geertz, *Peddlers and Princes: Social Change and Economic Modernization in Two Indonesian Towns* (Chicago: University of Chicago Press, 1963).
28. Clifford Geertz, "Suq: The Bazaar Economy in Sefou," in Clifford Geertz, Hildred Geertz, and Lawrence Rosen, *Meaning and Order in Moroccan Society: Three Essays in Cultural Analysis* (Cambridge: Cambridge University Press, 1979), pp. 123-310.
29. For *Negara*, see note 22 above. See also Clifford Geertz, "Deep Play: Notes on the Balinese Cockfight" *Interpretation of Cultures*, pp. 412-53.
30. Robert Redfield, *Peasant Society and Culture: An Anthropological Approach to Civilization* (Chicago: University of Chicago Press, 1956); the complementarity of Redfield's and von Grunebaum's views can be seen in their separate opening essays in *Unity and Variety in Muslim Civilization*, ed. Gustav E. von Grunebaum (Chicago: University of Chicago Press, 1955). Many of the same themes appear in Marshall G. S. Hodgson, *The Venture of Islam: Conscience and History in a World Civilization*, 3 vols. (Chicago: University of Chicago Press, 1974).
31. Clifford Geertz, "Ethos, World-View, and the Analysis of Sacred Symbols," *The Antioch Review* 17/4 (1957): 421-37; republished in Geertz, *The Interpretation of Cultures*, pp. 126-41.
32. Geertz refers to Susanne Langer, *Philosophy in a New Key*, 3d ed. (Cambridge, Mass.: Harvard University Press, 1957). The background to Langer's popular work is Ernst Cassirer, *Philosophie der symbolischen Formen*, 3 vols. (Berlin, 1923), trans. Ralph Manheim as *Philosophy of Symbolic Forms*, 3 vols. (New Haven, Conn.: Yale University Press, 1953).
33. S. Körner, "Cassirer, Ernst," in *The Encyclopedia of Philosophy* 2:44-46. See Geertz, "The Growth of Culture and the Evolution of Mind," in Geertz, *Interpretation of Cultures*, esp. sect. III-IV, pp. 70-83.
34. Geertz, "Religion As a Cultural System," see note 24 above.
35. Geertz, *Islam Observed*, p. 97; cf. "Ethos, World View, and the Analysis of Sacred Symbols," in *Interpretation of Cultures*, pp. 87-125.
36. Geertz, "Suq," see note 28 above, esp. pp. 198-212 subtitled "The Information Situation."
37. Geertz trades on Wilfred Cantwell Smith's discussion of Muslim theological concepts in the latter's pamphlet, "Orientalism and Truth," a public lecture in honor of T. Cuyler

Young, Princeton: Program in Near Eastern Studies, 1969.

38. Geertz, "Thick Descriptions," *Interpretation of Cultures*, p. 5.
39. Geertz, "Religion As a Cultural System," *Interpretation of Cultures*, pp. 87-88.
40. Paul Ricoeur, "The Model of the Text: Meaningful Action Considered As a Text," *Social Research* 38 (1971): 529-62.
41. Ricoeur, "Model of the Text," p. 332 is quoted and discussed but not cited by Geertz, "Thick Descriptions," *Interpretation of Cultures*, p. 19. See also Geertz's discussion of hermeneutics in "From the Native's Point of View," pp. 235-236 (see note 4 above).
42. Ricoeur, "Model of the Text," p. 529.
43. Ricoeur, p. 549; cf. E. D. Hirsch, as cited in notes 7 and 8 above.
44. See note 41 above.
45. Geertz, "Native's Point of View," p. 235.
46. *Ibid.*
47. Geertz, *Negara*, p. 136.
48. Schneider, "Theory of Culture," p. 203 (see note 4 above).
49. On this point, see Abdul Hamid el-Zein, "Beyond Ideology and Theology: The Search for the Anthropology of Islam," *The Annual Review of Anthropology*, ed. Bernard J. Siegel (Palo Alto, Calif.: Annual Reviews Inc., 1977), vol. 6, pp. 227-54, esp. p. 251. The operative notion for Geertz is "Symbolic Action." See "Thick Descriptions," p. 10, and "Ideology As a Cultural System," pp. 208-209, *Interpretation of Cultures*. In his discussions of "symbolic action" Geertz refers to Susanne Langer and Kenneth Burke; the utility of this notion is that it links to meaning both textual and social data. While it is useful to see that human actions express meanings, it is also important to recognize that actions remain a separate empirical matter, capable of eluding meaning, even for those by whom they are performed, in any given circumstances.
50. Suggestive of this tension between meaningful constructions of reality and reality itself is the essay by Jonathan Z. Smith, "Map Is Not Territory," in Smith, *Map Is Not Territory: Studies in History of Religions* (Leiden: E. J. Brill, 1978), pp. 289-309.
51. Moshe Piamenta, *Islam in Everyday Arabic Speech* (Leiden: E. J. Brill, 1979).
52. Paimenta, *Islam*, p. 1.
53. Geertz, "Religion As a Cultural System," *Interpretation of Cultures*, p. 100.
54. See the reference to Geertz's article on the *sūq*, note 28 above.
55. The problem of literary versus oral modes of cultural transmission, in partial reference to Muslim history and societies, has been discussed by Jack Goody, *The Demostication of the Savage Mind* (Cambridge: Cambridge University Press, 1977). See also Marilyn R. Waldman, "Primitive Mind/Modern Mind: New Approaches to an Old Problem Applied to Islam," in *Islam and the Study of Religion: Essays on the Study of a Religious Tradition*, ed. Richard C. Martin (Tucson, Ariz.: University of Arizona Press, forthcoming).
56. Clifford Geertz, "Art As a Cultural System," *Modern Language Notes* 93 (1976): 1473-99. See also "Suq," note 28 above.
57. See William A. Graham, "The Earliest Meaning of Qur'ān: An Islamic Contribution to the Understanding of Scripture," in *Islam and the Study of Religion* (see note 55 above), and Kristina Nelson, "The Art of Reciting the Qur'ān," (Ph.D. diss., University of California, Berkeley, 1980). Both works serve to orient Quranic studies toward speech-act conceptions of social meaning.
58. Richard C. Martin, "Understanding the Qur'ān in Text and Context," *History of Religions* 21/4 (1982): 361-84.
59. See John Wansbrough, *Quranic Studies: Sources and Methods of Scriptural Interpretation* (Oxford: Oxford University Press, 1977), and the following note.
60. Michael Zwettler, *The Oral Tradition of Classical Arabic Poetry: Its Character and Implications* (Colombus, Ohio: Ohio State University Press, 1978).
61. Sam D. Gill, *Sacred Words: A Study of Navajo Religion and Prayer* (Westport, Conn.: Greenwood Press, 1981), and Thomas A. Sebeck, *Structure and Texture* (The Hague: Mouton, 1974).
62. Mary Louise Pratt, *Toward a Speech Act Theory of Literary Discourse* (Bloomington, Ind.: Indiana University Press, 1977), pp. 80-81.
63. See note 51 above.
64. Erich Auerbach, *Mimesis: The Representation of Reality in Western Literature*, trans. Willard R. Trask (Princeton: Princeton University Press, 1953), pp. 14-15.
65. Wade T. Wheelock, "Ritual Language: From Information to Situation," *Journal of the American Academy of Religion* 50/1 (1982): 49-71.
66. Geertz, *Islam Observed*, pp. 96-97.

CHAPTER II

From Geertz's Ethnography to an Ethnotheology?

Joanne Punzo Waghorne

> . . . there remains, when he attempts to give a description of savage or half-savage tribes and their religion, the immense difficulty that not one of these religions has any recognized standards . . . there is no Bible, no prayer book, no catechism. Religion floats in the air, and each man takes as much or as little of it as he likes.
>
> — F. Max Muller

Historians of religions initiated into the line of F. Max Muller have inherited a curious behavioral trait: the tendency to act like theologians among anthropologists and anthropologists amid theologians. To theologians, historians of religion such as Joachim Wach and, more recently, Wilfred Cantwell Smith and Ninian Smart declare that normative text is but one medium of divine revelation.[1] Look, they say, to human behavior, to the products of human culture, to human history for a "a comprehensive but articulated inventory of the varieties of expression"[2] of the human experience of the divine. F. Max Muller's voice lingers directing the theologian toward the revelation of religion available from an anthropology: "The Divine, if it is to reveal itself at all to us, will best reveal itself in our own human form."[3] Yet when among anthropologists, the historian of religions offers versions of Max Muller's early theological critique of anthropology:[4] The anthropologists' inventory of religion is too small, too unconscious of text and of the normative traditions of advanced cultures, and too facile in its reduction of religion to a single encompassing behavioral definition. Ugo Bianchi restated this perspective recently: The history of religions continues to search primarily for an "identification of a religious 'quality' " in human behavior and a "sensitivity to the religious fact as such." This sensitivity rests with a broad based approach which must remain "in constant contact with the concrete data of religion" and also not be limited "to the mere immediate and reflected finalities" of simple common needs.[5] In the face of anthropologists, then, historians of religions look to text or to the kind of historical research which transcends any overly concretized study of behavior. But placed eyeball to eyeball with theologians, the historian of religions inevitably shouts for a consideration of concrete human expression and experience.

Until recently, this latent inconsistency in the approach of history of religions toward its two major "conversation partners"[6] remained masked by a careful balancing of the two perspectives. Historians of religions, like theologians, fundamentally studied the normative texts (and myth as if it were normative text) of non-western traditions. But like anthropologists, they regarded these texts not as unmediated divine revelation but rather as documents of human ideas, and of human actions expressing religious experience. This was Max Muller's initial approach, and the tradition of this method continues. Not surprisingly when historians of religions left their libraries and traveled abroad, they never engaged in the kind of field research of raw human behavior that came to dominate anthropology. To text, the historians of religions added "context". To their approach to text, they added the "insights" derived from the field research of anthropologists. Thus even in this present volume, the theories of Levi-Strauss, Victor Turner, or even Clifford Geertz are borrowed to aid the historian of religion in reading texts with the keener eye toward their cultural or social milieu. The historian of religions until recently has not confronted the raw, concrete, and highly particular data of religious behavior. As long as texts are available, as long as comparative material abounds, the historian of religions remains safe in this customary methodology. But what will happen when the historian of religions in search of data to investigate some key problem, is forced to face the anthropologists in the field bereft of any clear nominative texts or even comparative material, and then is forced to return to the theologian with little except concrete behavioral data to offer as an expression of "natural theology"?[7]

This paper could, in fact, be called the true confessions of an historian of religions in just such a dilemma. Seeking to uncover much needed data on sacral kingships in South India (a perfectly respectable topic for any historian of religions), I went to the former royal state of Pudukkottai and found myself in the arid backlands of Tamilnadu with numerous people who declared openly that they had regarded (and in some cases continued to regard) their raja as a god on earth. But there were no normative *texts* for this kingship. Brahmins called the system *pauranika* or not *vaidika* which they loosely translated into English as "popular" and not orthodox. But this state did not lack written records. There were over a century's worth of day-to-day orders, requisitions, and petitions which issued from the council and the palace of the king. And yet somewhere amid the orders for tennis balls and palace liveries was a functioning sacral kingship.

It is at this point and on this level of "ethnography" that the work of Clifford Geertz became important. For Geertz was the single most articulate defender of ethnography as *the* method of anthropology. Moreover, Geertz unlike the fieldwork textbooks does not speak in mere mechanical how-to language; he speaks fluent hermeneutics. For the historian of religions up the backcountry without a textual paddle, Geertz's "ethnography" began to provide a method for ordering the vast pieces of what he calls "the informal logic of actual life." His careful explanation of "thick description" as a hermeneutics challenges the historian of religions to take a second look at the very methodological assumptions that originally drove the discipline away from the study of immediate behavior and toward the once removed abstractions of text. But Geertz's clarity with his method of "ethnography" also allows the historians of religions to strengthen their theological eye and to begin to see through the assumptions of Geertz's own "ethnography" into the possibility of developing what might be called an "ethno-theology". But all of these issues should, by the very rules of field research, be discussed in the concrete context of an historian of religions engaged in "exceedingly extended acquaintances with extremely small matters" in the little kingdom of Pudukkottai.

I. ON THE BORDERS OF ORTHODOX INDIA

The kingdom of Pudukkottai was established in the seventeenth century on the fringe of three urban centers in one of South India's perennial hinterland regions. Ancient Tamil poets termed such areas *mullai*: unstable agricultural belts whose lords were often as uncultivated as the soil. Politically, Pudukkottai swung its alliance successively from the Telegu kingdoms of Vijayanagar to the Tamil lords of Tanjore and Madurai, and later to the British at Trichinopoly. By the nineteenth century, the vicissitudes of history left Pudukkottai the only semi-independent state within the Tamil speaking region of British India. Yet in spite of its longevity as a native state, the Pudukkottai rajas were never considered by those outside the state to be "real kings" and to this day are still termed by my informants as "petty chiefs of old time South India" who had "just some of this tribal religion".[8] The Pudukkottai rajas seem to have remained forever on the fringe.

This marginal quality of Puddukkottai's sacral kingship emerged as the most important feature of my own initial field research in the state. The peripheral nature of kingship was admitted even within the borders of Pudukkottai in many ways, some subtle and others overt. The semi-tribal Kallar caste origin of the Tondaiman family was never disguised either in present conversation or in the oldest court epic genealogies.[9] Other low caste founders of more central states often did make claims to true royal caste status.[10] In addition, the royal rituals in Pudukkottai such as the coronation *(pattabhisheka)* did not pretend to Vedic orthodoxy. The classification of these as *pauranika*, "popular" was enormously significant as an acknowledgement that Pudukkottai did not follow normative texts. *Pauranika* rites are those performed according to present custom and not according to eternal law. As the lack of normative texts for royal rituals became clear, so did the consistant choice to have this remain so. By the time of the last coronation in 1928, Pudukkottai, as the only Tamil native state, could have been expected to lay claim to a more orthodox legitimacy using Vedic or even normative Agama texts for the coronation.[11] Yet a priest who was present at this coronation confirmed that no normative text was used. Only the mantras from a late Sanskrit text were adopted.[12] Gradually I was forced to admit the possibility that Pudukkottai in the midst of Sanskritic texts and Tamil ideals of perfect kingship,[13] rejected absorption into *any* orthodox model thus overtly confirming what those from urban areas had always held — that they were hinterland chiefs still with "just some of this tribal religion."

The importance of the non-normative quality of kingship in Pudukkottai was confirmed by the findings of historians of Hindu polity who had turned their attention to such marginal areas in recent years. Burton Stein first described the long term phenomenon of fluctuant relationships between the "nuclear areas", stable urban centers, and the outlying forested regions in South India. Stein defined the distinction between the *periyanadu*, the "big states", and those smaller territorial units in forested areas as a distinction between "stable highly ordered regions" which were "centers of Hindu culture" and "the other type of power center" which "consisted of isolated, tribally organized, upland and forest people".[14] The nature of this "other type" of power center has been more closely defined throughout India and termed "hinterland regions" or "little kingdoms". In times of upheavel of central authority, these little kingdoms appeared to function as the base unit of Hindu polity and yet their own internal polity was far from stable. Richard Rox's description of "state-hinterland relationships" in north India posits a five-stage cycle in the constant rise and fall of dominant royal lines in these outlying regions: An adventurous clan conquers a wasteland area and establishes rule. A dominant member of the clan arises as king only to fall back into obscurity as new "adventurer-freebooters" return to make anarchy and to seed a new impermanent order.[15]

The marginality of such kingship was culturally expressed in marginal imagery. A powerful example is given by Thomas Metcalf in his study of the rajas of Oudh, "The physical symbol of this quasi-independent political status can be found in the sturdy mud fort, fortified with cannon and surrounded on every side with dense growths of jungle which lay at the heart of every talukdari estate."[16] Again in South India, Nicholas P. Dirk's description of epic genealogical literature confirms that hinterland kingship was set in the imagery of the movement between "Forest/Field, Disorder/Order, Nonritual/Ritual, Periphery/Center".[17] Thus, while kings over nuclear areas quickly legitimized their rule by the adaptation of a clear paradigm of stable kingship[18], there is good evidence that hinterland kings could no more settle into a single paradigm of stability than they could permanently settle themselves to the land.

The case of Pudukkottai, then, presents a special challenge for the historian of religions. Pudukkottai's hide-and-seek relationship with normative texts and stable polity is curious. This was not a primitive people without the tools of literacy to create texts. Likewise, the kingdom did not lack the intellectual resources to hammer its royal system into abstracted philosophical or even ritual discourse. Brahmins literate in Sanskrit had long been patronized by the rajas, yet the royal system in the kingdom continued to be defined in praxis but not in text.

Those historians confronted with a similar lack of historical texts in such hinterland regions have turned to "ethno-history" in order to define and analyze the nature of a praxis oriented system. Certainly historians of religions have often taken a similar route and borrowed from ethnography to supply data when texts fail. Yet here in Pudukkottai what is needed is a very special sense of the ethnographic method capable of including historical sources within the bounds of field research *and* able to deal with religious practice inside larger highly literate textually oriented systems. For here in Pudukkottai, it is not enough to abstract praxis into a simple formulation of the "hidden" structure of this or that ritual. Some careful account must be made of the fact that this sacral kingship system itself refused to create its own abstracted model. Enter Clifford Geertz.

Clifford Geertz has seen himself as a reformer within anthropology on that issue which is so relevant to Pudukkottai. Like the kings and people of this hinterland region, Geertz has refused to allow the domain of anthropology to move away from behavior into abstracted theoretical formulations. He has held to this position throughout his career. His first major methodological article spoke out against "abstract and rather scholastic arguments" on moral values in philosophy but already looked forward to a development of a "proto-theory" in which a new empiricism would provide hope to a stagnant academic world. "One almost certain result of such an empirically oriented, theoretically sophisticated, symbol-stressing approach to the study of values is the decline of analyses which attempt to describe moral, aesthetic and other normative activities in terms of theories based not on observation of such activities but on logical considerations alone."[19]

Geertz began by pulling the normative rug out from under pure "logical considerations" in philosophy but soon applied this same formulation to a critique of anthropology. "Normative" could not be defined as a thing abstractable from behavior especially in a discipline that began by examining behavior. Interestingly, he reserved his most savage attack on this "mistake" for his fellow anthropologist C. Levi-Strauss: "For what Levi-Strauss has made for himself is an infernal culture machine. It annuls history, reduces sentiment to a shadow of the intellect, and replaces the particular minds of particular savages in particular jungles with the Savage Mind immanent in us all."[20] Geertz's critique of the fallacy of abstraction reached the most articulate form in "Thick Description". For here Geertz finally developed his proto-theory beyond a limited critique of idea or scholasticism to a method defined over and against the very essense of the major methods of nineteenth century anthropology and history of religions: comparison.

In "Thick Description" Geertz never openly names comparison as the chief methodological obstacle to the development of a sophisticated ethnography. He simply draws a picture of a donkey without writing "ass" underneath. Assertions against much of the groundwork of comparison abound. For example, Geertz declares that anthropology can not gain empirical access to cultural systems by "arranging abstracted entities into unified patterns." Theory must remain close to the "bodied stuff" on which it feeds. For, cultural analysis is "not discovering the Continent of Meaning and mapping out its bodiless landscape" nor moving theory toward "some empyrean realm of de-emotionalized forms."[21] Geertz here never names comparison as the enemy because his argument is not with the possibility or even the necessity of cross-cultural comparisons but rather with comparison as a method of analysis which has tended to value the form over substance, the general at the expense of the particular, and the system above the subject.

Geertz's "ethnography", then, is a method oriented toward the study of behavior without ever subsuming that behavior into an abstracted model. This kind of ethnography may well suit the equally non-idealizing Pudukkottaiyans. Yet because Geertz pits his ethnographic method against the logic of the comparative method as practiced by both anthropology and the history of religions, the rise of this brand of ethnography requires a major mental effort for the historian of religions. No historian of religions can willingly adapt Geertz's methods in practice without fully realizing the impact of this upon some of the most basic working assumptions of the discipline. For abandoning the axioms of the comparative method to "ethnography" for the historian of religions may well be like rejecting the primordial authority of a father.

II. THE ETHNOGRAPHIC AND THE COMPARATIVE METHODS

A critique of the methods of anthropology at the level of ethnography has received little serious attention by historians of religions. The overriding emphasis given to comparison as "the very method of the history of religions"[22] has reduced ethnography to a data-collecting tool beyond the interests of a library oriented discipline. Of course, this same attitude was long shared by anthropologists who during the Victorian era were as much library theoreticians as the historians of religions. Anthropologists separated themselves from ethnographers whose work they used as the raw data on "the peoples of . . ." for their own manufacture of comparative theory. Max Muller's early critique of the rising new discipline of anthropology noted his concern over the unsophisticated methods used to collect raw data[23] but quickly turned to question the exclusive use of such material as a basis for the comparative study of religion.

At the turn of the century, L. H. Jordan granted that anthropology had proven invaluable in supplying "rich and undreamed-of discoveries" but quickly turned to critique the use of some of this new evidence in "the unskilled employment of a method which is still unfamiliar in its hand" – comparison. Anthropology created grand comparative theories about religion using only "very meagre and uncertain" sources from remote ages and ethnographic data from "the religions of savage communities." "Comparative Religion, on the other hand", Jordan affirmed, "insists that the spiritual impulses which reveal themselves in man can best be studied in their higher and more organized forms." Anthropologists could never become "leaders, in command of the field" because of their own doubtful skills at the logic of comparison and of course because, "They are prone to treat with contempt the theory that religion perhaps, after all, may owe something to an express divine revelation." No study of human behavior alone, especially of "savages" could yield a true understanding of the nature of religion which for Jordan as for Max Muller was bound to "organized forms" expressed, they assumed, in text.[24]

Anthropologists now have become their own participant-observers but two recent discussions of anthropology in relationship to the history of religions still echo Jordan's emphasis on the critical use of comparison and what could be called the theological openness of the history of religions. Jonathan Z. Smith's important historical overview of the use of comparison in scholarship classifies the ethnographic genre as one of the least sophisticated methods of comparison in use now and in the past. Smith traces the method back to Herodotus's Ionian ethnography of the land and the people type which merely sought to find the most humanly familiar in the foreign land. Smith argues that this ancient "traveler's eye" report still resembles the contents of a contemporary field research report. He chides this observer's vision for its lack of "apparent analytical mediation". Explicit in his critique is also the familiar lament of the historian of religions that such a mundane catalogue of customs often reduces the "gods or theology" of a society to those aspects of cultic life that "has been seen by the observer."[25] Ugo Bianchi's critique of the "Religio-anthropological Approach" begins by acknowledging that "in positive-inductive research, phenomenology, morphology and typology of religion must result from and be continuously nurtured by historical study and from the correct application of the historical-comparative method." While admitting the recent sophistication of field work in anthropology in providing reliable data, Bianchi turns away from any direct critique of the ethnographic method to question ". . . what the role of comparison may be . . . for the social anthropologist does not, today, renounce the method of comparison and the elaboration of general theories on the basis both of his work 'in the field' and of books and material concerning other cultures."[26] Bianchi then offers a delightful critique of the distinguished participant-observers, Victor Turner and Mary Douglas, at the point when they move from their particular areas to the formulation of general theories.

Both Bianchi and Smith clearly assume that comparison remains the major method for both anthropology and the history of religions. Bianchi further implies that no comprehensive theory on religion could ever arise from the particularism of field research alone. The "historical-comparative method" recommended by Bianchi allows the study of religion to "transcend that initial and insufficient level of enquiry (its functional level) which we would reach by limiting our consideration to the more immediate and reflected finalities of the practices of . . ."[27] Smith likewise remains certain that no thought is free from comparison — "the omnipresent substructure of human thought". In the shadow of comparison ethnography is reduced to the simplest level of "we/they" and hardly a major method of the study of religion. Thus as in the earlier dismissals of ethnography by historians of religions, these recent theoreticians likewise regard field work/ethnography as only one step toward the comparative method.

Historians of religions consider ethnography as adjunct tool, at best, to the primary task of comparison. And yet the exact reasons for this subordination of ethnography have never been clearly articulated. All are concerned that ethnography unearths a kind of data that is overly concrete – overly particular. Max Muller expressed this in his concern that "savage behavior" unbridled by the normality of text merely "floats in the air" and in the subjective tastes of each "savage". Smith implicitly views ethnography as an undisciplined, subjective meeting with "the other" and Bianchi worries over the particularism of any single event viewed outside of a full historical-comparative context. Implied in these concerns over the merely particular lies the essense of Geertz's own defense of ethnography. For Geertz, the single behavioral act is indeed neither particular nor subjective. For Geertz, the locus of culture is precisely in the particular – in an act of behavior.

For Geertz the ethnographic method implies more than an observation of behavior. Behavior itself, the particular act of acting, becomes the alpha and omega of both research and theory. Ironically, Geertz turns away from the search for morphological types which was the ground of comparison to avoid precisely the same problem that Jonathan Z. Smith and Ugo Bianchi see in unsophisticated uses of comparison. All are concerned that a universal theory of "religion" or "culture" overly idealize types at the expense of "the reality of concretes" in Bianchi's term, or the map without territory for Smith, or the "bodiless landscapes" feared by Geertz. Yet Smith remains certain that the basic logic of comparison "How am I to apply what the one thing shows me to the case of two things?" remains the key question for the study of religion.[28] Ugo Bianchi still hopes for a "concrete universal" which would save the morphological enterprise of the history of religions. Only Geertz, the anthropologist, is willing to leave the formulations of universal vs. the particular far behind. Geertz has turned back to "ethnography" as the starting point for a philosophical leap out of the baffling dualities of concrete/transcendent, subjective/objective, example/type.

At this point, the real shock value of Geertz's definition of ethnography as *the* methodology of anthropology can easily become lost amid the fast moving pace of his own sometimes all too fluid style. "Thick Description" clothes a sophisticated philosophical enterprise in highly readable prose. Geertz used "Thick Description" to sandwich his earlier theoretical writings into a tight packet with the earlier loose ends neatly folded inside. Yet, "Thick Description" is the culmination of two decades in which Geertz moved from a "vague and imprecise . . . kind of proto-theory" (by this own admission)[29] to a confident methodological position on the nature of culture. During these years, Geertz engaged in a kind of trilogue between his own ethnographic fieldwork, recent philosophy on the nature of symbolic action, and the growing field of cultural anthropology. Geertz was never willing throughout this period to leave any aspect of this three-way conversation behind. Anthropology had to adopt the clarity of philosophy in order to develop a "theoretical analysis of symbolic action comparable in sophistication to that we now have for social and psychological actions".[30] All this was to be accomplished without losing the discipline's ethnographic roots.

Geertz's earliest work openly acknowledged his own philosophical debt to Susanne Langer and as late as 1966 much of his theoretical language continued to adopt her formulations on the nature of symbol as a kind of embodied idea. Geertz then called symbols "concrete embodiments of ideas, attitudes, judgments, longings, or beliefs" with the empirical addendum that such concrete symbols are "social events like any other; they are as public as marriage and as observable as agriculture" and not ever abstractable from these events.[31] Geertz's formulation here leaves room for some transcendent "ideas" or "attitudes", to ultimately emerge from their supposed non-abstractable concreteness at the level of interpretation and theory-making. By 1973, however, Geertz had ceased to define symbol via this incarnational theory of ideas.

In "Thick Description", Geertz's understanding of culture as symbol had matured into a model of culture as the arch "semiotic"[32] enterprise. Now the language of behavior had no referent beyond itself. Action, thought, ideas are encompassed in "transient examples of shaped behavior".[33] Never explicitly but certainly implicitly, Geertz took anthropology into some rather new philosophical waters. By 1973, Geertz seemed conversant with the then nascent post-structuralist movement in France. In what has been called the "Saussure/Levi-Strauss/French-literary-critic-axis",[34] Geertz's ethnographic theory appears to develop the long sought philosophical sophistication.

Geertz's re-definition of ethnography when viewed in the context of post-structuralism comes alive as a serious revolt against the base logic of the comparative method. The essense of post-structuralism, the extension and yet the revolt against Levi-Strauss is described by T. K. Seung as "a reversal in attitude toward universality and particularity. Whereas formalists in general were enamored of universality and uniformity, post-formalists have tended to disdain them because of their obsession with particularity and diversity . . ."[35] This obsession with particularity has radically shifted the focus of study from the search for the universals *in* the various symbol systems generated by culture to a look at *sign* as the definition of culture itself. The particular power of this new analysis is its radical transcendence of the old dualities of subject/object, particular/universal, temporal/eternal within the context of theory-making, as well as data-collecting. The earlier logic of comparison assumed, as does J. Z. Smith's eternal question of how-is-one-like-another, that ultimately interpretation itself was possible only in the mode of object/universal/eternal and not in the mode of subject/particular/temporal. Post-structuralism denies this axiom and the implied dualities; hence, Geertz declares with full confidence that: "The interminable, because unterminable, debate within anthropology as to whether culture is 'subjective' or 'objective,' together with the mutual exchange of intellectual insights ('idealist!' — 'materist!'; 'mentalist!' — 'behaviorist!'; impressionist!' — 'positivist!') which accompanies it, is wholly misconceived."[36]

In "Thick Description" and later in *Negara*, Geertz sets his own discussion of ethnography in opposition to the unexamined nineteenth century philosophical assumptions about the nature of subjectivity and particularity. Geertz views with concern the scholarly worship of Culture as something transcendent to common sense existence. Thus Geertz aims his iconoclastic critique equally against those who run after brute behavioral patterns and those who ideate Culture as a "self-contained 'super-organic' reality."[37] The location of culture in patterns or in the mind are variants of a single misconception: the inability to understand that behavior itself already embodies "culture" or "religion". With an invocation to Wittgenstein, Geertz argues that since thinking must not be viewed as a mental process independent of the process of expressing a thought, so too culture can not be abstracted as a thing separate from the expression of culture. Declaring that modern philosophy has thrown down "meaning" and "culture" as "occult" entities,[38] Geertz chides anthropology to put aside such nineteenth century "fears of metaphysical ghosts."[39] Culture is no thing at all: nothing *in* the mind, and nothing *in* behavioral patterns. Culture *is* because and only because shaped behavior *is*.

Like the Saussure/Levi-Strauss/post-structuralist axis, Geertz has cast out a covey of assumptions which he feels had bewitched the nineteenth century mind. First, like Saussure, Geertz posits the independence of all linguistic phenomenon from dependence on either the perceiving subject or on the object of reference. Saussure had already included cultural expression within his semiology, according to a recent review, "via the notions that he shared with Durkheim about the role of language as the social phenomenon par excellence . . ."[40] But, with Levi-Strauss, Geertz shared the conviction that culture itself was a language — the ultimate linguistic phenomenon. And as a language, culture was not a *product* but the very *essence* of socialized life. However, Geertz went beyond Saussure and Levi-Strauss. Like the new French critics of both scholars, Geertz was not satisfied to abolish merely the old arguments that symbol-language is made — projected from the subjective needs of collective individuality (a la Freud); or that culture is *made* by some transcendent force (the theologian's God, or even Hegel's Geist); or that cultural symbols are made from the muddled experience of nature in an unscientific age (Taylor). Geertz's sense of the independence of the language of culture from subject or object referents is radical. Geertz would abolish any sense of transcendence, any abstraction from the concreteness of enacted behavior, even within the perimeter of independent language.

The early semiologists deny subject and object references outside of the sphere of linguistic phenomenon, but they did permit some older dualities to exist *within* the realm of language. Saussure allowed for a duality of *langue/parole* — the form of language in relationship to its occurrance in a specific speech act. Husserl allowed for a "transcendental subjectivity" to direct particular language and of course, Heidegger's Being moves beyond each particular expression of its own essence.[41] Like the post-structuralist Jacques

Derrida, Geertz atacks even this internal duality within semiology. In "Thick Description", Geertz carefully distinguishes his own methods from cognitive anthropology and the work of Ward Goodenough which "may look close enough to the one being developed here to be mistaken for it . . ." Cognitive anthropology commits the fallacy of identifying culture with the "systematic rules" that supposedly motivate it rather than defining culture as ongoing rule inseparable from enactment. Again Geertz's earlier critique of Levi-Strauss dwelt on this mistake of turning patterns of cultural language into "frozen reason — a coincidence of forms — not affective, not historical, not functional."[42] Here Geertz's insistence on the absolute inseparability of concept and action bears a striking resemblance to Derrida's theory on the absolute co-incidence of signified concept and expression:

> . . . the signified concept is never present in itself, in an adequate presence that would refer only to itself. Every concept is necessarily and essentially inscribed in a chain or a system, within which it refers to another and to other concepts, by the systematic play of differences. Such a play, then — difference — is no longer simply a concept, but the possibility of conceptuality, of the conceptual system and process in general.[43]

This post-structural sense of the ever-flowing process of language, the temporality and particularity of all conceptualization, marks Geertz's latest ethnographic portrait of Bali. In *Negara*, the inseparability of act-and-concept, of historical event-and-conceptual model is reflected intrinsically in the very organization of the book. Here Geertz's study of the "ritual state" begins not with a description of ritual per se but with three complex chapters on such hard core history as alliance forms, village polity, irrigation systems, and forms of trade! At last, Geertz discusses "spectacle and ceremony" with the cold insistence that the content of such ritual can not be the sole definition of symbol. The entire historical spectrum, the process and unfolding of all events was in Bali symbolic — "A structure of action, now bloody, now ceremonious . . ."[44] In *Negara*, there could be no concept above action nor action without conception. In a grand bow to the entire culture-as-semiotics theory, Geertz ends *Negara* with the statement: "The dramas of the theatre state, mimetic of themselves, were, in the end, neither illusions nor lies, neither sleight of hand nor make-believe. *They were what there was.*"[45]

In *Negara*, Geertz has implicitly re-introduced an empirical ethnographic context to the reliance on philosophical and logical considerations alone that have marked post-structuralism. Ironically, in his persistent drive to define all arguments for particularity and concreteness in terms of ethnography, Geertz has answered Levi-Strauss's own recent critique of post-structuralism as "sentimental pastimes which feed on badly digested summary knowledge."[46] Just as Saussure's initial model of language allowed Levi-Strauss to turn ethnographic experience into ethnographic theory, the new semiotic enterprise allowed Geertz to turn his ethnography from a method of research into a "form of knowledge." Ethnography a la Geertz could change from a tool into an epistomology only because semiotics had broken the metaphysical foundations of the old search for universal concepts. All behavior could now be termed "shaped behavior" – concept embedded in action. "Concept" had no ontological status outside of expression. Ethnography, as the study of action, was the only method that could suit this new philosphical position.

Given the new philosophical base, the old comparative method of both anthropology and the history of religion seems left without teeth and with little to chew on. Comparison assumed not only that culture was concepts but that such concepts could be isolated as universal phenomenon. Geertz and the poststructuralist do not deny that concept exists – they deny that concepts are ever free from expression and from particularity. The search for morphology of culture makes no sense unless the form is assumed to be abstractable from the living body. And that abstracted form comes to be the ultimate definition of the thing studied. Hence Geertz recoils against anthropology's isolation of Culture as "some mysterious entity transcending material existence".[47] For the new ethnography, there exists only cultural acts (plural); there is no Culture (singular).

A substition to the world Religion for Culture in the preceding paragraphs should send some serious shock waves into history of religions. The latent fear of the particularity and concreteness of ethnography in the discipline may indeed be related to an old unexamined but ever present need to protect Religion as a reality with purposes and forces of its own. What Geertz's ethnography proposes is a step into a dark area of our own theological unconsciousness where the intellectual pursuit of Religion merely masks an attempt to remain faithful to a transcendent God by avoiding the potential heresy that religions are fully embodied in human behavior. Even a quick glance at the language used to describe immanent religious experience begins to sound suspiciously Biblical. The early emphasis of Max Muller and Jordan on "revelation" clearly attempts to protect a sense of Something that can be revealed or Someone who reveals. Max Muller's major concern with the textless "savages" was their lack of any clearly identifiable "religion" which existed outside of their subjective needs. Jordan's bow to "divine revelation" also resisted the hidden heresy of a religion fully incarnate in human behavior. Joachim Wach's discussion of universals hedges at the point of materialized divinity. Wach willingly admits that "All human action will be *conditioned* by the physical *material* in which and with which alone it can work." But after a brief paragraph which begins to move in a direction similar to Geertz's emphasis on embodied culture, Wach feels compelled to add a warning: "Tone, word, colour, stone, wood and metal are universal media by means of which man has tried to give expression to the profoundest experience of which he is capable. He has become a *secondary creator*. The dangers which must accompany this development . . ." At this point Wach slips into a discussion of the Hebrew prophets.[48] Bianchi assumes a "religious fact as such" as well as "concrete univerasals." Even Jonathan Z. Smith, who more than any other recent historian of religion has abjured the religion-out-there model, still chides ethnography for ignoring those aspects of human culture "that can not be observed" in daily behavior. By Geertz's logic, then, the comparative method of the history of religions does not merely generate theory but identifies that theory with the "thing" studied: Religion. Thus the comparative method may provide an endless self-fulfilling proof of the existence of Religion — an entity extractable from the day to day transient examples of behavior or a divine essence revealed *in* but not identifiable *with* human behavior.

At this point it is possible to return to some direct questions: Why do historians of religions find it difficult to deal directly with observable behavior? Why do they seek normative texts where they may be found and shun those areas where texts are not and can not be made? Pushing Geertz's ethnographic logic a bit beyond Geertz may reveal an answer. The comparative method protects the silent ontology of history of religion's Religion. That "occult entity" of Religion, like Culture, seems to have the subtle nature of an idea or a thing so holy that it can never be revealed fully in visible form. In fact, the more obviously visible the expression, the less identifiable with the "true" nature of Religion it becomes. Hence the order of precedent established by Max Muller continues: those-who-do are not as close to the nature of Religion as those-who-imagine or conceptualize, and of course, those who-think-about are the keenest seers of all. Written another way, this formula yields the axiom that text, already in purer abstracted form reveals more than practice; and, interpretation, a step closer to pure form, reveals nearly all. Geertz's ethnography would radically reverse this order: action here speaks louder than words.

The most crucial difference in comparativist's thirst for texts and the ethnographer's eye for behavior is illustrated ironically in the context in which Geertz invokes "the model of a text" as an interpretive tool. In "Thick Description", Geertz describes any instance of "shaped behavior" as an "acted document" which must be "read like a text". In "Thick Description" and his book, *Negara*, the "model of a text" is explicitly and practially developed with acknowledgment to the work of Paul Ricoeur. Yet at the very moment Geertz invokes Ricoeur, he subtly but clearly denies an important aspect of Ricoeur's philosophy: the primacy of interpretation over ritual action. For Geertz, the emphasis forever remains on "acted" and not on "document", on "behavioral" and not on "text". Yet Ricoeur in *The Symbolism of Evil* theorizes a movement from symbolic actions to the rise of "thought" in the movement from primitive to modern. The modern interpreter of symbolic action in fact knows more of the meaning of the action than the actor himself. (Here Ricoeur follows Heidegger.) In "The Model of the Texts", this is explicit: "Henceforth, only the meaning 'rescues' the meaning, without the contribution of the physical and psychological presence of the author. But to say that the meaning rescues meaning is to say that only interpretation is the 'remedy' for the weakness of discourse which its author can no longer 'save'."[49]

Geertz, indeed adopts Ricoeur's logic that action can and must be interpreted and that each behavioral moment has much to say. But Geertz, the ethnographer, will not acknowledge that his interpretation, that his pen, is ever mightier than the deed: "Nor have I ever gotten anywhere near to the bottom of anything I have ever written about . . . Cultural analysis is intrinsically incomplete. And, worse than that, the more deeply it goes the less complete it is . . . But that, along with plaguing subtle people with obtuse questions is what being an ethnographer is all about."[50] Geertz may translate the meaning of action, but he never will release "meaning" from that action in a way that makes "meaning" more important than the action itself for "to divorce it from what happens – from what, in this time or that place, specific people say, what they do . . . is to divorce it from its applications and render it vacant".[51] Ethnographers may " 'inscribe' social discourse", they may "fix" and hence preserve what is said, they may read this fixed behavior as a text, and interpret it on the model of a text, but ethnographers must not make normative texts: "In short, anthropological writings are themselves interpretations, and second and third order ones to boot. (By definition only a native makes first order ones: It's *his* culture) . . ."[52] For Geertz, any behavior holds meaning in full; all the rest is translation and "experiment" with understanding . . . even the native "texts" are less potent than native behavior, and the scholar's interpretation sits on the ring farthest from the real source of power – action itself. In Geertz's ethnographic hands, behavior-as-text affirms the primacy of behavior and ultimately reduces the status of text.[53]

The value of Geertz's own ethnographic method becomes strikingly important for those regions like Pudukkottai in which text has in fact been rejected in favor of action. Here in very practical terms, ethnography as defined by Geertz, and not comparison, matches the action-oriented system in Pudukkottai. For when "action" is viewed as embodied religion, when each religious action is viewed not as an element in a pattern but as a wholistic event and when existing texts are viewed only as "native interpretation" and not the primary data, then religion in the hinterland regions begin to make sense.

III. MEANWHILE BACK IN PUDUKKOTTAI . . .

In very practical terms, what does Geertz's ethnographic eye correct in the vision of an historian of religion seeking to understand royal rituals through the historical records and the living memory in the kingdom of Pudukkottai? The first error that ethnography corrects occurs in the most seemingly simple task: the identification of the primary sources for the study. The tendency of the historian of religions to give precedent to texts over actions translates in Pudukkottai into a serious case of mistaken identity. A number of types of records in libraries and government files in Pudukkottai could easily have been mistaken for the central fact in the interpretation of royal rituals but for the nagging of Geertz's ethnography which reminds the investigator to carefully distinguish in an action-oriented system between interpretations, even "native" models, and the actual locus of ritual.

On the most obvious shelf of the old government files called the Darbar Records, stood a well bound book *The Standing Orders of the Pudukkottai Darbar*.[54] Neatly catalogued was a section to delight the textualist's heart: "Festivals – Conduct and Arrangement". Then even more seemingly solid data appeared. The former Palace Head Harikar, the official in charge of arranging all state rituals, offered the old printed programs for the most important state rituals. These programs detailed the exact ritual order for specific festivals in 1930, 1938, and 1945. In addition, printed almanacs for various years during the 1930s contained outlines of festival programs. At last in an old chest of palace records, the tattered pages of the Harikar's 1935 diary emerged. Here the Harikar had carefully recorded and described each ritual held that year specifically for the raja or supported by the raja. All of these written sources could have provided all of the material necessary with which to commit the comparativist's mistake number one: Always find or at least reconstruct a "text" as the primary data and bracket all the rest.

At this point, Geertz's argument that "culture" exists only at the co-ordinates where model meets history become important for Pudukkottai. The *Standing Orders of the Pudukkottai Darbar* was only one description among many of the numerous ceremonials which year after year occupied the major attention of officials of the state. In the context of a record file beginning as early as 1856, the Standing Orders of 1937 appeared only as the final attempt of a British trained and British led administration in Pudukkottai to find some concise envelope in which to seal once and for all the bulky and carefully recorded precedents of a century. This last year of logic had been added to Pudukkottai at the turn of the century when the British sought to "bring order" through a Brahmin regent whose Brahmanical need for normative statute matched the British love of definition and precision in polity. This early attempt at normalizing Pudukkottai extended to the careful education of the young raja to his duties as a leader. The experiment had comic-tragic results. The sophisticated, educated, carefully trained gentleman-king married an Australian woman and soon left a realm too superstitious and disordered for his tastes. The 1937 Standing Orders was yet another attempt by the ever persistent British-Brahmin mind to clarify things in Pudukkottai. History, itself, reveals the failure of this example of nineteenth century logic abjured by Geertz. For an interpreter of Pudukkottai to again try to bring order by creating another idealized, another third level interpretation and mistaking that for the "essence" of the royal ceremonials here would be another sad repetition of an old mistake.

The lesson of the Darbar files, the almanacs and the Harikar's diary is an ethnographic lesson in the meaning of precedent as distinct from text: the difference between event and pure model as the locus of culture/religion. The officials of the kingdom of Pudukkottai kept surprisingly careful records for a place with "just some of this tribal religion". Certainly the demand for records for the East India Company and later the British Government of India could account for such record keeping. Yet, very early land grant documents attest to the long employment of Brahmin scribes for the king's library.[55] The habit of listing and keeping all correspondence in a yearly diary seems to have been well established by the time the Darbar files were housed in a single office.[56] Each event, each ceremony, year after year, was recorded. In a sense, the records indicate an intense interest in particularity. Just as, year after year, the Harikar recorded and described *each* ceremonial in his diary, and the astrologers set the exact time and place for the key religious events of each calendar year in the state almanacs. Moreover, no ceremony could be performed without the yearly petition to the king and council for funds and the permission granted never for more than a single year at a time.[57] This was not the rote repetition of a paradigm but a clear consciousness of the importance and the distinctiveness of each time, each ceremony, for each year.

The logic of precedent reverses the logic of normative text in the same manner that Geertz's ethnographic method reverses the status of text and behavior. Each year a ceremony was performed in a manner similar to the previous year. Therefore records had to be kept to indicate how the ritual was done on that occasion. The next year's ceremony, however, did not have to be a replica of the last. Something could be added, something else removed. The numerous petitions to the king to grant such changes in the personal ceremonials, the marriage and death rites, in the family of court officials illustrate this process of precedent well. The raja lent a specific set of "honors" in the form of the loan of ceremonial animals, troops and court musicians from the palace for us in the family rituals of his state officials. On the occasion of a marriage, the head of the family would petition for his rightful share of these honors but the requests often bade for more honors than were in fact granted at the last marriage occasion. The Harikar would be requested to check his diary. The person involved would plead for his "rights". The raja usually granted only what precedent allowed but occasionally the raja sanctioned an extra black horse to be added to the family's growing marriage parade. Each ritual was an occasion not just for repetition but for a new claim to new status, a new honor, and a new precedent.[58] The raja himself played his own game of add-an-honor. In the conduct of his own great ceremonials, the raja added to his ritual parade in a continual attempt to reformulate the exact nature of his own rule. The status which he held vis-a-vis other kings and his changing relationships with personalities in his own court fluctuated in the year by year expression of kingly rule. In the records of the British administration in the regional capital of Madras or in the Crown Records in London, the petitions of the Raja of Pudukkottai to his own liege, the British sovereign, to add to his ceremonial regalia now rest with the petitions of so many other hinterland rajas who had survived as ruling princes long after the center of India came under the direct rule of the British government.[59]

In Pudukkottai the only rule was precedent, and precedent did not rule as law, form or structure. Nothing in Pudukkottai was done once and forever the same. The earliest rajas, before "reforms" based on British law, sat in state in their ceremonial alcove in the old palace and judged one by one, case by case, the crimes and controversies in their realm.[60] No land was owned forever, but only by the continued grant of the king. No ceremony was forever funded except on a day by day, event by event relationship with a particular raja sitting in his particular court. Precedent was particular; precedent was personal; precedent was acutely bound to history and to the ever flowing passions and promises of daily life. What was sure, indeed, was the single event — that which happened then and there for all to see then and there only. The nineteenth century British desire for permanence did little to really change this logic of precedent. The historian of religions, working in turn in Pudukkottai, must acknowledge this "informal logic of actual life" which seems to have long internalized the very arguments of Geertz's ethnographic methods.

This logic of precedent extends in Pudukkottai to yet another kind of "text" often "discovered" by the historian of religion — myth. Indeed there was in Pudukkottai a set of documents which looked enough like "normative myth" to tease the historian of religion into committing the comparativists' mistake number two: If all else fails to produce structure, seek for the myth "behind" any ritual system. Pudukkottai also abounds not only in records but in "myths". The raja had patronized musicians and poets granting his weight in gold to the best. This production of poetic word and music left several extant "myths" about the founding of the Tondaiman family dynasty in Pudukkottai. There were also other "songs" in which the rajas of Pudukkottai were mentioned as patrons in stories about the temples within Pudukkottai State. These legends were all set in classic Tamil poetic forms which resemble "myth".[61] The Tondaiman Vamsavali,[62] the most famous of these "myths", portrays the ancestors of the Tondaimans slaying fierce lions and single-handedly taming wild elephants in episodes that seem to mimic the exploits of heroic gods. And indeed parallels are easy to draw between the ancient god Indra's own taming of the demons of chaos and the first Tondaiman's valiant surpression of wild jungle beasts. The Tondaiman legends also closely resemble similar tales told of the exploit of the founders of little kingdoms in other Tamil hinterland regions. In some sense, the Tondaiman Vamsavali is indeed an example of a type of "myth" which Nicholas Dirks has well described as existing throughout the entire region of Tamilnad. Yet Dirks, an historian, argues convincingly that such myth "can be seen as an integral historiographic possibility, a distinctive way of establishing sequence and relevance in the understanding and representation of the past . . . Anthropologists must realize both that myths have histories and that they are histories."[63]

The genre of "myth" then in Pudukkottai cannot be compared to those cosmogonic paradigmatic productions which historians of religions mean by Myth. David Shulman has terms this tendency of all Tamil "myth" to be attached to very particular persons and places as "the phenomenon of localization."

Shulman's study of Tamil temple myths (*sthalapurana*) concludes that this genre of myth always balances "the localization of the deity and the universalism proclaimed by the god's devotees . . ."[64] Shulman views the essential message of all such particularized myth-histories as sacred places as "God is present in man's life; he is rooted forever in the very soil of the Tamil land."[65] The *Tondaiman Vamsavali*, like the *sthalapurana*, was written in this mode of localized myth. The message of all such myth is not to convey model or law nor to ask for imitation. The Tamil "myth" seems rather to celebrate the face of particularity — of the embodiment of universality in the observable world.

In *Negara*, Geertz's ethnographic method seems again to capture the importance of the process of particularization in relationship to a universal model. For all myth has a common pattern, a seeming model and yet the question of the ontological relationship of model to supposed copy intrigues Geertz. Characteristically Geertz warns of the all too easy western analysis of this type of model and copy into a formulation that might easily become "rather too neoplatonic". The model and copy in a Balinese sense, just as in Geertz's own thenography, must never be reduced to "heaven-in-a-grain-of-sand turn of mind"[66] which separates idea from material, or mind from matter. Geertz rather argues that each king is both "an image of power" and "an instance of it." In other words, each copy of the model becomes in itself another model for yet another level of manifestation of the copied model. "The basic idiom is again emulative. Seeing Siva as the exemplary shape and the king as its activation, the people see the king as the exemplary shape and the state as its activation, the state as the exemplary shape and society as its activation . . ."[67] The neoplatonic mistake, and by inference the comparativist's mistake, would be to assume that the model was more important than the copy or worse, that the model and the copy could be separated. The activation is model-and-copy.

The ethnographic axiom to observe the concrete in context and not in relationship to a generalized model does separate Geerz's definition of the function of "myth" from "myth" as paradigm or text. Again Pudukkottai and South India seems to follow Geertz. Indeed the narrative movement of the *Tondaiman Vamsavali* as a history of the Tondaiman family presents each succeeding raja as doing the same type of exploits which marks him as another true king, *but* each raja is mentioned by name and each exploit is narrated again in full as if each deed remained important not as an example but as a fact. In this sense, it would be a mistake to regard this genealogical tale as a repetitive summary of the essence of "kingship". For clearly this history itself intends to convey the message that a king dies and another king rules, history flows, and each king is for that time and place the only king. The present raja rules not as a copy of a model. In this sense, Dirks is right: the *vamsavali* is a history — an acknowledgement of an unfolding process, and an affirmation of the importance of each king reigning in his own time and place and ruling in the here and now. This genre, then, of myth-history follows the same logic of precedent as do rituals in Pudukkottai. This little kingdom again declares in its "myths" that it is a government of men and now laws.

Because law cannot be abstracted from religious actions in ritual or in myth, Pudukkottai created no texts of its own and merely flirted with the normative texts of orthodox Hinduism by using them pragmatically but not paradigmatically. Geerz's ethnography makes clear the difference between the myth-ritual act as precedent and not paradigm. Pudukkottai does not divide conceptualization from the religious act. Ritual and myth are neither revelations of Something else nor enactments of a timeless model. This is not a culture of revelation or of models or of texts. Each religious act embodies concept in the form of precedent which can now be understood to function similarly to Derrida's description of the chain of signified concepts in the perpetual play of difference or in Geertz's terms of the model-and-copy process. There are no normative texts in Pudukkottai because there can not be such an abstraction given the logic of the culture.

Taken a step further, there can also be no normative theology here in the "nineteenth-century" dictionary definition as "rational inquiry into religious questions." Abstracted rational inquiry seems the very opposite of concept embodied in action. For the historian of religions, the nature of "theology" in Pudukkottai becomes the truly important question. For now, the interpretor of Pudukkottai's "religion" must look to behavior not only as embodied culture but as embodied theology as well. It is at this point where Pudukkottai's own "informal logic of actual life" parts company with ethnography and Clifford Geertz. The parting takes place at exactly the point where any anthropology by its very name must fear to tread.

IV. ETHNOGRAPHY AND ETHNO-THEOLOGY

In spite of his acknowlegment that modern scholarship has entered an era of "blurred genres", Clifford Geertz remains quite literally an anthropologist. Geertz was more than willing to leave behind outdated ontologies and nineteeneth century metaphysics to plea for a serious consideration of cultures and not Culture. Geertz argues with such passion for the careful consideration of each distinct cultural event. "The native's point of view" must be taken seriously. No overriding definitions of culture should obscure the particular person or place. And yet, as much as Geertz denies the universal laws of Culture, he feels compelled to formulate a universal definition of the "human" in homo sapien. His understanding of the ultimate needs and desires of humankind do not clearly appear to develop from his own long studies of culture. Adopting a tone of scientific truth in place of his more usual relativistic language, Geertz felt able quite early in his career to define the nature of human nature.

Geertz defines the human species as "a meaning-seeking animal" whose need of an ordered sence of existence is written into the very genetic code of this species. In "Transition to Humanity"[68] Geertz subtly argues against the last of the unconscious carry-overs of Judeo-Christian theology into anthropology:

the notion that humanity moved from animal to human at a single "critical point" when the mind or spirit "like the flare of a struck match, leaped into existence." Circumventing this position, Geertz insists that "Whether or not human minds or souls come in degrees, human bodies most assuredly do."[69] The neurological development of the humanoid, says Geertz, forced the human to forfeit the instinctual skills of animals and develop culture in order to survive: "Without the guidance of the public images of sentiment found in ritual, myth and art we would, quite literally, not know how to feel. Like the expanded forebrain itself, ideas and emotions are cultural artifacts in man."[70] Religion is indeed "real" as an intrinsic part of the human being's biological equipment for survival.

In this anthropo-logy, Geertz implies a definition of religion that is far more important to the history of religions than his often quoted and very explicit definition of "religion as a cultural system". For in his anthropology, Geertz has embedded a hidden theology that both opens and yet closes the doors to a place like Pudukkottai. Geertz's anthropology gives "religion as a cultural system" a firm footing in the universe. Religious imagination has become true public space — the uniquely human environment created by homo sapiens in order to survive as a species! Hence both religion and culture and indeed "real" as a biological necessity. Geertz seems to breathe a sigh of relief that he has found a solution to the now almost ancient problem in anthropology: How to provide a modern humanistic view of religion that does not insult the stark sense of reality that such a system creates.

By the time Geertz completed *Negara*, he had fully affirmed the ontological status of what could be called *intra-space* — the public level of consciousness that extends beyond individual projections of the psyche and between the stark impact of the external world on our naked senses. This public imagination is home for homo sapiens. By adopting the ontological stand of semiology, Geertz was now able to attribute an independent status to this space. For *intra-space* is the world of communication: "language" raised to the level of Being. In *Negara*, Geertz has clearly set aside the nineteenth century metaphysics, but he has subtly replaced this with a new ontology — an ontology that resembles a theology. He makes no distinction between the public imagination in the sense of world-view and the manifestation of public image in what is more literally an image — an image of god.

In his description of sacral kingship in Bali, Geertz posits an equation between public imagination and public image: "the aim of higher politics was to construct a state by constructing a king" and "a king was constructed by constructing a god."[71] Yet, at this point Geertz becomes unwilling to take his ontology into deeper theological waters. In a disappointing retreat to his own brand of neo-platonism, Geertz further defines the nature of this divine image as "a constellation of enshrined ideas." And alas here all of Geertz's careful arguments for the public image as non-abstractable, totally embodied, totally empowered reality fall back into that nineteenth century axiom of the social sciences (and the humanities as well) that in making "gods", human society is engaged in an endless process of self-reflection. Geertz, the anthropologist, can not imagine that in a place like Pudukkottai, the public divine image, be it king or icon, can have an ontological status beyond embodied social ideas.

In Pudukkottai, ethnography has an importance beyond Geertz's own anthropology. Ethnography releases some serious theological issues in Pudukkottai which would otherwise remain masked by the comparativists' search for transcendent categories. Indeed ethnography makes possible an understanding of religion as a serious human product created in a highly concrete media of daily life. Ethnography can affirm the "reality" of each concrete ritual action and of each product of that ritual action — such things are necessary for the very life of the human species. There is no need here to protect religion by appealing to concepts of a transcendent reality *behind* the human "experience of the sacred", or an "infinite" above the mere finite expression of religious experience.

Ethnography, then, allows the historian of religion to leave behind our latent fear of "idolatry" and accept the clear fact that no one in Pudukkottai would be stunned by the statement that god is embodied fully within the human world. Nor would anyone even balk at the suggestion that an image of god is "made" by human hands out of human need and through the agency of human power. Such statements can be found explicitly stated in the occasional formal "second-level" interpretations of temple priests on ritual issues of how to properly "make god". In this explicit "how-to" theology, the ingredients needed to embody god are listed.

> Divine spirit (takes a seat) is embodied within the icon through the power of the divine energy (*tapas*) of the priest's own body, through the beauty of the image body itself and through full ritual worship.[72]

Here god comes to be embodied in this world out of the power engendered by community worship. Yet in this same document an order of precedent is clear. There is no community without the real presense of god and yet *devata*, the divine spirit, does exist beyond the bounds of community life. For Pudukkottai, society remains a sub-category of the divine world. The embodied god, the holy image or the sacral king, remains primarily a theological construct.

An understanding of "image" and "imagination" demands a theological eye in a place like Pudukkottai. The very ontological order that Geertz defends constitutes not *social* space but *divine* space in Pudukkottai. Geertz indeed admits this to be true in Bali. The *negara* is the holy state both as a state of consciousness and as the definition of the political state as well. But attention must be focused on the fact that at least in Pudukkottai the "ritual state" never escapes its marginal quality. Pudukkottai and its icon-king are never subsumed into the stable social world of the city state. Marginality here does not simply imply freedom from permanent encasement into stable social paradigm, marginality also implies that the social world is created and destroyed within the larger sphere of divine space. Social space is not always coterminous with divine ritual space. Semiotics in a place like Pudukkottai remains a "theological" enterprise.

The historian of religion's own hereditary position as the middle person between theology and anthropology is an ideal location from which to interpret a place like Pudukkottai. Once freed from the need to search for "texts" and once released from the fear of fully embodied god, the historian of religions can accept the fact that we have always been "ethno-theologians." That is, scholars who, like the Pudukkottaiyans themselves have assumed that there is indeed a revelation of god in human behavior. But the definition of that revealing of god now must be extended to include a far more radical sense of revelation — the embodiment of a god that can be seen, tasted, and felt as living in the very space that also defines our own humanity.

Notes and References

1. See Joachim Wach, "The Place of the History of Religions in the Study of Theology" in *Types of Religious Experience, Christian and Non-Christian* (Chicago: University of Chicago Press, 1951). Wach declares here that "God has at no time left himself without witness." This "divine self-disclosure . . . is recorded in the history of the religion of mankind." (p. 28) Wach understands this type of revelation to occur in practice as much as in text. Wilfred Cantwell Smith argues that a world theology may be possible once we recognize that "God reveals to men not propositions about Himself or institutional structures or specific dance patterns, let us say, but Himself; to contend this is to say that such propositions or structures or patterns as some have deemed revealed may more generally be interpreted as revelatory." See *Towards a World Theology* (Philadelphia: The Westminster Press, 1981) p. 173. Ninian Smart's understanding of the nature of theology in a world context is based on "world-view analysis" and not limited to textual analysis. "The Implications of the History of Religions for Christian Systematic Theology" Lecture at Harvard University, April 29, 1982. See also, *The Phenomenon of Christianity* (London: Collins, 1979) and *Beyond Ideology: Religion and the Future of Western Civilization* (New York: Harper and Row, 1981).
2. Wach, *Types of Religious Experience*, p. 28.
3. F. Max Muller, *The Origin and Growth of Religion* (Reprinted by photo offset; Varanasi (India): Indological Book House, 1964. Original date of publication, 1878) p. 371-372.
4. Ibid.
5. Ugo Bianchi, "Religio-anthropological Approach" in *Science of Religion: Studies in Methodology: Proceedings of the Study Conference in the International Association for the History of Religions,* held in Turku, Finland, August 27-31, 1973. edited by Lauri Honko. (The Hague: Mouton, 1974) pp. 317-319.
6. A term used by Ninian Smart for his lecture "The History of Religions and Its Conversation Partners", conference of the Institute for the Advanced Study of Religion, University of Chicago, May 8-10, 1983. Not all historians of religion are at present willing to include theology as a major conversation partner. For example, Jonathan Z. Smith defines the partners as "anthropology (in its broadest sense), humanities, and history." *Imagining Religion: From Babylon to Jonestown* (Chicago: University of Chicago Press, 1982.) p. 102.
7. This term was adapted from early Christian theology by early twentieth century historians of religions who sought to re-establish the field within the theological disciplines after the initial separation from theology in the mid-nineteenth century. See Wach, *Types of Religious Experience*, p. 10-25 and J. Z. Smith, *Imagining Religion* pp. 102-105.
8. These opinions were expressed in personal interviews with government officials at state libraries and record offices, and by university trained scholars. Interestingly, the majority of these informants were Brahmins trained in urban universities in the classical textual definitions of kingship.
9. The *Tondaiman Vamsavali* traces the origin of the Tondaimans (the dynastic name of the Pudukkottai royal family) to one of the god Indra's sexual adventures on earth. The story

is an exact parallel to the caste origin stories told by the Kallar community itself. These epics stress the martial character of the Kallars and thus claim the function of the warrior but not classic *kshatriya* status.

10. Louis Dumont points to the numerous incidents in which "power" forced a recognized mobility within the caste system. "Dominance over a large territory could even open the gate to Kshatriya varna." *Homo Hierarchicus An Essay On The Caste System* (Chicago: University of Chicago Press, 1970) p. 198. There does seem to be some distinction, however, between rulers who claimed *kshatriya* status and those who did not. The nearby Ramnad rajas also acknowledged with considerable pride their Marvavar Sudra status. See Pamela G. Price, "Raja-dharma in the 19th century south India: land, litigation and largess in Ramnad Zamindari" *Contributions to Indian Sociology* N.S. Vol. 13, NO. 2, 1979.

11. There are texts written locally in South India in Sanskrit which are now considered to be normative. This Agama tradition also includes model rituals for the installation of the king. Neither the Vedic nor the Agamic models were duplicated in Pudukkottai.

12. Verses were chanted from the *Shantiratnagara* – a text classified as *joshisha:* relating to the astrological sciences.

13. The earliest Tamil language poetry were poems by court bards which extolled the model king. The Pudukkottai rajas are not easily placed even in this "native" model, since they ruled over the wasteland and not over the centers of early urban Tamil culture.

14. Burton Stein, "Integration of the Agrarian System in South India" in *Land Control and Social Structure in Indian History* edited by Robert E. Fykenberg. (Madison: University of Wisconsin Press, 1969) p. 185-187.

15. Richard Fox, *Kin, Clan, Raja and Rule: State-Hinterland Relations in Preindustrial India* (Berkeley: University of California Press, 1971) p. 58-128.

16. Thomas Metcalf, "From Raja to Landlord: The Oudh Talukdars, 1850-1870" in Fykenberg, *Land Control and Social Structure*, p. 124.

17. Nicholas P. Dirks, "The Pasts of a Palaiyakar: The Ethnohistory of a South Indian Little King." Journal of Asian Studies, Vol. 41, NO. 4 (1982), p. 679.

18. See Arjun Appadurai and Carol A. Breckenridge, "The south Indian temple: authority, honour, and redistribution." *Contributions to Indian Sociology* N.S. Vol. 10, No. 2 (1976).

19. Clifford Geertz, "Ethos, World-View and the Analysis of Sacred Symbols" in *The Antioch Review* Vol. 18, NO. 4, (1957) p. 437.

20. "The Cerebral Savage: On the work of Claude Levi-Strauss" in *Interpretation of Cultures:* Selected Essays (New York: Basic Books, 1973) p. 355.

21. "Thick Description: Toward an Interpretive Theory of Culture" in *Interpretation of Cultures*, pp. 17, 20, 30.

22. Bianchi, "The Religio-anthropological Approach", p. 299.

23. Origins and Growth, p. 86.

24. Lewis Henry Jordan, *Comparative Religion: Its Adjuncts and Allies* (London: Oxford University Press, 1915) pp. 3-8.

25. "Adde Parvum Parvo Magnus Acervus Erit" in *Map is Not Territory: Studies in the History of Religions:* (Leiden: E. J. Brill, 1978) pp. 244-249.

26. "Religio-anthropological Approach", p. 302.

27. Ibid., p. 319.

28. Jonathan Z. Smith, *Imagining Religion*, p. 35.

29. "Ethos, World-View and the Analysis of Sacred Symbols", p. 436.

30. "Religion as a Cultural System" in *Anthropological Approaches to the Study of Religion* ed. by Michael Banton (London: Tavistock Publication Ltd., 1966) p. 42.

31. Ibid., p. 5. Compare this to Langer's *Philosophy in a New Key*. Mentor Book (New York: New American Library, 1951 (1942), pp. 131-133.

32. Geertz claims his entire concept of culture is "a semiotic one" in the initial pages of "Thick Description", p. 5.

33. Ibid., p. 10.

34. David Kronenfeld and Henry W. Decker, "Structuralism" in the *Annual Review of Anthropology*, 1979 (Palo Alto: Annual Reviews Inc., 1979) p. 504.

35. T. K. Seung, *Structuralism and Hermeneutics* (New York: Columbia University Press, 1982) p. 177.

36. "Thick Description", p. 10.
37. Ibid., p. 10-11.
38. Here Geertz paraphrases Wittenstein almost verbatim. Compare "Thick Description" p. 10 with Ludwig Wittgenstein, *The Blue and Brown Books*, Harper Torch Books. (New York: Harper and Row, 1958) pp. 73-74.
39. *Negara: The Theatre State in Nineteenth-Century Bali* (Princeton: Princeton University Press, 1980) p. 135.
40. Kronenfeld and Decker, p. 505.
41. See Werner Marx, *Heidegger and the Tradition* translated by Theodore Kisiel and Murray Greene with an introduction by Theodore Kisiel (Evanston: Northwestern University Press, 1971) pp. 243-256 and the preface xxviii-xxix. See also Seung, p. 236-238 on Husserl.
42. Geertz, the Cerebral Savage", p. 354.
43. Quoted in T. K. Seung, p. 151 from "La Differance" translated in *Speech and Phenomenon and Other Essays on Husserl's Theory of Signs* translated by David Allison (Evanston: Northwestern University Press, 1973) p. 140.
44. Ibid., p. 135.
45. My emphasis, Ibid., p. 136.
46. Quoted in Edith Kurzweil, *The Age of Structuralism: Levi-Strauss to Foucault* (New York: Columbia University Press, 1980) p. 242.
47. "Thick Description", p. 11.
48. Wach, *Types of Religious Experience*, p. 44.
49. "The Model of the Text: Meaningful Action Considered as a Text", *Social Research* Vol. 38 (1971) p. 535.
50. "Thick Description", p. 29.
51. Ibid., p. 18.
52. Ibid., p. 15.
53. Interestingly in his "Model of a Text", Ricoeur actually had Derrida's emphasis on "writing" (trace) in mind but ironically rather than directly using Derrida, Ricoeur quotes John Searle, *Speech Acts* (London: Cambridge University Press, 1969) who understood or rather "misunderstood" Derrida's "writing" to imply permanance (see Seung, p. 141). Here Geertz's own model of a text may well be truer to Derrida's original sense of "writing" as fixing sentiment for a moment already past and hence empty of ontological status. Geertz, of course, quotes only Ricoeur in "Thick Description".
54. 2 vols. (Pudukkottai: Sri Brihadambal State Press, 1937).
55. Recorded in the records for title deeds confirmed at the time the British-directed "reform" of the old land tenure system by which the raja "owned" all the land and "gave" it in lieu of salary for special service. These Inam Settlement Records of 1888 contain numerous grants to Brahmin scribes.
56. In the remains of the palace's own records, I found an Old Tamil diary from about 1856 which had carefully listed incoming correspondence for the year. Correspondence from as early as the 1750's had also been preserved in several bound volumns called the Huzur Records.
57. Interestingly, old land grants on copper plates from this part of India often record royal grants to temples as given "as long as the sun shines" but clearly in Pudukkottai approval for palace controlled temple grants was on a year by year basis.
58. The Palace Records in Pudukkottai consist mainly of such petitions for honors. By the twentieth century, the granting of such honors constituted the raja's major civil duty.
59. The Crown Records in the India Office Library in London abound with petitions for new titles and honors from the "native chiefs" to the British government. The British took the granting of honors very seriously also. The major source book and manual for political practice in the "Native States" devotes a full chapter to "Titles and Ceremonials". See C. L. Tupper, *Indian Political Practice: A Collection of the Decisions of the Government of India in Political Cases.* 3 vols. (Calcutta: Office of the Superintendent of Government Printing, 1895). vol. III., p. 203ff.
60. The central feature in the oldest palace complex in Pudukkottai is an alcove-platform opening into a large courtyard where the raja held public audience. The pre-British Darbar, the official court meeting, was not merely ceremonial but also seemed to serve as a viva voce decision making body for day to day problems.

61. By Tamil literary logic, however, there is no classification "myth". Stories told of both gods and kings are rather classified according to the type of poetic meter and general poetic form in which the praise or tale is set.

62. The official court *vamsavali* was composed in Telegu by the court poet Venkanna in about 1750.

63. Nicholas B. Dirks, "The Pasts of a Palaiyakar", p. 658.

64. David Dean Shulman, *Tamil Temple Myths* (Princeton: Princeton University Press, 1980) p. 41.

65. Ibid., p. 352.

66. *Negara*, p. 109. Here Geertz seems to paraphrase post-structuralist Roland Barthes who critiques the "whole landscape in a bean" notions of the formalists. See Seung, p. 177.

67. Geertz, *Negara*, p. 109.

68. In the *Voice of America Lectures, Anthropology Series 3*. (n.d.) Later republished as "The Growth of Culture and the Evolution of Mind" in *The Interpretation of Cultures*.

69. Ibid., p. 2-3.

70. Ibid., p. 8.

71. *Negara*, p. 124.

72. From the Proceedings of the Pudukkottai Darbar No. 3089/c of 1913 dated December 14, 1914. A decision on the state pandits on the necessity of the temple dancers in the definition of "full worship" to maintain gods presence in the temple. My translation of the Tamil text.

CHAPTER III

"Thick Description" and Psychology of Religion

Judith Van Herik

I will do two things: descend into Clifford Geertz's writings to discern the data, topics, methods and purposes of interpretive cultural anthropology as he presents himself practicing and reflecting on it; and use this formulation of his approach to indicate how it might inform conceptualization of the psychological study of religions.

I. GEERTZ
METAPHOR AND PERSPECTIVAL MOTION

The difference between reading Geertz's works piecemeal and reading them chronologically and systematically, as I've done for this essay, is that, doing the latter, one encounters two intertwined characteristics of his thought that, one gradually realizes, are everywhere and in increasingly complex forms. These are his concerns with metaphor and with methodological perspective. Perspective is altered by movement between immediate closeness and mediated distance and is related to the difference between data and topic.

First, one notices Geertz's own use of metaphor becoming more apt and complex as he becomes more explicit about the metaphorical structure of others' enacted documents, their lived texts — of the minute assays of the "flow of social discourse" that are his data. Geertz is using metaphor; they are living metaphor, and the guiding metaphor for what Geertz is doing becomes "reading behavioral texts." One sees increasing convergence (and increasing reflectiveness about the convergence) between what Geertz is studying and how he is studying it, or, more exactly, between how he construes his data and how he construes his construal — how he describes his interpretive activity. (To construe something is "to understand not just what it means but how it does so."[1] His term for ethnographic activity is "thick description." So, after discussing metaphor and perspectival motion, I will turn to his discussion of thick description to see how it is related to his concepts of culture and symbols, and to look, with it, more carefully at the methodological metaphor of reading texts.

To remark on convergence between the way Geertz construes his data as metaphorical and his use of metaphor to express this construal is not meant as criticism. This reflexiveness is central to the power and cogency of his work. It emphasizes his view that students of religions (or other cultural systems) are in a tangle of interpretations: we interpret the interpretations of those whom we study to see what they say (to themselves and us) about them and us. Interpretation is all we can do; the problem is to do it intelligibly. Intelligibility is Geertz's view of the aim of interpretive cultural anthropology. Metaphor understood makes the nonrational intelligible without either rationalizing or "theologizing" it.

When Geertz writes about construal of his construals, the issue of perspective as a function of interpreter's movement arises in relation to the difference between what one studies — the data — and what one is trying to learn about using these data — the topic. Perspective is also related to the difference between what his subjects are engaged in (the lived manner of that engagement) and what that engagement is a message *about*. In both cases, he distinguishes between event and meaning — meaning for the actor and for the interpreter.

Geertz describes his data as different, exotic, particular, specific, concrete; the topic as familiar, generic, general, more abstract. Data is various, irregular and, on the face of it, an unordered mess of detail; the topic admits of patterned uniformity. Data are parochial, narrow, and intimate; the topic is comprehensive, broad, and of general scholarly and existential concern. Data are observed at close range; the topic is addressed on the basis of a "judgment at great distance."[2] The objects of study are tiny slices of social life: exchanges in bazaars in Moroccan villages, costumes in Barong dances in Bali, speeches prior to elections in small Indonesian towns, and, within these, minutiae such as "lexical antitheses, categorical schemes, morphophonemic transformations."[3] Such droplets of the flow of behavior, snippets of social action, are treated as "enacted documents" which are windows opening on "the informal logic of actual life."[4] But the data that are used are already interpretations: "our own constructions of other peoples' constructions of what they and their compatriots are up to."[5]

The topic of inquiry is more generic. "In ethnography," Geertz writes, "the office of theory is to provide a vocabulary in which what symbolic action has to say about *itself* — that is, about the role of culture in human life — can be expressed."[6] The "essential vocation of interpretive anthropology" is, after providing this vocabulary, to allow particular human messages to be spoken using it: not "to answer our deepest questions, but to make available to us answers that others . . . have given, and thus to include them in the consultable record of what man has said."[7] When general categories are appropriate, they should order variety, not dissolve it.[8]

His purpose is not to develop an interpretive method as an end in itself, but to develop a vocabulary in service of making an inventory of human answers to human questions. Without this vocabulary, which is more than translation and less than a new language, we are unaware that the questions are being asked. Geertz writes that the problems regarding which cultural patterns provide orientation, "being existential, are universal; their solutions, being human are diverse. It is, however, through the circumstantial understanding of these unique solutions, and in my opinion, only in that way, that the nature of the underlying problems to which they are a comparable response can be truly comprehended." So the task ("the road to the grand abstractions of science") takes one through a "thicket of singular facts"[9] because "there is no route to general knowledge save through a dense thicket of particulars."[10] "There is no ascent to truth without descent to cases."[11] Truth, here, seems to be the comprehended human problems — diagnosis of the human condition. It is not a presupposed solution or system of solutions, whether theoretical or theological.

Speaking of the sociology of religion, Geertz comments that generalities (in this instance, association of religious change with social change attendant upon modernization) are generally known, but the particulars are not, and only the particulars take us beyond the "easy banalities of common sense."[12] Geertz's dedication to the particular has not waned over the years; one need read only his 1979 "Suq: The Bazaar Economy in Sefrou" or his 1980 *Negara: The Theatre State in Nineteenth Century Bali*[13] to suspect that it has perhaps increased. He is not resting on particularities ordered in the past to provide general knowledge. He is, though, deepening his reflection on the problem of interpretation of detail — vocabulary creation — and he is doing so increasingly in literary metaphors.

I mentioned that these two issues, metaphorical complexity and commentary on perspective — small and large, distant and close, particular and general — are intertwined. Four instances of his discussion of aspects of perspective that use metaphor to discuss it may clarify this. In *Islam Observed* (1968), we read that anthropologists, always "inclined to turn toward the concrete, the particular, the microscopic," are the "miniaturists of the social sciences, painting on lilliputian canvases with what we take to be delicate strokes." Why? Because they hope to "find in the little what eludes us in the large, to stumble upon general truths while sorting through special cases."[14] One is reminded of Bachelard's observation: "Thus the miniscule, a narrow gate, opens up the entire world."[15] And, returning to *Islam Observed*, Geertz tells us that anthropology is a "sly and deceptive science," for when it seems "most deliberately removed from our own lives, it is most immediate." It appears to be telling stories about "the distant, the strange, the long ago, or the idiosyncratic" (the data) but is in fact also saying something about "the close, the familiar, the contemporary, and the generic."[16] The metaphor of the miniaturist opens up the methodological problem we face in studying religions: if the data are utterly strange, we can know or say nothing of them; if they are entirely familiar, we are probably either mute about them or uncritical, so that we reduplicate rather than interpret them. One needs intelligible terms for otherness and metaphor becomes, for Geertz, this mediation.

In "The Politics of Meaning" (1972), the problem is the relationship between recent Indonesian politics and perduring Indonesian culture. The first

Geertz likens to a "clutter of schemes and surprises"; the second to a "vast geometry of settled judgments." The juxtaposition of metaphorical contrasts — clutter and vast geometry, schemes and surprises and settled judgments — is the point. Geertz's summation is metaphor more general: "chaos of incident, cosmos of sentiment."[17] Here the contrasts are *in* the data, not between data and topic. In the data one construes chaos and cosmos, each tied to the particulars of incident and sentiment. The metaphor suggests the method: the way to see their connection is "to frame an analysis of meaning at once circumstantial enough to carry conviction and abstract enough to forward theory." The topic of this essay is larger than the material it examines: a specific answer, in one case, to the question of how every people "gets the politics it imagines."[18]

In "From the Native Point of View" (1974), Geertz shows how notions of personhood are expressed in publicly accessible symbols and are comprehensible as cultural in three instances. He then describes "the intellectual movement, the inward conceptual rhythm" of what he has just done as a "continuous dialectical tacking between the most local of local detail and the most global of global structure." In addition to dialectical tacking, we have "hopping back and forth" between the whole conceived through the parts which actualize it, and the parts conceived through the whole which motivates them, this hopping seeking to transform them, "by a sort of intellectual perpetual motion," into "explications of one another."[19] Here, the whole is, again, their cultural whole, not ours. The parts are those vehicles — publicly accessible symbols — in which the whole, a general form of life, is carried. Neither can be understood without the other. The interpreter must tack in this particular wind, which means construing others' symbol systems as they are publicly available, and not becoming one of them ("achieving communion") *or* leaving them inaccessible, strange, not understood. They do have a notion of person, but just as importantly not our notion of person. The familiar, general, and abstract refer to notion of person; the unusual, particular, and concrete are the contents and cultural contexts of variant notions, apprehended through symbolic vehicles. We all have such vehicles; their passengers vary. Calling them vehicles of meaning is part of the new vocabulary. (See Martin, in this volume, for discussion of its intellectual sources.)

In "Common Sense as a Cultural System" (1975), metaphor is converted almost to allegory and is used to illuminate a point similar to the one just discussed: that we, the interpreters, have public, intersubjective, cultural notions, too. Geertz quotes Wittgenstein's comparison of language to an old city: "a maze of little streets and squares, of old and new houses, and of houses with additions from various periods; and this surrounded by a multitude of modern sections with straight regular streets and uniform houses."[20] He extends these — the old city and the new suburbs — to compare them to how anthropologists tend to view the contrast between the kinds of societies they study and those they inhabit. The latter have suburbs — systems of thought and action like physics, existentialism, jurisprudence, Marxism, Christianity — that are "squared off and straightened out."[21] He then turns this back on us to argue that "districts of the soul" usually seen as unsystematized old quarters – in this case, common sense – are ordered, cultural realms – suburbs, cultural systems. What seems to us a highly particular and dense overgrown thicket – someone else's common sense – and what seems obvious and therefore not culturally patterned – our own common sense – are both cultural systems, which means accessible to interpretation.

THICK DESCRIPTION

Geertz's (metaphorical) term for what one does to move from data to topic, expressed in an accessible vocabulary, is "thick description." In his essay of this title (1973), he presents it as a way to get responsibly from "a collection of ethnographic miniatures to wall-sized culturescapes" without confusing the locale of study with the object of study or the discipline with its subject matter.[22] Thick description accentuates the local, particular, and parochial and also is available to the questions of outsiders who want to know what this local behavior *means*. The four characteristics of thick description are (1) that it is interpretive; (2) it interprets the "flow of social discourse"; (3) its interpreting consists in rescuing the "said" of such discourse from fleeting occasions and fixing it in perusable terms; and (4) it is microscopic.[23]

The point is neither to study specifics in order to "codify abstract regularities" *nor* just to inventory particularities. Thick description, like clinical inference, leads to generalization within cases: "rather than beginning with a set of observations and attempting to subsume them under a general law, such inference begins with a set of (presumptive) signifiers and attempts to place them within an intelligible frame."[24] Thus particulars are made to speak to larger questions: How are society and culture related? How do different social forms support different faiths? How does each people get the politics it imagines?

To understand thick description, one must understand Geertz's semiotic view of culture. Because this is presented elsewhere in this volume (Martin), I will here repeat only some major points. Culture is not a power but a context of meanings within which particulars can be intelligibly (thickly) described.[25] It is not private, subjective, or mental (all of which for Geertz are often synonymous with psychological); culture exists in human behavior, which is socially enacted, and is therefore discoverable therein.[26] Human nature is indelibly and specifically cultural. One finds nothing human before or outside or beyond culture. Stripping away the particulars would leave only a concept, not human life.[27] Culture is an accumulation of the totality of cultural patterns, the latter being "ordered clusters of significant symbols" through which humans make sense of the events through which we live.[28] Cultural analysis searches out these clusters of symbols ("material vehicles of perception, emotion and understanding") and "the statement of the underlying regularities of human experience implicit in their formation."[29]

A symbol is anything that "denotes, describes, represents, exemplifies, labels, indicates, evokes, depicts, expresses, e.g., signifies." Symbols are intersubjective public vehicles of meanings. Ideas are envehicled meanings, as are arguments, melodies, formulas, maps, pictures, rituals, palaces, technologies, and social for-mations.[30] The vehicles are socially determined, and social life is itself mapped by the conceptions carried in symbols, that is, by culture.[31] Culture and social relationships are mutually interpretive: "to rework the pattern of social rela-tionships" is to rearrange the "coordinates of the experienced world." Those coordinates are culture; therefore, society's forms are culture's substance.[32] Culture is like a program, a genetic code, a map, a template, a blueprint,[33] although Geertz qualifies these. Adequately to understand anything human is to understand it in this context, because its meaning for both the experiencer and the interpreter is established therein. The anthropologist is an interpreter who, through ethnography, is capable of perceiving, not *what* his or her infor-mants perceive, but "what they perceive 'with' or 'by means of,'" or 'through,'..."[34]

This brings us back to "thick description." Geertz adopts the term from Gilbert Ryle, who uses "rapidly contracting the right eyelids" as an example of a thin description—one that cannot distinguish between a twitch and a wink, and hence does not indicate significance. To counter it, Ryle's final example of "thick description" is "practicing a burlesque of a friend faking a wink to deceive an innocent into thinking a conspiracy is in motion." This thick description contains "piled up structures of inference and implication," of signification: parody, rehearsal, etc. Geertz's point is that the object of ethnography is "a stratified hierarchy of meaningful structures" that lies "between" thin and thick and in terms of which social actions are produced, perceived, and interpreted.[35] This object of ethnography is what I have been calling topic; not the raw data-events (which are moving eyelids), or the construed data (thickly described), but that which one aims to construe *in, from* the data. Ethnography *is* the thick description; its *object* is these meaningful structures. The point is not, finally, what happened, but the meaning of what happened, and more finally still, what those meaningful structures are which give it *that* meaning. Analysis (inter-pretation) is "sorting out the structures of signification . . . and determining their social ground and import."[36]

The two steps of interpretive anthropology are not description and explana-tion, for description is already construed, interpretive. They are "inscription" (of meaning), that is, thick description (doing ethnography) and "specification": deciding, diagnosing, what is inscribed. Inscription is setting down the meaning that particular social actions have *for the actors* whose actions they are—winks or twitches? Specification, like clinical diagnosis, is stating what the knowledge thus attained "demonstrates about the society in which it is found and, beyond that, about social life as such." The former task, discovering what this knowledge demonstrates about the society of the actor, is "uncovering the conceptual structures that inform our subject's acts." These conceptual structures are parts of culture—some of the coordinates of that actor's experienced world. The latter task, stating what the knowledge thus attained demonstrates about social life as such, is to "construct a system of analysis in whose terms what is generic to these structures, what belongs to them because they are what they are, will stand out against the other determinants of human behavior."[37]

To recapitulate: the data of cultural anthropology are social actions—local, parochial, concrete. The construed data are thickly described (inscribed). The point of interpreting (specifying) the thickly described data is to get to the object (topic) of ethnography—piled up structures of signification that lie between thin and thick description—but not precisely *in* either. As I read this, such structures are like invisible filters; thick description, interpreted (specified), makes them visible. So specification is the action that moves one from lots of local detail, however thickly described, to the general, to conceptual structures, to the coordinates of (their) experienced world. Further specification is needed to see what is *"generic* to those structures." This further specification, which Geertz does not tell us how to do, is clarified in his discussions of metaphor (and other tropes) in behavioral texts. Geertz's semiotic anthropology emphasizes the cultural particularity *of* coordinates, or conceptual structures, and their generality *as* coordinates. We are left neither with complete cultural relativism (because structures of signification are humanly generic) nor with absolute, perhaps god-woven, structures (because structures are indelibly and particularly cultural). Rather, Geertz's view is reflexive: he also interprets the filters (metaphors) which the interpreter uses to understand others' enacted tropes.

READING TEXTS

The issue is raised in "Deep Play: Notes on the Balinese Cockfight" (1972). A functionalist argument treats cockfight as reinforcing status discrimination. Geertz finds it more illuminating to show, first, that cockfight "provides a metasocial commentary" on social hierarchy and, second, to specify the message of the commentary: that status is a matter of life and death. Cockfight is interpretive, a "Balinese reading of Balinese experience, a story they tell themselves about themselves."[38] It is an art form that "renders ordinary, everyday experience comprehensible by presenting it in terms of acts and objects which have had their practical consequences removed and been reduced (or . . . raised) to the level of sheer appearances." Cockfight "catches up" themes (death, masculinity, status, chance, loss, gain) and orders them into an encompassing structure that "puts a construction on them."[39] The construction is "visible, tangible, graspable" in social drama.

The metaphoric content of cockfight (a "mock war of symbolic selves") is enactment of a dimension of Balinese experience that is usually unmarked. The fight joins "pride to selfhood, selfhood to cocks, and cocks to destruction."[40] Metaphor is the agency of such joining. The Balinese commentary formulated in cockfight does not replicate literal Balinese being but depicts how they are imaginatively. They are imaginatively what cockfight is literally and, oppositely, cockfight is a figure of social action that depicts what Balinese really are. Geertz explains that expressive form works "by disarranging semantic contexts" so that "properties conventionally ascribed to certain things [cocks] are unconventionally ascribed to others [human status divisiveness], which are then seen to actually possess them." Phenomena are "clothed in signifiers which normally point to other referents."[41] Interpretation of behavioral texts reverses the metaphoric process.

In previous writings, Geertz had analyzed figurative language to understand social action (see his discussion of the Taft-Hartley Act likened to a slave labor law in his 1964 "Ideology as a Cultural System"). He had also understood social structures in linguistic terms. (In *Kinship in Bali*, he and Hildred Geertz wrote that "kinship is a social idiom, a way of talking about and understanding and hence shaping some aspects of social life.")[42] But the methodological discussion in "Deep Play" heralds explicit analysis of what is gained and implied by construing interpretive activity as textual analysis. What is gained is retaining specificity, particularity and variety. What is implied seems to be a still provisional reunion of social scientific and humanistic understanding of the human. Data, topic, and method converge in metaphor (and other tropes). The Balinese are enacting metaphor: they transfer perceptions from "the collision of roosters" to "the divisiveness of status."[43] Metaphor is just such a "stratification of meaning, in which an incongruity of sense on one level produces an influx of significance on another."[44] Metaphor is the way Geertz inscribes the meaning of cockfight in thick description. His specification is that cockfight is a metaphor that says something in particular, of something particular, to somebody in particular. His further specification is that social life consists in "collectively sustained" symbolic structures that can be construed as texts ("imaginative works built out of social materials").[45]

So Geertz's analogy for his own undertaking becomes closely reading an ensemble of texts over the shoulders of those to whom they properly belong.[46] He calls this a "metaphorical refocusing" of the anthropologist's project. One no longer draws methodological analogies from physical processes (one no longer dissects an organism or diagnoses a symptom, which fragment and condescend) but from symbolic form.[47] One reads texts, interpreting whole and parts in terms of each other, which implies decently distant respect for internal textual meanings *and* the interpreter's interest in their generic significance. Refocusing the method makes it more appropriate to the particularity of anthropological data and the genericity of its topics.

Geertz addresses his metaphorical refocusing in a 1980 article entitled "Blurred Genres: The Refiguration of Social Thought." Having thought about what others perceive with, by means of, or through, he is also thinking about what social thinkers perceive with, by or through. This is an obligation, for, with Dewey, Geertz understands thinking as a form of conduct, a moral act.[48] Theory moves by analogy, "a 'seeing-as' comprehension of the less intelligible by the more." Geertz suggests that social scientists' increasing treatment of social action as analogous to (serious) games, (sidewalk) dramas, and (behavioral) texts, while humanists are "mumbling about motives, authority, persuasion, exchange and hierarchy," indicates that "something is happening to the way we think about the way we think." An alteration of the social thinker's principles for mapping the relation between thought and action in social life, not just a redrawing of the map, is underway.[49]

In this article Geertz plays down his own influence on this alteration and draws on Alton Becker's study of Javanese shadow puppetry to discuss what he believes is happening. Becker names it a "new philology." "Old" philologists (humanists) studied language within individual texts to discern meaning, while social scientists studied the activity of creating texts in general.[50] Humanistic interpretation of fixed inscriptions has thereby been severed from social scientific study of the activity of inscribing; study of fixed meaning has been isolated from study of the social processes that fix it. The "new philologist," who understands social action as texts to be read, reunites the study of "meaning-form" aspects and of "practical contexts that give them life."[51] This is the "great virtue" of treating social actions as metaphorical texts: "It trains attention on . . . how the inscription of action is brought about, what its vehicles are and how they work, and on what the fixation of meaning from the flow of events—history from what happened, thought from thinking, culture from behavior—implies for sociological interpretation."[52]

This is a step towards reflexive specification, towards "uncovering the conceptual structure" revealed by the text metaphor in social thought. The metaphor suggests construal of social actions as intersubjective, tangible carriers of inscribed meaning. Social thought (like all thought, as discussed below) is construction and manipulation of symbol systems as models of other systems. The new model is literary; thinking with it, we seek to understand "how action is connected to sense rather than how behavior is connected to its determinants."[53] The reflexivity is that Geertz is looking at his own metaphor, now widely used, to ascertain the coordinates of his own universe of thinking.

II. PSYCHOLOGY AND THE STUDY OF RELIGION

This metaphor for social thinkers' activity, closely reading behavioral texts over the shoulders of those to whom they belong, has implications for thinking about what psychologists of religion could be about. Before addressing this, I will outline Geertz's use of a psychological theory of the "extrinsic" nature of thought and his understanding of what one is studying when the topic is religion.

THE EXTRINSIC THEORY OF THOUGHT

From Geertz's semiotic position that meanings are encoded in public texts, it follows that culture is public, not intrasubjective. If thinking is cultural, it too is available to textual analysis on the basis of Geertz's use of a psychological theory of the extrinsic nature of thought. This theory treats cognition (and in Geertz's hands, mood, motivation and affect) as manipulation of public materials. Geertz uses Walker Percy and others to argue that mental functioning is not fundamentally private, but is an "overt, public act, involving the purposeful manipulation of objective material," that is, of cultural symbol systems.[54] Thought is constructing and manipulating symbol systems by matching the "states and processes of symbolic models against the states and processes of the wider world." It uses symbol systems as models of other systems (physical, organic, social, psychological) so that the structure of these other systems is understood.[55] In short, cognition, like cockfight, is metaphorical: attributes from one referential system (symbolic) are transferred to another (physical, etc.) to understand the second in terms of the first. Again, the interpreter may reverse the metaphoric process to make available for analysis particular, public, structures of signification. This is Geertz's psychology directed against psychologism. It is neither introspectionist, because it studies manipulation of extrinsic "materials," nor naively behaviorist, because it studies traffic in public symbols that are carriers of meaning and indices of conceptual structures rather than determinants, causes, or explanations. It keeps the meaning that subjectivist psychologies accuse objectivist ones of sacrificing, and it bases its construals of meaning on intersubjective data rather than on posited invisible entities that are "inside" minds.

RELIGION AS TOPIC

As Geertz's often-quoted definition of religion declares, it is a cultural system: "A system of symbols which acts to establish powerful, pervasive and longlasting moods and motivations . . . by formulating conceptions of a general order of existence and clothing these conceptions with such an aura of factuality that the moods and motivations seem uniquely realistic."[56] The key here is twofold: conceptions, and "of a general order of existence." Symbols formulate conceptions that are models for and models of reality (templates and maps). As models for it, conceptions shape moods and motivations. As models of it, they come with an "aura of factuality." The conception formulated is of a "wider world" (Geertz uses William James's term) than the commonsense one. What differentiates religious conceptions is that they "glow" with their own authority, are "intrinsically coercive" and "immediately persuasive." They are prior to, rather than conclusions drawn from, experience.[57]

Let me underscore the point that, for Geertz, the topic of study of religion is conceptions. In *Islam Observed*, he writes that, understood secularly, "religion is not the divine, nor even some manifestation of it in the world, but a conception of it."[58] It is used, not to cope with, but to conceive of, the world.[59] Religious perception is the "actual employment of sacred symbols to activate faith," which is "steadfast attachment to some transtemporal conception of reality."[60] Sacred symbols, for those for whom they are sacred, "formulate an image of the world's construction [world view] and a program for human conduct [ethos] that are mere reflexes of one another."[61] Studying religion, then, comes down to specifying conceptions—imaginations and cognitions of the *really* real. Both are metaphoric.

The task that Geertz assigns to psychological study of religion in *Islam Observed* is to explain why particular individuals are susceptible to workings of particular sacred symbols by explaining how individual needs and capacities are met and used by them.[62] This view limits psychology to the understanding of individuals by restricting it to idiosyncratic needs and capacities. It presupposes prior identification, by someone other than the psychologist of religion, of the relevant symbols and the conceptions that they formulate. The psychologist then enters the scene with an already formulated roster of needs and capacities and proceeds to explain. Psychology works within the old model of tying behavior to its determinants.

A related view is implicit in "Religion as a Cultural System." There, discussing the two cultural functions of religion as model *of* reality (a source of conceptions of world, self, and world-self relations) and model *for* reality (a source of rooted "mental" dispositions—mood and motivation), Geertz comments that the psychological functions of religion flow from the latter.[63] That is, religious conceptions as "templates" are cultural sources or shapers of moods and motivations; the latter give rise to psychological functions of religion. Presumably, the psychologist of religion would identify and account for these functions—for needs and capacities being met and used. These are fair indications of how many psychologists of religion have understood their task.

RELIGION AND PSYCHOLOGY: VARIETIES

Psychology *of* religion, though, is one of several overlapping but distinguishable approaches within the larger area of religion *and* psychology. Areas with "and" in their titles require definition because the "and" serves to specify neither which is the method and which the datum in a particular instance nor which, if either, contains the topic. My preliminary sorting of approaches here is undertaken to identify methods, data, and topics within some influential approaches, in order to clarify what Geertz's views about data, method and topics in anthropology can bring to our thinking about psychological study *of* religion.

Psychology *of* religion is the best known approach, both because it can refer to classical founders (at least William James and Sigmund Freud) and because its mission seems readily understandable. It uses psychological methods and terms to explain data from religious lives. Discussion about method among psychologists of religion is often about the relative merits of established, more-or-less scientific, psychological vocabularies (Freudian, neo-Freudian and object-relations, humanistic, existential, Jungian, behavioral). Discussion of data often centers on which already-abstracted dimensions of religion should be psychologically explained (i.e., ideas, myths and symbols, ritual acts, experiences, emotions). Arguments for the methodological superiority of a vocabulary are often based on their merits for understanding one or more dimensions. Geertz's work questions both discussions. Instead of studying dimensions, one might read particular behavioral texts in their own contexts to learn, in particular cases, which particular conceptions they formulate. This would free the student from the dubious presuppositions that dimensions are cross-cultural slices of some generic religion and that the thing to do with them is to subject them to an explanatory scheme that is foreign to (at least some of) their cultural soil. "Dimension" is a falsely generic term—it collapses our conceptual categories into lived data. If lived data—snippets of symbolic action—were thickly described and read for the conceptual structures that they reveal (that is, specified), they would suggest their own interpretation.

Discussions about method in psychology of religion have also been about the relative advantages of an idiographic approach, based on in-depth study of one or more unique cases, and a nomothetic approach, which establishes correlations among characteristics identified in large populations in order to discover regular, lawful relationships between things "psychological" (e.g., measured or reported self-esteem) and things "religious" (e.g., denominational selection). When psychology *of* (or social psychology *of*) religion meets contemporary behavioral science standards for research methodology, its findings necessarily remain within the model of tying behavior to its determinants (actually, more often correlates). It sacrifices understanding of the meaning of behavior to the actors within their conceptual coordinates. Nor can this approach specify these coordinates, because pre-identified factors determine them by fiat. Many nomothetic studies investigate which already-understood psychological factors are associated, under what conditions, with reported religious experiences or behaviors. This topic is generic, if culture-bound, but so are such data: particularity is lost in translating experience into identifiable "factors."

An idiographic approach, which is necessarily more humanistic and can therefore more closely approximate a "new philology," varies widely in its data, methods, and topics. William James, in *The Varieties of Religious Experience*, worked first as an old-fashioned natural historian by gathering and classifying verbal accounts of religious experience. He also thought as a psychologist to tie some of these classes (i.e., instantaneous and gradual conversions) to psychological determinants, using an associationist psychology which hypothesized subliminal regions of consciousness and subconscious selves. But James also made clear that, as a pragmatist and an empiricist, his interest was not in diagnosis but in significance. His topics were, first, whether religious experiences changed anything psychological (i.e., energy) in experienced human lives and, second, whether they provided new knowledge, or hypotheses, about human nature (his subtitle was "A Study in Human Nature") and the nature of the cosmos or "wider world." James's topics were thus generic, his data were thickly described, and he looked in them for what Geertz might call "conceptions." But James's data, reports of experiential interactions between individuals and the divine, were rarely inscribed in such a way that cultural or social particularity is readable in the texts.

Much in Freud's data, method and topic is also formally similar to Geertz's approach. Freud's data are symbolic actions (speech, behavior, writing, fantasy, ideation), understood as symptomatic of his topic: unconscious psychical dynamics and structure. However, Freud's interpretive method differs from Geertz's when Freud dissolves the particular (unconscious) conceptual structures that he uncovers into intrapsychic universals (they are universal because they are collective). Freud unifies, not locale of study (symbolic action) and topic (unconscious mental life), but methodological vocabulary and topic. The method interprets religious phenomena as indices of mental reality-construction—i.e., oedipal dynamics, pleasure-principle thinking—and Freud's view is that these are what religion *is* in psychological terms. The strength of this view is its steady focus on the inner mental world. But, what is being studied becomes identical to the methodological vocabulary. Those who take the conceptual structures of religion to be more real than, prior to, or more valuable ("higher") than those of a psychology of the unconscious (or of consciousness) name this reductionism. (Viktor Frankl's claim, in his *The Unconscious God*, that God is the human model of paternity instead of fathers being models for God is an example of the logic of this charge.)

A crucial difference between Geertz's and Freud's approaches is that Geertz does not share Freud's conviction that distortion systematically occurs in the passage from unconscious to perceived, enacted, or symbolized. Or, if Geertz shares it, he does not draw on it in interpretation. Freud's notion of systematic distortion (repression) is the basis for his dissolution of dense thickets of particulars into generic, theoretically undistorted, universals. Geertz, in specifying structures of signification, does sometimes identify what in Freudian terms is descriptively unconscious, but not what is dynamically unconscious (repressed). Geertz's subjects are aware of their symbols (though not necessarily *as* symbols) but not of the "conceptions that they formulate." The coordinates of one's own experienced world, when they are functioning *as* coordinates, are not themselves objects of awareness.

If Jung is treated as a classical founder of psychology of religion (which is justifiable if one's criterion is the number of studies that call themselves psychology of religion and use his methods), his work is also a transition to another sort of approach within religion and psychology. This sort can be called psychology *as* religion and religion *of* psychology. These are conceptually distinguishable but closely related, and often are not distinguished by those who take them. Both treat religious conceptions as either privileged over, or equal in status to, psychological ones, so that a psychological method is no longer being *applied* to explain religious data. Because a transition from psychology of religion to this approach often goes unremarked, I will discuss it in more detail.

For Jung (for example, in his 1937 *Psychology and Religion*), data are symbols in dreams, visions, fantasies, and creeds. He calls his method "amplification," which means looking for analogies to these symbols in the larger (textual) world of comparative religions and discovering to what, in these analogous cases, the writer understood the symbols to refer—usually god, self, or some aspect of either. Jung then concludes, on the basis of posited archetypes of the collective unconscious, that the contemporary symbolizer also "means" this referent, although it is consciously unknown. So Jung's topic is the god within (self) and the god without, which are psychologically indistinguishable and are both actually religious and actually psychological. For Jung, an adequate psychology demonstrates that the most important psychological contents (archetypal symbols) and processes (individuation) are really religious. Jung's approach, then, could be named psychology as religion. It is also a religion of psychology, because he understands the goal of the discipline of psychology as making authentic experience possible. Psychology will restore our spiritual lives by being a system of guidance of the inner life that restores its true meaning.

For all of his methodological and theoretical differences from Jung, Abraham Maslow, the American humanistic psychologist, takes similar formal positions. In his *Religions, Values, and Peak Experiences*, he equates "core" religious experience (which is explicitly stripped of cultural particularities) with "peak experience." The latter is a psychological concept, an index of self-actualization, which is the highest form of human psychological life. Hence, Maslow unifies the most authentic religious phenomenon and one of his central psychological concepts. In addition, for Maslow, humanistic psychology will not just study but also provide values, meaning and orientation to those who no longer respond to their religious providers. There are other examples of psychology as religion and religion of psychology. Claudio Naranjo, in *The One Quest*, takes the position that transpersonal psychology (which is closely related to humanistic psychology) and religion are functionally identical: they provide information about and guidance for the basic human quest for wholeness. Transpersonal psychology does so by studying *and* encouraging "higher" states of consciousness.

In these instances, method and subject-matter are unified. In Jung's case, data may be thickly described, but cultural particularity is omitted and the conceptions formulated by symbols are presupposed to be universal. In most humanistic and transpersonal writings, particular religious ideas or experiences are not presented in their particularity nor thickly described. Maslow's substitution of an acultural construct, "core" religious experience, for thickly described data, is typical of such approaches. Data are already generic (i.e., mystical experiences in general) and are matched with the already-generic psychological (i.e., peak-experiences). The topic in this approach is psycho-religious *truth*, discovered and then recommended.

Two other approaches merit brief mention here. The "dialogue" between (mostly liberal Protestant) theology and (mostly dynamic depth) psychology, of the 50's and 60's, took psychological and theological concepts as its data in order to enrich comprehension of generic human phenomena such as guilt, anxiety, and hope. Its topics were such phenomena, often abstracted from particular occurrences, and, secondly, the relative adequacy of theological and psychological conceptions of them. A theology of psychology (or sometimes theology and the social sciences) approach accepts a normative theological position and adopts and/or criticizes psychological concepts and presuppositions.

Finally, a religion and culture approach treats both religions and psychologies (actually, selected aspects of them) as data—as assays of culture. Both religions and psychologies are understood as cultural systems which express, bestow meaning on, save, liberate, order, or constrain humanity. Both are seen, not necessarily as competitors in providing norms or as mutually reinforcing therein, but as historically and socially conditioned variants of cultural systems, so that the topic is culture. At the least, both religions and psychologies are treated as indices of culture (Geertz would belong here if he studied psychologies as cultural systems); at most, a critical component is introduced and one or both are treated as ideology. This approach provides scholarly interpretation *of* psychologies; it neither works wholly within a psychology nor does it recommend one as truth-giving. Examples of this approach are Philip Rieff's *The Triumph of the Therapeutic: The Uses of Faith after Freud*, which he understands as a step towards a sociology of culture, and Peter Homans' *Jung in Context: Modernity and the Making of a Psychology*, which looks at sociological, personal (psychological) and religious (theological and experiential) factors to interpret and criticize Jung's psychological and religious ideas. Their methods are not exclusively psychological, but both use psychological ideas as interpretive tools (Rieff uses Freudian notions of repression and instinctual gratification; Homans, Freud's and Kohut's understandings of narcissism).

A REFIGURED PSYCHOLOGY OF RELIGION

I believe that Geertz's method can help us conceptualize a psychological approach to religion that could become a new philology. This approach would retain the emphasis on the religious as data found in the psychology of religion. It would make particular, behavioral religious texts its data, and would look in them for conceptions to ask: what do religious conceptions demonstrate about psychological life as such? Its topic would be psychological *life*, so its data would not be confounded with its own methodological vocabulary. This approach would also retain the strong point of the religion and culture approach, which is the capacity to interpret psychological ideas themselves, to specify conceptions entailed in them and to understand them as cultural systems. Thus, it could also ask what psychological conceptions demonstrate about psychologies, not just religions. More specifically, were we to think with a Geertzian metaphoric refocusing about psychological thought about religion, we could conceive of psychology as reading behavioral texts *for* and *with* metaphors. Enacted, linguistic, cognitive, and emotive religious texts to be read are metaphoric. Just as important, psychology works metaphorically, transferring referents from one system to another to help us comprehend the less intelligible in terms of the more.

This metaphoric refocusing of psychology could do at least three things. First, it could provide a way to mediate a major impasse that has haunted religion and psychology, an impasse often called the problem of reductionism. Second, it could give us a way to resolve, in particular instances for particular instances, the empirical problem that is related to this theoretical one, the problem of which, if either, system, psychological or religious, is the symbol system and which the nonsymbolic system. Third, such a metaphoric refocusing could provide impetus for developing a psychology which is again part of social thought— part of new philology—which I believe is necessary in order for a psychology to be adequate to the study of lived religion. I will briefly address each of these in turn.

1) In order to address the impasse over reductionism, it will help to look more closely at Geertz's distinction between the model for and the model of aspects of religious conceptions. For Geertz, "true symbols" are characterized by the *intertransposability* of the model-of and model-for aspects. Such symbols both "express the world's climate and shape it."[64] In the "model-of" sense, symbol structures are manipulated to make them match pre-established nonsymbolic systems. A theory or a chart is developed to model (imitate) physical reality. The symbolic is altered; the nonsymbolic is given. The model-for aspect of symbol structures entails manipulating (conceptualizing) the "nonsymbolic systems in terms of the relationships expressed in the symbolic." Here, theory guides understanding of nonsymbolic relationships. Symbolic sources of information have "an intrinsic double aspect: they give meaning, that is objective conceptual form, to social and psychological reality by shaping themselves to it and by shaping it to themselves."[65] Nonsymbolic sources of information (i.e., genes) have only the model-for aspect.

Between psychology of religion and psychology as religion, there is disagreement about whether religious conceptions or psychological conceptions are symbolic or nonsymbolic. Psychologies that view what they study as symbolic, for example, the idea of God as father, tend to view the psychological as nonsymbolic, as "given" like physical reality. They interpret religious ideas as functions or results of these supposedly nonsymbolic, psychological givens. Hence religious data are seen as epiphenomenal; psychological conceptions are placed on them when religious conceptions could also be read in them. And users of supposedly nonsymbolic psychologies often confuse their psychological conceptions, which are themselves symbolic of a nonsymbolic realm, with that realm itself. Thus Freud sees Oedipal complexes as (very complex) models for submission to or rebellion against gods; Jung sees archetypes as analogous to genes, as models for religious symbols; Maslow sees peak experiences as the actual psychological states onto which religious, culture-bound particularities are glossed. The religious is seen as resulting from psychological reality, and the psychological theory is treated as if it were nonsymbolic like the reality it maps.

Those who see religious reality as the model for psychological reality name this reductionism. They point out the symbolic nature of "scientific" thought systems which do not understand themselves as symbolic. But this argument about reduction is an argument about the direction in which metaphoric thinking is working, about which system contains the primary referents, about which system of symbols is actually understood in terms of the other. As Geertz shows, this is an issue that "thick description" can help us resolve empirically. The charge of reductionism is an index of prior valuation of the vocabulary of what is being analyzed (religion) over that of the psychological interpretation. Geertz's work is part of the resolution of this impasse, for with it we can comprehend *both* as symbolic culture systems. If we need a clue that both psychological and religious systems are cultural systems of symbols, it is to be found in their intertransposability; psychology of religion easily becomes psychology as religion, or religious psychology.

2) What we need, and what I believe Geertz's work can offer stimulus towards, is a psychology that, like the psychology of religion, makes the intersubjective symbols of lived religion its data and, like the religion and culture approach, understands both religions *and* psychologies, including itself, as texts in which conceptions can be construed. If psychology were to take metaphor and other tropes seriously at all the levels that Geertz analyzes and uses them, it would be in a position to inventory when and understand how religious conceptions are models *for* understanding other realities and when and how they are models *of* other realities. It need not and should not expect the same answer in each instance. That is, psychology would be in a position to sort out what is a commentary on what.

3) In conclusion, I find in Geertz's thought some guidelines for a psychology adequate to the study of religion. It must be a symbolic, cognitive, and interpretive psychology that aims to construe religious *and* psychological conceptions, "coordinates of the experienced world," rather than uncritically working within one or both of them. This means it must be reflexive, engaged in examining its own metaphors as it examines others' metaphors. Stratified structures of signification, "coordinates of the experienced world," are surely proper objects of psychological inquiry. Thick description (inscription and specification) would yield accounts of specific religious conceptions and of their relationship to specific psychological ones. This psychology would be asking what religious conceptions and psychological conceptions demonstrate about religious and psychological life as such. In this way, the "and" in "religion and psychology" would be defined for specific instances of particular cultural lives, that is, *in* the data, and not just in scholars' disciplines.

There is a certain historical appropriateness to imagining such a psychology, which would be part of "refigured" social thought. When psychology was explicitly part of social thought (as Freud's, Jung's, and James's were), psychologists knew that psychology ought to be methodologically adequate to the interpretation of religions. An adequate psychology must still be adequate to the construal of lived religions. This adequacy would locate it again as part of social thought.

Notes and References

1. Clifford Geertz, "Blurred Genres: The Refiguration of Social Thought," *The American Scholar* 49 (Spring, 1980): 176. I am grateful to Emily R. Grosholz and Kathryn Hume, The Pennsylvania State University, for criticisms of and helpful suggestions for this chapter.
2. Geertz, *The Social History of an Indonesian Town* (Cambridge, Mass.: The MIT Press, 1965), p. 13. Other references in this paragraph are to discussions in *Islam Observed: Religious Development in Morocco and Indonesia* (Chicago & London: The University of Chicago Press, 1968), pp. vi, 4.
3. " 'From the Native's Point of View': On the Nature of Anthropological Understanding," reprinted in *Symbolic Anthropology: A Reader in the Study of Symbols and Meanings*, ed. Janet L. Dolgin et al. (New York: Columbia University Press, 1977), p. 491.
4. "Thick Description: Toward an Interpretive Theory of Culture," in *The Interpretation of Cultures: Selected Essays by Clifford Geertz* (New York: Basic Books, 1973), p. 17. *The Interpretation of Cultures* is hereafter abbreviated as IC.
5. Ibid., p. 9.
6. Ibid., p. 27.
7. Ibid., p. 30.
8. *Islam Observed*, p. 24.
9. "Person, Time, and Conduct in Bali," IC, p. 363.
10. *Islam Observed*, p. 22.
11. Ibid., p. 21.
12. Ibid.
13. In Clifford Geertz, Hildred Geertz and Lawrence Rosen, *Meaning and Order in Moroccan Society: Three Essays in Cultural Analysis* (Cambridge: Cambridge University Press, 1979), pp. 123-244; Princeton: Princeton University Press, 1980.
14. *Islam Observed*, p. 4.
15. Ibid., p. 155.
16. Ibid., p. 22.
17. IC, p. 311.
18. Ibid., p. 313.
19. *Symbolic Anthropology*, p. 491.
20. *The Antioch Review* 33, 1 (Spring, 1975): 5; quotation from *Philosophical Investigations* (New York, 1953), p. 8.
21. *The Antioch Review* 33, 1 (Spring, 1975): 6.
22. IC, p. 21.
23. Ibid., pp. 20-21.
24. Ibid., p. 26.
25. Ibid., p. 14.
26. Ibid., pp. 10-13.
27. See "The Impact of the Concept of Culture on the Concept of Man," IC, pp. 40-41, 43, 49-50, 52-54; "The Transition to Humanity," in Sol Tax and Leslie G. Freeman, ed., *Horizons of Anthropology*, 2nd ed. (Chicago: Aldine, 1977), pp. 30-32.
28. "Person, Time, and Conduct in Bali," IC, p. 365.
29. Ibid., p. 408.
30. *Negara: The Theatre State in Nineteenth-Century Bali* (Princeton: Princeton University Press, 1980), p. 135.
31. "Ideology as a Cultural System," IC, p. 212. Here Geertz explains that the vehicles, but

not the nature, of conception are socially determined.

32. "Thick Description," IC, p. 28.
33. "Ideology as a Cultural System," IC, p. 216.
34. " 'From the Native's Point of View,' " Symbolic Anthropology, p. 483; italics mine.
35. "Thick Description," IC, p. 7.
36. Ibid., p. 9.
37. Ibid., p. 27. Geertz uses "inscription" in a related sense when he draws on Paul Ricoeur's use of "inscription of meaning" to explain how social action is like a written text in that both are interpretable repositories of meaning. In Freud and Philosophy, Ricoeur points out that, for Freud, "interpretation is concerned not only with a scripture or writing but with any set of signs that may be taken as a text to decipher, hence a dream or neurotic symptom, as well as a ritual, myth, work of art, or a belief" [Freud and Philosophy: An Essay on Interpretation (New Haven: Yale University Press, 1970), p. 26]. In this respect, Geertz's project is more like Freud's, as understood by Ricoeur, than Ricoeur's (a point on which Geertz does not comment). Geertz discusses Ricoeur in "Thick Description," IC, p. 19, "Deep Play," IC, p. 448, n. 36, and "Blurred Genres," p. 175.
38. "Deep Play: Notes on the Balinese Cockfight," IC, p. 448.
39. Ibid., p. 443.
40. Ibid., p. 444.
41. Ibid., p. 447.
42. In IC, pp. 209-213; Hildred Geertz and Clifford Geertz, Kinship in Bali (Chicago: The University of Chicago Press, 1975), p. 169.
43. "Deep Play," IC, p. 447.
44. "Ideology as a Cultural System," IC, p. 210.
45. "Deep Play," IC, p. 449.
46. Ibid., p. 452.
47. Analogy from physical process vs. symbolic form is from "Blurred Genres," p. 178; dissecting and diagnosing are from "Deep Play," IC, p. 448.
48. Geertz, "Thinking as a Moral Act: Ethical Dimensions of Fieldwork in the New States," Antioch Review 28, 2 (1968): 139-158.
49. "Blurred Genres," pp. 166, 168, 175.
50. Ibid., p. 176.
51. Geertz, "Found in Translation: On the Social History of the Moral Imagination," The Georgia Review 31 (Winter, 1977): 803.
52. "Blurred Genres," pp. 175-176.
53. Ibid., p. 178.
54. Geertz, "The Growth of Culture and the Evolution of Mind," IC, pp. 76, 78. See Walker Percy, "Symbol, Consciousness and Intersubjectivity," Journal of Philosophy 55, 15 (1958): 631-641 and "The Symbolic Structure of Interpersonal Process," Psychiatry 24, 1 (1961): 39-52; Eugene Galanter and Murray Gerstenhaber, "On Thought: The Extrinsic Theory," Psychological Review 63, 4 (1956): 218-227.
55. "Ideology as a Cultural System," IC, p. 214.
56. "Religion as a Cultural System," IC, p. 90.
57. Islam Observed, p. 17, 98.
58. Ibid., p. 56.
59. Ibid., p. 93.
60. Ibid., p. 108.
61. Ibid., p. 97.
62. Ibid., p. 100.
63. "Religion as a Cultural System," IC, p. 123. Geertz follows Gilbert Ryle in defining motivation as "a persisting tendency, a chronic inclination to perform certain sorts of acts and experience certain sorts of feeling in certain sorts of situations, . . ." Motivations are neither acts nor feelings, but "liabilities to perform particular classes of act or have particular classes of feeling." Motivations are interpreted in relation to their intentions; moods in terms of "the conditions from which they are conceived to spring" (ibid., pp. 96-97).
64. Ibid., pp. 94, 95.
65. Ibid., p. 93.

Part Two

The Work of Victor Turner

CHAPTER IV

Victor Turner's Theory of Religion: Towards an Analysis of Symbolic Time.

Dario Zadra

The processual symbolic analysis developed by Victor Turner is one of the operative concepts which have given anthropology a capacity of critical innovation in the methodology and theoretical interpretation of religion. Turner's analyses have greatly enlarged our knowledge of the processuality of the symbolic system and have made a major contribution to our understanding of the interconnections of symbols in the ritual process and the relation which may be observed between ritual and social structure. This chapter will outline the main elements of Turner's method of symbolic analysis and theory of religion, its main conceptual formalisation and epistemological perspectives; the last part of our study observes the implications of this theory with particular reference to the concept of Symbolic Time.

In the religious system, time results from the co-ordination of two main parameters, the epigenetic and the performative, which create a periodical order within the symbolic system. It will be shown that Turner's performative model of the ritual process is a constitutive element of the definition of periodicity in the symbolic system in that it explains the ritual elaboration of the epigenetic paradigm. The epigenetic theory of the symbolic function is necessary for a definition of Sacred History and Symbolic Time: to this purpose we will analyse the concept of Symbolic Intentionality and will observe the periodical character of Christian symbolic time.

I. ANTHROPOLOGICAL APPROACHES TO THE STUDY OF MEANING IN RELIGION

Following the school of Durkheim and Mauss, a common theoretical assumption in anthropological studies has been that religious facts should be analysed with reference to the concept of 'fait total', that is, in terms of the totality of cultural and social forms in which they arise. As Evans-Pritchard has suggested, religious facts should be seen "as a relation of parts to one another within a coherent system, each part making sense only in relation to the others, and the system itself making sense only in relation to other institutional systems, as part of a wider set of relations."[1]

When explained in systemic terms, society acquires a structural form in which every fact and institution is defined in terms of its function within the whole. Analytical categories such as 'collective conscience' and 'collective representation' are used, within this theoretical framework, to explain, in terms of social function, the relation between religion and social nascent state, structures of reciprocity and forms of thought.

The ethnological and cultural analyses undertaken by Victor Turner have introduced into this approach a new set of relations in the study of religion and society. Concepts such as 'social drama', 'the processual view of society', 'social antistructure' and the observation of ritual symbols in terms of multivocality and polarisation of meaning have significantly modified both the understanding of the 'fait total' and the approach to the analysis of religion.

For Turner, the paradigmatic event of social life is the 'social drama'. Ritual process is embedded in the event of social drama as its performative symbolic feature but develops a function which is at variance with the dynamics of the structural system. These concepts, which inform Turner's anthropological and cultural studies, sustain the idea that "human social life is the producer and product of time, which becomes its measure."[2] The theoretical perspective that society is characterised by process is delineated, not by a description of social structures as such, but by the structural transformations considered as 'semantic transformations' which indicate and give meaning to the flux and changeability of culture and society. The process of social life has movement as much as structure, persistence as much as change which give to it the features of 'processual units'. These 'processual units' often display a dramatic form in that they orchestrate the resolution of conflicts and tensions which menace fundamental aspects and values of society.[3] It is with reference to conflict resolution within the social drama that Turner has studied the religious symbolic function.

Between the 1950s and 1970s, there has been a significant reworking of the concept of religion in primitive and literate cultures, for example, in the writings of Levi-Strauss, Eliade, Geertz, Turner, Douglas and Bellah. The dominant theoretical concern which has characterised this shift in the anthropological study of religion has been the conceptual analysis of the symbolic with reference to social action and social structure.

Victor Turner's specific contribution to the study of symbolic meaning has been to develop a method of symbolic analysis which directly relates the symbols to the performative process of the ritual. Ritual processes are related to individual and specific dominant symbols which operate as structures of meaning within the event of social drama. Dominant symbols show a particular stability of meaning which is relatively independent within the ritual performative elaboration of the event. This siting of symbols within the performance has enabled Turner to study symbolic meaning in its relation to time, to the ritual performance, and to social processes or events. Turner's analysis relates the meaning of symbols to their semantic fields as well as to their linguistic transformations, to their relative predominance through the sequence of ritual performance and to the articulation of symbols into architectonic forms. The analysis of symbolic forms is undertaken to show their internal structure of signification which has a performative function in the sociocultural process.

The shift in anthropological studies towards symbolic analysis is attributable to several factors. The evident limitations of structural and functional analysis of social institutions have clarified the need for studies of the dynamic aspects of culture and have also directed anthropologists to the study of the forms of mental activity of the individual actors. This new focus of attention has been facilitated by theoretical progress in the linguistic and psychological sciences which offers possibilities for the integration of cultural features, linguistic and semiotic, with institutional and sociological forms. The recognition of the formation and interpretation of symbols as a significant problematic in the study of meaning has provided a more adequate theoretical framework for the definition of the religious function. As a result, structures and processes internal to the religious fact and to its elaboration and interpretation can be analysed with a greater degree of conceptual precision.

Turner's theoretical and methodological writings reflect this shift and development in anthropological studies of religion. His early field-work among the Ndembu people of north-western Rhodesia led to the description in *Schism and Continuity* (1957) of processes of village social life, in which he concentrated especially on the forms of crises and their resolution. In particular, Turner studied those crises induced by tensions between matrilineal descent and village membership and by the schismatic activities of individuals and factions who manipulate social relations to their own advantage. Turner examined the different types of conflict by observing the changes and breaches in social relationships over a period of time. He looked for the "systematic interconnections in successive interactional events within a single spatial system" with the aim of showing how the "general and the particular, the cyclical and the exceptional, the regular and the irregular, the normal and the deviant, are interrelated in a single social process".[4] By studying the jural and ritual activities set in motion by representatives of social groups as modes of crisis resolution, Turner developed the concept of social drama as a device for describing and analysing episodes that manifest social conflict. This emphasis on the dramatic structure of social processes represents a transition from the structural-functionalist forms of explanation of social process to a processual analysis of social structure.

In *Drums of Affliction* (1968) and *Forest of Symbols* (1967), Turner gravitated towards the explicit study of symbolic processes in Ndembu culture in order to analyse the forms of meaning and the dynamics present in the collective and individual condition of social drama. Symbols are studied in the context of their performance and at the different levels of meaning which may be derived from their internal structure and articulation. Turner distinguishes three levels of symbolic meaning: exegetic meaning derives from the interpretations available to those within the ritual system; operational meaning is the actual use of the symbol and its manipulation by the different social groups within the ritual; the positional meaning of the symbol may be observed from the interrelation of symbols within the ritual system considered as a whole.[5]

In the later work, for example *Ritual Process* (1969), *Dramas, Fields and*

Metaphors (1974), *Image and Pilgrimage in Christian Culture* (1978), *Process, Performance and Pilgrimage* (1979) and *From Ritual to Theatre* (1982)[6], Turner has taken the model of social drama, of ritual performance and symbolic activity as comparative paradigms and applied them to a broader field of religious and cultural analysis in literate societies. In this enlarged approach, 'structural analysis' is based not so much on institutional forms but, instead, on the ways in which "social actions of various kinds acquire form through the metaphors and paradigms in their actors' heads (put there by explicit teaching and implicit generalisation from social experience) and, in certain intensive circumstances, generate unprecedented forms that bequeath history new metaphors and paradigms."[7] At this point, the model of social drama has become, for Turner, the processual structure of social action itself.

As Turner's areas of analysis have varied, there has been a corresponding variation in his definition and characterisation of the meaning of religion. In his first ethnographic studies, Turner defined the meaning of religion primarily with reference to the diachronic features of social drama in the structural system. In the later work directed towards literate societies, the meaning of religion is analysed with explicit reference to the condition of reflexivity within the structure of mental and social experience. Reflexivity introduces into the concept of ritual process and social drama a systemic dimension which had not previously been explored. In the earlier ethnography, these systemic features seemed to rest upon custom and habit and therefore to be below the level of conscious awareness present in the elaboration of social drama.

EPISTEMOLOGICAL PERSPECTIVE

Turner's theoretical approach and his description of religious forms and processes is guided by two sets of epistemological relations. One set relates sociocultural forms to a condition of particularity of the individual historical event; it is expressed in Blake's line from *Jerusalem*, "General Forms have their vitality in Particulars, and every Particular is a Man."[8] The second set of epistemological relations connects the general forms of the historical event to a "condition of indeterminacy" which Turner relates to liminality and antistructure. This condition of indeterminacy, present below the General Form in every Particular is, for Turner, the source of constant change and of social and cultural innovation.

This dual set of relations puts the different data which Turner examines into a temporal paradigm which simultaneously connects historical particularity and innovation, thereby reducing the rigidity and determination which structural and symbolic articulations display when observed simply as functions of a social system.

An order of relation is therefore brought into evidence between events and the sociocultural system and between social structure and symbolic processes which is different in articulation and complexity from that observable within a primarily functional or simply structural form of analysis.

Turner's two epistemological perspectives evince the historical particularity of structures as functions of human action; they also enable him to present social forms not as definitive or unchangeable but, rather, as related to an original condition which is intrinsically capable of change and therefore has a dynamic structure. The interrelation of form and indeterminacy is a significant pattern within Turner's theoretical formulations. This combination of themata allows him firstly to observe the social fact as an historical structural formation within a field of plurality of facts and secondly to connect structure to process and to time. This is a significant possibility for the theory and analysis of religion because it enables the observation of features of religion which are intrinsically dynamic and related to the condition of change and innovation.

SOCIAL DRAMA AND RITUAL PROCESS

"At its simplest, the (social) drama consists of a four stage model, proceeding from the breach of some relationship regarded as crucial in the relevant social group . . . through a phase of rapidly mounting crisis in the direction of the group's major dichotomous cleavage, to the application of legal or ritual means of redress or reconciliation between the conflicting parties which compose the action set. The final stage is either the public and symbolic expression of reconciliation or else of irremediable schism."[9] These social processes in which normative breaches are redressed and crises are resolved or recognized in their permanently schismatic character "occur within groups bounded by shared values of persons and interests and having a real or alleged common history. Their main actors are persons for whom the group which constitutes the field of dramatic action has a high value priority."[10] Social rules and cultural paradigms are transformed in the social drama into metaphors and symbols which enable the mobilisation of political power and which determine a trial of strength between influential paradigm bearers in the sociocultural settling.[11] When social drama irrupts into the normal course of social life, it forces the group to assess its own pattern of behaviour and the relation to values enunciated by the group. In other words, "dramas induce and contain reflexive processes and generate cultural frames in which reflexivity can find a legitimate place."[12]

In Turner's ethnological studies, ritual process appears primarily as a mechanism for the redress of social tension; in the later works, ritual is understood to be a source of innovation. Although the ritual process is related to the phases of crisis resolution in the social drama, it reveals and differentiates in symbolic form, a modality of meaning which cannot be identified as the expression or reflection of social structure. Ritual inverts the forms of perception, the dynamics and the order expressed in the structural system; it articulates a vision of reality which becomes the test of legitimation within society.

RITUAL FORMALISM AND INDETERMINACY

Turner understands ritual to be a performance structured by symbols which have a relation with structures of meaning elaborated within the processual unit of the social drama. Ritual has a dramatic processual structure and an inherent temporal form which co-ordinates three stages of symbolic performance. The first stage is that of destructuration, the second is a symbolic and structural condition of liminality, the third consists of a condition of differentiation. As Turner describes it with reference to van Gennep's definition of rites of passage, "the first phase detaches the ritual subjects from their old places in society; the last installs them, inwardly transformed and outwardly changed in a new place in society".[13]

The three stages of the ritual process are correlated into a dramatic unity. This unity is a complex fact which shows, on one hand, a high level of formalisation and is, on the other, related to innovation and change. For Turner ritual is a "prescribed formal behaviour for occasions not given over to technological routine having reference to beliefs in mystical beings or powers."[14] Both the performative rules of ritual and the systematisation of its symbolic features reveal a high degree of formalisation. The objects, events and words of ritual are each incorporated as a 'performative genre' and are employed under circumstances related to the resolution of the dramatic conditions of social life and specific to the communication with invisible powers. The formalisation of ritual, that is the synchronisation of many symbolic features, and of their performative genres within the sequential dramatic structure, is essential to the efficacy of ritual although the level of systematisation varies with each society together with the style of correlation of the many different kinds of symbolic features and of their generative grammars.

At the same time, throughout the formalisation of the ritual, the performative connection of the symbols and of symbolic action serves to contrast and to evaluate or re-assess major sociocultural classifications and contradictions in such a way that change and a condition of transformation may be developed within the social structure itself. "Performances of ritual are distinct phases in the social process whereby groups adjust to internal change and adapt to their external environment."[15] Turner's approach sharply differentiates ritual from social ceremony which is linked with social status; he shows the modalities by which ritual, in terms of its own internal structure, far from being a simple memory and re-enactment of cultural values, is a generative structure within the process of life and the conditions of existence and experience.

The question then arises of how these apparently opposed characteristics of formalisation and change may be seen at work together in ritual and in religion. We would suggest that a balanced theoretical description of the structural and dynamic features of religion should avoid both rigid formalism and the assumption of radical sociocultural indeterminacy.

Structural-functionalism and cultural rationalism seem to compress life within the limits of a rigid formalism. Whether the form of determinism applied is political, economic or cultural, these models for the definition of social structure cannot comprehend the complex dynamics of the field of action or of the symbolic structures of a culture. These models also display a tendency to explain change or variation and temporal transformation simply as forms of permutation and combination within a socially related and culturally differentiated code. A rigidly formalistic approach does not provide theoretical space for religious facts or for specifically religious forms of life. Affective processes are not included within the theoretical framework which is applied to cognitive structures; furthermore, formalistic models discount or undervalue the subjective and individual contribution to cultural and religious forms in favour of the function of the collectivity as the determining source of symbolic structures.

The contrary approach of sociocultural indeterminacy is unable, however, to offer a satisfactory explanation of the function of structure and system. It emphasises the deep spontaneity of the human process of life to the point of devaluing the phylogenetic function of the symbolic system and of its logical and cognitive structures. Accentuating the unpredictable character of the symbolic elaboration within the sociocultural process, indeterminacy comes close to being identified as an originary condition of freedom and creativity. This assumption undermines the historical character of the symbolic function as well as the fact that the performative and structural modalities of the symbolic function embody historical continuity in addition to the creative tension of existence. This historical development is sedimented in the symbolic function as it develops specific symbolic structures within the performative order.

In the case of both rigid formalism and of cultural indeterminacy, it is impossible to understand how the public and the individual, the general and the particular may be unified in the religious symbolic function. What is Turner's solution to the problem of understanding the relation between structural pluralism and change in the ritual symbolic performance? For Turner, the structure and function of the ritual shows in paradigmatic form what may be said of the religious system as a whole; that it is a performative structure which is highly formalised but which is innovative in the process of social relation; it is bound to an apparently repetitive form but is predicated upon the originary and nascent state of motivations and structures operative in the sociocultural condition.

Turner, therefore, locates the religious function in the ritual process rather than in the systemic formations and elaborations of the symbolic function. At the same time, he binds ritual to the historical particularity of the 'social drama' which he considers to be the creative condition of sociocultural life and the point of encounter of human motivations. In his most explicit formulation, Turner has seen "social action as systematic and systematising but culture as a mere stock of unconnected items."[16] In this way, ritual function is related to processuality as well as to historical particularity; the symbolic function is not formalised by a rigid code ruling the symbolic structure nor by direct correlation with social institutions. Symbols are multivocal functions simultaneously combining, by multiplicity of reference, affectivity and cognition. They operate in different conditions of social drama and of ritual performance; more importantly, they have a liminal character which is dynamic and structural and therefore distinguishes them from those forms which are articulated by the social structure.[17]

We will return to a discussion of the adequacy of this set of analytical relations after delineating the main features of Turner's analysis of symbolic processuality.

II. PROCESSUAL SYMBOLIC ANALYSIS

LIMINALITY

Turner's work on the processual form of ritual is indebted to van Gennep's discovery of sequential structure in his comparative work on rites de passage. Van Gennep was able to demonstrate the existence of a "tripartite movement in space-time" showing that rites of passage "accompany transitions from one situation to another and from one cosmic or social world to another."[18] These ritual forms were subdivided by van Gennep into rites of separation, threshold rites and rites of re-aggregation for which the terms pre-liminal, liminal and post-liminal are also used. Through this analysis, van Gennep was able to define a common processual form of symbolic performance within the sociocultural system.

In the first phase, which is one of separation, symbolic behaviour demarcates the sacred from the profane and indicates the detachment of the ritual subjects from their previous social statuses. During the next phase of transition or limen, the ritual subjects pass through a period and area of ambiguity with reference to the social structure, in which few of the features of the preceding and subsequent profane statuses or cultural states are present. The symbolic phenomena and actions of the final phase of re-aggregation or re-incorporation represent the return of the subjects to newly defined positions in society. These three phases of van Gennep's model vary, both in relative length and in their degree of elaboration, according to the types of passage effected through the ritual process. Thus Turner has observed that "rites of separation are prominent in funeral ceremonies, rites of incorporation at marriages. Transition rites may play an important part . . . in pregnancy, betrothal and initiation."[19] The symbolic features of rites of separation and rites of aggregation demonstrate different forms of connection with the structural system. But van Gennep emphasised that in all these rituals, there is a specific time and condition of liminality in which the ritual subjects are freed from normative structures and are, therefore, in a condition of 'betwixt and between' positions in the sociocultural order. The dichotomy between sacred and profane is marked by this relation of opposition between the condition of liminality and the sociocultural system. In liminality, the social order is suspended or inverted and, instead, a sequence of symbolic actions defines the performance within a sacred space and time.

The work of Victor Turner contains an extensive analysis of the liminal phase in rites of passage. One of the most significant aspects of Turner's contribution to the study of religious forms, is the integration which he is able to make, in the analysis of ritual performance, between the historical dimension of 'event' and the character of passage noticed by van Gennep. By connecting the tripartite structure of ritual to the development of social drama, Turner extends the understanding of liminality by defining the processual character of its sociological, symbolic and experiental features. It would seem that Turner understands the ritual symbolic process to be the paradigmatic structure of the religious function.

'COMMUNITAS' AS SOCIAL ANTI-STRUCTURE

Liminality is characterized by a high degree of symbolic elaboration and, at the same time, by simplicity of social structure. This counterposition is underlined by the relation between the symbolic mediators in the liminal phase of the ritual and the liminal subjects among whom there is often a "complete equality of non-status."[20]

Turner defines communitas as "a relational quality of full unmediated communication, even communion, between definite and determinate identities which arises spontaneously in all kinds of groups, situations and circumstances."[21]

An indissoluble link is posited between the condition of communitas and social structure although each is defined in contrast with the other and in terms of structural opposition. This linkage which occurs within the existential condition of the ritual process is revealed in the observation of sets of dyadic symbolic features and in the antonymic classifications of structure and antistructure. Turner understands social structure as a "patterned arrangement of role sets, status sets and status sequences consciously recognised and regularly operative in a given society and closely bound up with legal and political norms and sanctions."[22] The form of a generalised social relation is intrinsic to communitas understood not merely as the antithesis or inversion of symbolic or social structure but, instead, as a condition of potentiality linking the individuals involved in a 'total confrontation of human identities' within nontransactional forms of experience. The antistructural aspect of communitas is, therefore, directly related to events which are experienced as being out of both normal time and social structure. These events bring possible and contrary forms into prominence, thereby engendering a potential reflexivity for the social and cultural system as a whole. Oppositions which may be clarified or formalised within the 'flow' of communitas by its irruption into the sociocultural process are those of equality and inequality, homogeneity and heterogeneity, absence of property and rank with the presence of property and rank, simplicity and complexity. Turner states that communitas is the "fons et origo of all structures and at the same time their critique . . . The bonds of communitas are undifferentiated, egalitarian, direct, extant, non-rational, existential, I-Thou (in Buber's sense). Communitas is spontaneous, immediate, concrete, not abstract. It is part of the 'serious life'."[23]

Communitas may break into society through the interstices of structure in liminality, at the edges of structure in marginality, and from beneath the structure in inferiority. Nevertheless, communitas has a constant tendency towards structuration. In the attempt to preserve its existential character, what Turner describes as spontaneous communitas may become normative through the elaboration of a system of ethical precepts and legal rules. Alternatively communitas may develop ideological forms through the elaboration of egalitarian or utopian concepts of society.[24] According to Turner, communitas may, in its function as the source of non-transactional experience, be propelled into cultural prominence and may become instrumental in the development of mediatory structures within the sociocultural system. Turner regards this propensity of communitas in the light of Sartre's remark that structures are created by activity which has no structure but suffers its results as structure.

The introduction into sociocultural analysis of the concept of antistructure has been a significant innovation. The definition of the creative process at the public level in the form of communitas and its antistructural features has given theoretical shape to dynamics which are also of central importance to the study of religion. The observation of these dynamic features at their points of emergence in cultural areas and at times of institutional void has brought attention to neglected aspects of social and religious formation and change; these aspects have often been omitted from the analyses of structural functionalists amongst whom there has been a marked tendency to restrict value and factual status to forms of social organization.

RITUAL SYMBOLS

Turner's model of symbolic analysis is coherent with his processual model of social fact. For Turner, symbols are essentially dynamic systems of signifiers which operate in the context of temporal sociocultural processes.[25] In processual symbolic analysis, attention is brought to the 'way of performance' of the symbol as well as to its relation with formal structures of meaning. Turner studies symbols "in a time series in relation to other 'events' . . . for symbols are essentially involved in social process."[26] The significance of symbols and their dynamic properties as factors in social action, becomes evident when ritual performances are viewed as intrinsic to those social processes whereby groups adjust to internal change and adapt to their external environment. Turner observes the temporal dimension of the symbolic function by correlating the sequence of the symbols in a given ritual process with the relative dominance of particular symbols within the ritual system.

Dominant symbols represent or refer to 'non-empirical' beings, powers or types of efficacy. They appear in the rituals of affliction and those of life crises which Turner studied among the Ndembu. Two types of dominant symbols are distinguished: the first (for example a series of specific trees, plants or other natural objects or colours) attains its significance through relative position in the ritual sequence. The second type (for example the shrines at which particular rituals take place or the medicines administered to ritual subjects) acquire meaning from their configuration and integration of several distinct symbolic elements within a single form of symbolic unity. Dominant symbols are distinguished, by Turner, from instrumental symbols: the latter lack the stability of meaning and extension of reference to more general forms of semantic articulation observable in the dominant symbols; instrumental symbols have a more limited reference to the ostensive purposes and teleology of the particular ritual.[27]

The position of the dominant symbols within the ritual process characterizes the whole symbolic function. The dominance of a symbol may be observed, according to Turner, from the frequency of its appearance in the ritual system, from the constancy of its meaning and from its performative structure. A dominant symbol may preside over a particular ritual in its entirety or it may be manifest only in one particular phase of the ritual; in both cases, the dominant symbol represents a crystallisation of the pattern of 'flow' within the ritual process.

Although dominant symbols may be studied as factors of social action within distinct ritual processes, they may also be studied within a more general frame of reference. As points of juncture between cultural forms and social structure, and as indicators of primary values, dominant symbols also possess an inherent continuity of meaning and therefore some considerable degree of independence from the aims of the particular ritual in which they may appear. This dual aspect of semantic continuity and internal dynamic structure specific to the individual ritual, explains the propensity of dominant symbols to give unity to the different symbolic elements of ritual behaviour "whether associated with an object, activity, relationship, word, gesture or spatial arrangement."[28]

The performative structure of the dominant symbols in the ritual process emerges from the co-ordination of different planes of classification which can be expressed in spatial or biological terms, in binary oppositions such as above-below, cooked-raw, masculine-feminine, death-life or in the triadic forms of colour sets such as black-red-white. The different sets of paired or triadic values are not to be regarded as analogous or equivalent: the symbolic values transect one another so that the performative structure of the dominant symbols is constituted by the points of interconnection between separate planes of classification through the different phases of the ritual process.[29] When understood in isolation within a single plane of classification, or within a binary opposition or in a triadic relation, the individual symbol may appear to be univocal. If, instead, the symbol is seen in the complex interrelation of classificatory planes, its multivocality is apparent so that the symbol may be construed as a point of integration for diverse significations. By means of a holistic analysis of this 'nodal' function of the symbol in terms of the classifications which structure the semantic of the ritual, the function of the dominant symbol may be observed in its full complexity of meaning within the context of the processual form of social drama.

Within the ritual unity of performance, the dominant symbols change through time according to the sequential order of the performative stages. When one symbol co-ordinates the whole performance, the order of connection and the planes of classification are subject to change. In the phase of destructuration, for example, the symbols move from connotations of death to those of life and re-birth: "caves, tunnels, seclusion huts or camps, may represent simultaneously tombs (or former social-structural selves) and wombs of new identities."[30] It is in the temporal dimension of the symbolic function as defined by the semantic structure of the ritual symbols and by their performative connection in the sequence that symbols appear as multi-vocal, dynamic structures which connect and elaborate the conflictual tensions at work within the social drama. Since symbols are intrinsically related to action, they are understandable only as dynamic structures of meaning within an action frame of reference. Processual symbolic analysis in this way, allows for the description of the specific structures of symbols as modes of the dramatic elaboration of social meaning.

This approach redefines the function of the individual symbol with reference to the symbolic system as a whole. Because symbols possess these performative structures of signification, Turner argues that the character and structure of the symbolic function is revealed, not by the systemic elaboration of the symbols but by the features of the dominant symbols in their specific autonomy within the varying but interrelated processes and conditions of social drama. In this way, Turner distanciates himself from primarily synchronic or systemic descriptions of the symbolic function which tend to reduce symbolic forms to a-temporal cognitive maps of social and cultural features. His diachronic analysis of the symbolic performance shows, instead, that it is the individual symbol which elaborates the structure of meaning within the social drama and which defines the semantic character, both dynamic and cognitive, of the historical event.

EXPERIENCE AND SYMBOLIC PERFORMANCE
THE INDIVIDUAL DIMENSION OF THE SYMBOLIC PROCESS

Although Turner does not offer a theory of the mental structures which relate individual and public forms of meaning and action, he does provide an extensive phenomenology of the mental features of the symbolic process and shows how social drama results from the tension induced by the individual will and motivation.

Turner has stressed that symbols have an experiential character related to the mental life of the individuals who participate in the ritual process. Symbols are directly related, not only to structures of cognition, but also to affectivity and motivations which are present in the social drama and in the liminal condition. The performance of ritual differentiates symbolic transformations which reflect specific modalities of meaning and structures of experience.

Symbols are intrinsically related to processes of meaning and interpretation which the individual actors express in the social drama. The symbols do not, however, define individualistic dimensions of experience but, rather, ethos and morality as they are generated and specified within the liminal condition of communitas.

In this regard, Turner's theoretical position is consonant with that of Durkheim in sustaining that ethos is related to the condition of social bond. Turner differs radically from Durkheim, however, both in his definition of the order of relation between the individual and society and in his description of the dynamics internal to the ethos of society. For Durkheim, it is the order and normativity of society which structure value and transmit it to the individual. Social anomie, as absence of norm, is also absence of value and therefore entails destructive consequences for the individual. In contrast to this position of Durkheim, Turner suggests that morality is mediated not primarily by the structures of social normativity but by a condition that is interstitial to structure and which he describes as antistructure, a condition of liminality and communitas elaborated through symbolic processes. Furthermore, Turner does not understand social dynamics purely in terms of a set of performances which enact a systemic programme. For Turner, social actions acquire their form through the metaphors and paradigms which are operative in the mental life of individual actors and not through the external imposition of structure.

MENTAL CHARACTER OF THE SYMBOLIC PERFORMANCE

The performative connection of symbolic structure to the individual in the social drama brings into evidence the theoretical problem of an adequate understanding of the symbolic function in its dual aspect as the vehicle of both public and individual meaning. Although the symbol may be a function of meaning for the individual actor, when the public dimension is taken into consideration, it is clear that the significance of a symbol may not be described simply in psychological terms.

A primarily psychological analysis constrains the meaning of symbols to functions of the mental life of individuals. In the anthropological analysis of symbols, it is, however, the public character of symbolic meaning and its function as the mediating form of public action which is of primary concern. An exclusively psychological level of analysis is therefore inadequate to the form of explanation required. Turner states that "symbols refer to social facts that have an empirical reality exterior to the psyches of individuals."[31] The understanding of the public symbol in its operation as mental function for the individual presents special difficulty for the study of religion.

Turner resorts to psychoanalytic categories to define symbolic structures of meaning, but he does not adopt these categories in terms of causal psychology; rather, he incorporates them into a phenomenological description of the symbolic process in order to define the movement of experience within the social bond. Turner conceptualises dominant symbols as having two poles of meaning, namely ideological and sensory. At the ideological pole, a cluster of connotations is found which refer to the moral and social order. At the sensory or oretic pole, the connotations are usually physiological phenomena and processes which may be expected to have links with the unconscious. The unity of these two poles, in one symbolic object "gives the dominant symbol its transforming power. In ritual performance, the dominant symbol brings the ethical, jural norms of society into close contact with strong emotional stimuli."[32]

Turner puts himself at variance with those psychoanalytic interpretations of culture which "tend to regard as irrelevant the ideological pole of meaning and to focus their attention on the outward form and sensory meaning of the symbol."[33] Turner similarly distances his symbolic analysis from that of traditional social anthropology in which there is a tendency to ascribe social relevance only to conscious, verbalised, indigenous interpretations of symbols. Instead, his analysis concentrates upon those forms of social behaviour which are directly related to the total dominant symbol taken as a unity of action, conscious and unconscious. Properties which are significant to the description of symbols as 'forces' in a field of action, are polarisation of meaning, transference of affectual quality, discrepancies between meanings and condensation of meaning. Turner has suggested that the form of symbolic analysis available to the anthropologist does not enable the discrimination between the "precise sources of unconscious feeling and wishing, which shape much of the outward form of the symbol."[34]

Turner's analytical categories of the symbolic recall Freud's description of 'dream work' but the connection which Turner makes between affective and cognitive structures in the symbol is correlated to the resolution of conflict within the social drama. In distinction to the Freudian theory of symbols, Turner does not hold that symbols are the censored expressions of conflictual dynamics and wishes. Symbols are, rather, related to value and creativity. They are not the expressions of dynamic determinism but, instead, forms which are related to freedom and innovation. Symbols are not to be understood as the repressed forms of individual self-interest, but, on the contrary, as the public forms which evaluate and re-address the self-interest.

THE FUNCTION OF AWARENESS

The value of awareness and consciousness in the formation and elaboration of the symbolic function has been given greater weight in Turner's later writing. In the earlier ethnographic studies, Turner tends to treat consciousness as a relatively minor influence in the symbolic performance which he relates to the more powerful and autonomous forces of liminality and to its unconscious dimension expressed through the oretic feature of symbols. Conscious elements in the social process are seen to counteract, to some degree, the creative autonomy and unconscious forces present in the symbolic articulations which promote a more dynamic development of the social process and are able to elaborate in a more effective manner the tension of social drama. Turner seems to suggest that conscious forms and structures induce a degree of inertness and of exterior imposition to the autonomous movement of liminality and the spontaneity of communitas; consciousness, when related to control and programme limits the adaptability and creativity of social life.

In the later books, especially *Process, Performance and Pilgrimage* (1979) and *From Ritual to Theatre* (1982), there is a new emphasis on the participation of consciousness in the function and development of symbolic performance. Turner recalls Wilhelm Dilthey's concept of *Erlebnis* to describe the structure of experience within the social drama and to define in processual terms the formation of meaning in experience. Turner delineates the movement from the perceptual core of the images of past experience to the perception of interconnectedness with events which is not completed until it is expressed through representations capable of bringing into a structural unity the different elements of experience. These moments in the formation of *Erlebnis* correspond to an "act of creative retrospection in which 'meaning' is ascribed to the events and parts of experience."[35] Creative retrospection corresponds to performance, and it is therefore performance which creates unity of experience. Turner correlates this movement of reflexivity within the development of *Erlebnis* to the function and structure of the ritual process within the development of social drama. In its full formal development, in its full phase structure, social drama is a "process of converting particular values and ends, distributed over a range of actors, into a system (which may be temporary or provisional) of shared or consensual meaning. The redressive phase, in which feedback is provided by the scanning mechanisms of law and ritual, is a time in which an interpretation is put upon the events leading up to and constituting the phase of crisis. Here the meaning of social life informs the apprehension of itself."[36] The relation which has been stated by Turner between symbolic performance and reflexivity within the structure of experience lends to the concept of symbolic function and to liminality a systemic dimension which is both structural and temporal.

III. THE HISTORICAL CHARACTER OF EVENT AND THE SYMBOLIC FUNCTION

From our discussion of the dramatic processual model of social action developed in the work of Victor Turner, it is possible to appreciate both the innovative nature of his model as well as some of the theoretical problems which it raises. Turner's achievement has been to bring the dimension of time within the concept of social fact and to maintain this connection in an immediate relation to the motivations and actions of individuals.

The psychologistic schools of social action have failed to achieve this integration, nor is it to be found within the materialistic or idealistic models of sociocultural time and historical development.

The two parameters of time and space, process and structure which constantly inform Turner's method of analysis are both necessary to the definition of social fact. Turner's model of performance brings these two sets of parameters within the frame of the dramatic structure of social action at those points where structural and antistructural forms of relation are interconnected into a temporal, processual unity. The introduction of the concept of ritual performative time represents, as we have suggested, a distinct innovation in the description of the social fact: it redesigns the order of connection and articulation of the different structural features and also provides an understanding of sociocultural processes which improves upon definitions of social facts which are based primarily on systemic descriptions. If the previously available models were chiefly structural and provided spatial, systemic forms of description, Turner's model, on the other hand, poses the social condition not as a systemic unity but as a condition of plurality of events. Within each event, Turner draws attention to the existence of a constant creative tension between structure and antistructure. By their location within the dramatic articulation of the social fact, the temporal features have become the primary character of Turner's model; he has been able to relate them specifically to the dynamics which are differentiated by the symbolic function.

It will be suggested in the following discussion that Turner's method and concept of ritual process is essential to the understanding of the historical character of religion. As Raffaele Pettazzoni and other scholars have noted, the meaning and significance of religious structures can only become apparent from the study of their relation to historical context. Although this is a valid requirement, it is also clear that the possibility of making a theoretical definition of the relation between historical context and religion depends upon an adequate knowledge of the temporal model of social fact. 'Historical context' should not be taken simply to refer to a 'frame' for religious facts; nor may an explanation adequate to the problem be derived from the application of an explanatory model which relates in terms of external causality context and religious function. For this purpose of analysis, it is, instead, necessary to define how the structures and dynamics of the historical context and of religion are interconnected within the historical process and within the individual historical event.

As an expansion of van Gennep's study of 'fact coming into being' in rites of passage, Turner's temporal model allows for the definition of the relation which exists between social drama as paradigm of social fact and the ritual symbolic process. With reference to this problem, we will observe how Turner's approach may help to requalify the thematic distinction which has been made in religious studies between the sacred and the profane.

In the last part of this discussion, we will outline a possible development of the analysis of the temporal features of the symbolic function. We will move from an exegesis of some of the fundamental concepts in Turner's work to a specific formulation of the problem of symbolic time in the context of the religious system.

The processual character of liminality and antistructure, the 'between' in social drama, as described by Turner, enables us to raise the question of the temporal character of the symbolic function. Although the response to this problem, as it will be outlined below, will introduce a new paradigmatic dimension into the theoretical model of time, it is explicitly indebted to Turner's conceptual framework of the temporal character of the social fact.

Turner and van Gennep have each indicated the problem of the "between" of liminality as the area of the sacred and of symbolic performance. We will bring this question of the 'between' into a more comprehensive frame of reference than that of social structure and show that symbols, by their specific character and structure, are the 'intentional between' of subjects in a polar relation. In this reference, symbols are the mediating structures, the 'between' of relation defined by a specific condition of the reality principle. We will see that the symbolic time of the religious function is directly related to the dynamics of the bond which exists within a condition of religious intentional object relation. Symbolic Time specifies not only the structures of the ethos of the bond, but also those of perception and action within the historical process. The intentional analysis of the symbolic function will enable the observation of temporal paradigms other than the performative which are present within a temporal model of social fact.

SACRED AND PROFANE

Turner offers a set of formal categories and operative features which are of importance for the description of the way in which the sacred is related to the profane in the historical process.

Traditional attempts to define religious systems of practice and belief have often understood religion to be an expression of 'ultimate meaning', a form of resolution for anxiety, or a function of social or mental systems. These definitions are not analytically operative. They do not specify the relation of religion to the process of existence; nor can they give an adequate account of the complex data pertaining to the interrelation of the sacred and of the profane which have appeared from the study of both primitive and historical religions.

An analysis of religion should be able to account for the principle and condition which give rise simultaneously to the differentiation of religious structures and to their co-ordination into a processual and structural unity within the specific historical context. The analysis should be capable of explaining the way in which time is articulated within the religious symbolic system and also how religion is intrinsically related to time understood to be the processual structure of existence.

Part of the traditional definition of religion is the assumption of a separation between the 'sacred' and the 'profane'. If this assumption of separation is understood to refer not simply to a distinction, but to an absence of intrinsic relation between the sacred and the profane, or to opposition between them as two conflicting orders of reality, then the study of religion is confronted with a problem of significant dimension. Studies of both primitive and historical cultures show that clear distinctions are drawn between what is regarded as being sacred and that which is profane: sharp contrasts in social dynamics, differences in social structure and institutional forms, different systems of reference and objects of relation, distinct forms of legitimation and discrepancy of time orders may be observed. In spite of these distinctions, it is evident, however, that what are referred to as sacred and profane may be seen to coexist within the same frame of human action.

A theoretical position which sustains that there is an absence of intrinsic relation between the sacred and the profane implies the absence of dynamics which are specific to the religious symbolic system as such. If, according to this view, the qualification of the sacred is understood to depend upon the model of structural dynamics present within the profane system, then religion becomes a formation on the surface of the socioeconomic system or a projection of mental forms. The positive effects of religion tend to be restricted, within this perspective, to the reduction of social tensions or to the heightening of activity within the institutional system.

The theoretical view which holds, on the other hand, that the sacred and the profane are mutually exclusive or extraneous to each other in the fundamental sense of defining unrelated conditions of reality, has the disadvantage, in theoretical terms, of implying two, quite distinct, orders of reality which, although connected to the same individuals, are, in fact described without any common basis of interrelation.

Both these theoretical approaches to the problem of the sacred-profane dichotomy and their concomitant disadvantages result from the absence of a unifying theoretical principle. A unifying theory should be capable of defining both the specificity and the correlation of different forms of human action without having to appeal to separate theories for the explanation of divergent forms of action. If we may cite a possible analogy from physics, this is as if we were to have a physical theory of solids and another, autonomous, theory of liquids. What would be needed, instead, is a physical theory which could explain both the solid and the liquid status of matter.

Turner's answer to the problem of the distinction and correlation of the sacred and profane is given within this analysis of structure and liminality. They are distinct as structure and anti-structure, but, as we have noted, they are inextricably related to the development of social drama. Turner's analytical model captures the social fact in its making at the point of the connection and processual unity of the structural and the symbolic in a condition not only of change but also of structural differentiation. This approach offers a greater degree of specificity in clarifying the nature of the interrelation of the sacred and profane in terms of the temporal performance and structural articulation of the individual event.

Although Turner affirms that ritual has reference to beliefs in invisible beings and powers regarded as the first and final causes of all effects, he does not provide a theological qualification of the sacred nor does he offer an analysis of the theological articulation of the symbolic function. Instead, Turner differentiates the structural and processual features of both sacred and profane within the model of performance and within the development of social drama.

In this theoretical frame, the two sets of features (sacred and profane) emerge with reference to the concept of performance which unifies process, structure and symbolic transformation. In the language of performative analysis, then, these two sets of features are compared and defined in terms of universality and particularity, rigidity and processual flow, structure-antistructure, distinction-union of the opposite, structural differentiation and semantic function. The conceptual unity of the performative analysis of social drama does not imply identity of reference or equivalent dynamics and structures in the sacred and profane. The performative analysis is, instead, a unified theoretical model of social fact in which structure and antistructure are correlated into the central form which elaborates meaning and experience.

Turner's method makes the enquiry into the relation of the sacred with the profane more operative than previous approaches. If the history and study of religion are brought into a more direct relation with the complexity of their data, there will be a weakening in the credibility of problems such as whether religious forms are analogies or reflections of social institutions; whether the sacred is entirely anomalous when compared with the secular; whether the sacred is to be regarded simply as a 'natural' form of human emotion or a set of conventions based upon human interest or utility.

Although Turner does not explicitly tackle these general questions about the nature of religion, he is nevertheless able to bring them, to some significant extent, within a conceptual frame which is more analytically adequate. The question of the coincidence between symbolic modes of signification and modes of being, is transformed into the study of the necessary connection between symbolic features, symbolic performances and structural change at the individual and collective level. Turner has made a particular study of liminality within the ritual process to which he ascribes a special hermeneutical relevance for the understanding of religion. The result of this has been to bring into evidence the affinity between the 'centre' of sacred time and the 'outside' of sacred space. The structural and symbolic similarity which liminality has with inferiority and structural exclusion allows for the definition in more general terms of antistructure and of the dialectical relation which communitas has with structure. By considering human society, as Turner does, to be human process, instead of an a-temporal system constructed like an organism or mechanism, it is possible to bring into relief the complex relations which exist at every point and at every level of action and symbolic articulation between communitas and structure.[37]

EVENT, SYSTEM AND SYMBOLIC TIME

Performance and Epigenesis

It has been suggested above that Turner has placed his work within two epistemological perspectives: that of the historical particularity of forms and that of their function with regard to an original condition of indeterminacy and change. Turner's concept of religion moves within these two epistemological qualifications of social fact whilst avoiding both rigid formalism and radical indeterminacy. Nevertheless, the definition of the dynamic of change in the sociocultural process remains incomplete.

Two points of continuity throughout Turner's entire work are the theoretical primacy given to symbolic process as performance and an emphasis upon the event rather than upon the system. This theoretical approach has led to a redefinition in Turner's work of the concept of society as a field of social events and of the concept of event itself, bringing into evidence its character of 'processual unit'. On the other hand, such an emphasis lends itself to the explanation of change in terms of performance rather than in terms of epigenesis. The structural opposition and processual alternation of liminality and structure are, therefore, stressed rather than the creative dynamics of relation and of conflict resolution within the social bond. We will define below the concept of epigenesis in terms of the internal dynamic and structural differentiation of the nascent state of the social bond.

Turner connects change and innovation to an original condition of indeterminacy which emerges within liminality, and counterposes liminality to structure.[38] In this perspective, structure and system seem to exhibit an intrinsic ambivalence with regard to the original condition of indeterminacy and freedom; in order to allow the emergence of liminality in the individual and collective experience, structure must be periodically suspended or abrogated.

The counterposition between structure and liminality within the event is modulated to a counterposition between event and system. Turner describes system more in terms of an interpretation which is brought to bear upon the event of experience rather than an original condition of social fact. The system, therefore, appears to Turner to be detrimental to the variation of dynamics and plurality of events which is revealed by the dramatic model of social process and social condition. When the system attains priority over the processual character of social life, form constrains the creative character of liminality and indeterminacy; performance is turned into programme and ritual into repetitive ceremony.

But the insistence on the opposition between structure and liminality instead of on their dynamic linkage, in order to explain the dynamic of the event is problematic. Structure and liminality are, in fact, constitutive features of the event both in their structural specificity and in their processual interconnection. Liminality, as it is related to a phase and modality of destructuration, is also a matrix of restructuration. The processual feature of the event cannot, therefore, be seen simply as the result of tension emerging between structure and liminality. Change and innovation have characters which may not be explained by the performance of the ritual process, nor can conflict be described primarily in structural terms when it is values and not merely rules of interpretation which are at issue. Although conflict may originate and find expression at the level of structure, the innovative dynamics within social drama and in ritual process are intrinsic to the dynamics of relation within the social bond. The problem remains of how and why this elaboration of the dynamics of the social bond, from its nascent state to its full articulation, is located in the liminal condition and within its internal symbolic structures. The performative paradigm describes the structural transformation of the 'fact coming into being', the formal transformation related to change and nascent state; it also explains the contrast between discrete structure and processual flow, the opposition between individualistic and universal, but performance does not provide an adequate definition of the dynamic tension and structural elaboration which are the origin of the nascent state. The description of such a condition of epigenesis calls for an enquiry into the dynamic formation of the social bond.

To explain and study change in terms of epigenesis, and to explore its structure, it is necessary to extend the definition of the liminal condition which is the main area of the symbolic elaboration of conflict and value. In addition to examining the relation between liminality and structure, it is necessary to define how the symbolic structure of the liminal condition is itself the original structure of the nascent state. The epigenetic aspect of liminality should, therefore, be studied in its constitutive, symbolic articulation. We suggest an expansion of the analysis of liminality, moving the focus of inquiry from the study of liminality as the "in-between" or the antistructure with reference to the structural system, to the character of 'between' of the symbolic structure of liminality.

It will be shown, further on, that the character of 'between' is intrinsic to the symbolic function defined as intentional relation and also determines its dynamic and structure. The symbolic character of 'between' and its dynamic cannot be explained simply in terms of counterposition to structure in a social drama. The function and dynamic of the 'between' should instead by related to a condition of reality which is at the origin of the social bond itself. We will see that the paradigm of intentional epigenesis replaces the concept of indeterminacy with the concept of nascent state. The epigenetic paradigm defines change and innovation by differentiating the processes and dynamics which lead to the formation of a new social bond. In this sense, the system is not counterposed to event, nor does it become an abstract structure which is extraneous to the process of events. Instead, the system is itself brought within the explanation of 'event' and may be seen to qualify its temporal articulation and processuality.

In the last section of this discussion, we will describe some of the points of linkage between symbolic intentionality and Turner's processual symbolic analysis, indicating the integration which may be brought to the concepts of symbol, ritual process and event by an analysis which is epigenetic as well as performative. The model of symbolic intentionality has been derived from an observation of the symbolic function as the mediatory temporal structure within the object relation at both the mental and collective level. This theoretical descrption will be joined to a summary of the conclusions from a study undertaken to analyse the periodical structure of the symbolic function in the Christian Liturgical Year.[39]

The Periodical Character of Christian Symbolic Time

The organization of the religious symbolic system is sustained by three temporal forms of co-ordination: the chronological succession of time units (sun/year/day;moon/week), the set of festivals which represent specific ritual performances, and the symbolic *ordo* defining a set of rules which co-ordinates the performance of the festivals. In the Judaeo-Christian calendar, the lunar year, which is related to Easter, and the solar year which is related to Christmas and the sanctorial cycle are the axes along which two set of festivals are organized.

The temporal articulation of the symbolic function in the religious calendar has two main features: the unequal distribution of symbols through time, and the periodical form of the symbolic performance.[40] When the symbolic performative system of festivals is compared with the continuous, chronological succession of time units, the festivals located on the lunar axis appear in an uneven distribution over the sequence of the year. The temporal significance of Easter is not a function of a chronological sequence, rather Easter is the centre around which the entire calendrical performance of the symbolic system is organized in terms of preparation, and in terms of the new forms of intentional existence which are introduced by Easter. This shows that the organization of symbolic time follows a specific internal logic related to the nature of the symbolic function, independent of the frame of cosmic time reckoning, and quite different from the abstract concept of time as a continuous quantity infinitely divisible into successive, homogeneous parts.

The features of the three temporal orders, namely chronological succession of time units, processual character of the symbolic performance and the rules of performance, are all functionally correlated so that a condition of time is created which is periodical in nature, that is to say, a time in which change is connected to duration. Periodicity is, therefore, the essential fact for the understanding of the internal logic of the symbolic function as it is articulated through the symbolic time system. The symbolic order of periodicity is, in fact, the structure of intentional time.

From a general point of view, the period or cycle, is an interval of time in which a phenomenon, such as the position of the stars, changes value with the condition that it will be repeated in its initial value, and with the same characteristics, at the same point in the interval. Periodicity, therefore, incorporates within the 'event' both change and duration. They are the constitutive features of the concept of time and are correlated to sustain continuity which is perceived as movement from past to future. Without the existence of such a correlation between change and duration, there would be no time. Without duration, time would disappear with each instant but without change; time would be a perpetual static present. Duration within an event-interval, therefore, implies change, and both change and duration sustain the possibility of continuity.

We will see that the symbolic structural and performative features of time connect change and duration, and give us an understanding of 'intentional time'. It will appear that change is related to the nascent state of an intentional bond, while duration is the performance of the nascent state, that is the performance constitutive of and internal to the intentional bond.

Symbolic time as the periodical order internal to the religious symbolic system differentiates a specific dynamic; it defines how intentional change is related and connected to intentional duration by correlating into a temporal unity the dominant symbols, in this case the sacramental system with the central dynamics of the sacrifice.

We may define symbolic periodicity with reference to a theoretical model of symbol which correlates the structural and dynamic aspects of the symbol to a condition of intentional object relation.

The Periodical Features of Symbolic Intentionality

Within this frame of reference, symbols are the processual structures which elaborate the forms and dynamics of intentionality. The concept of intentionality defines the condition of 'being in relation' which is the constitutive feature of thought, affectivity and value orientation. Intentionality is a polar relation; it implies not only the orientation of the subject towards the object, but that the object is determinant and active in the dynamic processes and structural articulations of the intentional life of the subject. It indicates the way in which the subject and the object are constituted by 'being in relation' and also indicates the character of mediation proper to cultural and institutional forms. It may be seen in this theoretical perspective that the intentional bond, that is, the way of being intentional, progressively forms and transforms the structure and dynamics of the human being.

The polar character of intentionality is qualified by the object relation which defines the concrete conditions of the reality principle within an historical event. These conditions are the limits of existence and of relation which determine the possibility and development of the intentional life of the subject with reference to the conditions and values intrinsic to the specific object relation. To bring those limits of existence into a condition of total intentional reciprocity requires a dramatic elaboration of the form of relation which may be inadequate in terms of its dynamic and structural differentiation for a condition of total intentional reciprocity. An intentional position qualifying the relation between subject and object is unviable if it corresponds to a subjective appropriation of the object or to a subjective projection of negativity towards the object. This position may undergo transformation in the form of intentional epigenesis.

The paradigm of epigenesis indicates, on the one hand, the nascent state, that is the development of every new intentional bond; on the other hand, epigenesis defines, in the subject, the passage from a primarily subjective perception and dynamic with the object of relation to a condition of total reciprocity. More than developmental transformation, intentional epigenesis implies a dynamic and structural change which initiates and sustains, through symbolic forms, an intentional condition generative of the social bond. The condition of 'being in relation' may be studied directly in the structural articulation and processual forms of the symbolic function; it emerges most clearly in the analysis of the dominant symbols which are, in the theological system, referred to as sacraments.

A symbol is the structural and processual unit of mediation of the intentional relation; it differentiates the intentional character and process of the object relation. This concept of the symbolic as the function of intentionality brings into evidence the radical limitation of understanding the symbol as a representation, in the sense of something which is in place of something else. When understood within the conceptual framework of intentionality, the symbol may, instead, be seen to differentiate the direct expression of relation with the intentional object as well as the features of the intentional function.

This perspective reveals in the symbol a feature of polarity which is essential to the definition of its performative character. A symbol is polar in that it expresses the intentional positions of the poles of relation and performative because the symbol defines the dynamic structure of the relation itself.

In its structural features, a symbol is simultaneously physical entity, activity and word. The meaning of the symbol is not necessarily or exclusively conscious: it emerges through the performance, through the correlation of one symbol with other symbols in the intentional process and through the interpretation of the actors.

Symbols are often defined as 'unconscious' manifestations or as related to 'unconscious structures'. But this definition would seem, in the present frame of reference, to be inadequate; symbolic patterns may be more correctly described as 'intentional' rather than 'unconscious'. These binding patterns are not simply functions of the psychological apparatus; they are the mediation with reality, and as such they are specifically intentional. The symbolic performance touches conscious as well as unconscious structures, but these conscious and unconscious structures are those of the intentional relation as it is defined by the symbolic mediation. The symbolic performance refers to the bond of relation in which the object, the 'other' as well as the subject is the inspiration and dynamic source of an intentional form of life. It is this bond which is expressed in the symbolic performance which may be characterised as 'public'; that is a performance which elaborates the intentional relation (the 'between') as such. Through the symbolic articulation, cognition, perception and value orientation, as mental dimensions of human existence, are historically engaged and qualified by the intentional relation with the object. Symbols are the forms of such engagement with reality; they are its vision, its dynamics and judgment; in their systemic and processual articulation, symbols are the structures of vital relation which forms and sustains intentional life.

A religious system implies a selection of types of symbols which are specific within an intentional order. The system is ruled and specified by two combinatory models, the performative and the epigenetic. The performative model constitutes an order of relation between sets of symbolic positions. The epigenetic model defines a structural and dynamic sequence of active and passive exchanges of the subject with the object; the sequence is co-ordinated with a complementary line of action of the object towards the subject, initiated by gift, elaborated through a creative intentional crisis specified in the sacrifice, and conducive, at the end of the process, to a differentiation of a total object relation. Together the two complementary models, the epigenetic and the performative, constitute the temporal order which sustains the dynamic of the intentional relation.

Intentional epigenesis as it is developed within the symbolic function cannot be reduced either to the subjective dimension of symbolic action or to the biological character of symbolic mediation. The definition of the epigenetic paradigm of the symbolic system may recall the theory developed by the 'object relation' school of psychology; but in the model of symbolic intentionality it is public symbols which are observed and which define and differentiate not primarily the psychological dimension of the subject or of the object in the relation, but the relation as such. Symbols differentiate the public dimension within the order of perception, the structural and dynamic features of the constitutive condition of 'being in relation'. Furthermore, the concept of epigenesis does not refer to a biological denotation of the temporal order of the symbolic function but to the intentional sequence of symbolic positions which create a generative condition of object relation.

The ritual process, as a formalized paradigm of symbolic action, defines the epigenetic transformation of the relation as well as the form of total intentional reciprocity. Furthermore, the ritual process differentiates an intentional bond in its 'coming into being' (nascent state) by connecting symbols and elaborating their features in sequential phases of destructuration, liminality-communitas and restructuration. The ritual process may be described as a performative sequence which has an epigenetic structure and function.

When considered within this unified conceptual framework of the ritual process, symbols are seen to be epigenetic in the sense that they are the mediation in the transformative tension which arises in both the subject and the object in the encounter and which is conducive, together with the dynamic structure differentiated by the dominant symbols, to an intentional creative relation, a condition from which both the social bond and symbolic time originate. Symbols in their epigenetic and performative modalities are the features of the processual relation within the intentional-social bond.

The Periodical Structure of the Event

A system of symbols defines the temporal order of interrelations of symbolic elements which sustain an intentional vision and processual articulation of reality. The mythical figura is the system of symbols seen in its intentional, temporal unity, that is, in its epigenetic features and performative actions.

The pattern of the Christian symbolic system, as differentiated by symbolic time, is a configuration of sets of symbolic intentional positions which define types of reciprocity, negative and positive, ranging from a condition of opposition to one of union. The dynamic sequence of the intentional transformation is assumed to be initiated by God and is characterised by a vital form of mutuality. The symbolic sequence is directed towards a structure of total object relation, theologically defined as transcendence, and to this end it reveals, challenges and resolves the conflictual dynamics of the total object relation in man.

Easter, as the epigenetic center of the whole symbolic system, is the crucial time of resolution of the conflictual dynamics; it is the sacrifice, in its connection with resurrection, which constitutes the passage towards a new form of intentional relation. Thus in theological terms, through the position 'mors mea-vita tua' the sacrifice reveals the complementary value 'vita tua-vita mea'. Easter, as the ritual performance of the whole system, elaborates the passage from one intentional position to another by correlating the intentional transformation with the sequential order of the sacraments; as dominant symbols, the sacraments articulate into a unity the constitutive epiphanies of the symbolic system such as creation, covenant, law and incarnation. Through the performance, the religious polar symbols, God and man, receive their intentional qualification from the condition of their relation (e.g. creator-creation-creature) from the type of intentional position in the relation (e.g. father-son; friend-enemy; judge-sinner; redeemer-redeemed) and from the modalities of symbolic performance of the intentional relation (e.g. law of Moses-law of Christ).

In Easter the epigenetic and performative paradigms may, therefore, be seen to have a temporal complementarity: the performative model constitutes an order of relation between the set of symbolic positions differentiated in the symbolic system; the epigenetic is the dynamic model of transformation which, in its central function, guides the performative process and correlates into a new form of life, the specific intentional structures differentiated by the three performative stages. The integration of these two temporal models generates the structure of the Liturgical Year as well as the symbolic and mythic structure of the figura.

When seen in correlation, the epigenetic and performative paradigms delineate the periodical order and structure of the symbolic function. The performative pattern of Easter builds into the whole symbolic system an epigenetic structure with a periodical form.

In fact periodicity indicates primarily an order which connects the different features of the symbolic system into structures of 'intentional event' at the level both of the individual and of the collectivity. The intentional dynamic and the structural articulations of the intentional event are differentiated by the processual form and structural co-ordination of the symbolic figura. The figura, therefore, simultaneously displays aspects of epigenesis and performance. For these reasons, the periodicity of the symbolic function should not be read in terms of a sequential order or as a merely repetitive cycle, although the formal unity and internal temporal articulation of periodicity denote repetition and replicability. Instead, periodicity should be understood to define a 'dynamic status' within the intentional relation of the event. The discrete symbolic features of the event differentiate specific structures of intentional action. Periodicity, therefore, is the condition from which intentional historical continuity and sacred history may develop. Through the periodical temporal order the symbolic system becomes an intentional function of the event, that is, as the General Form which shows its vitality in the Particular so that the Particular is differentiated by the form and structure of intentionality.

Conclusion

Turner's operative concepts and analytical methods have the advantage of showing how religious meaning as well as the semantics of different cultural forms, far from being a-temporal schemes or exclusively the expression of innate structures, are the elaboration and structure of human drama in the social bond.

In the last part of this chapter we have indicated how the epigenetic temporal paradigm is interrelated with the performative paradigm in constructing the periodical temporal order of the symbolic system. The two paradigms define the way in which the symbolic system is interior to the intentional condition of human existence and how religious symbolic time elaborates the performance of a specific generative form of intentional relation and social bond. The principle of symbolic intentionality brings to evidence the epigenetic temporal order of the symbolic system, and the theoretical primacy of the intentional character of symbolic time. The 'systemic periodical order' of the Liturgical Year is not a 'representational model', nor is it a system imposed on the process of life, an external programme of meaning and action designed outside the process of events. The Liturgical Year is the 'periodical intentional structure' itself of the event within a sacred history. This 'periodical intentional structure' is not simply a 'model for' or 'model of', nor simply a powerful root metaphor, but an 'organon' of intentional perception and action. The periodical features of the symbolic function are constitutively related to the intentional character of the event. The dynamic internal to the symbolic system builds the meaning of religion at the center itself of time and of the social bond.

Notes and References

1. Edward Evans-Pritchard, *Theories of Primitive Religion* (Oxford: Clarendon Press, 1965), p. 112.
2. Victor Turner, *Dramas, Fields and Metaphors: Symbolic Action in Human Society* (Ithaca: Cornell University Press, 1974), pp. 23-24.
3. Ibid., p. 35.
4. Victor Turner, *Schism and Continuity in an African Society: A Study of Ndembu Village Life* (Manchester: Manchester University Press, 1957), p. 328.
5. Victor Turner, *The Drums of Affliction* (Oxford: Clarendon Press, 1968), pp. 81-83; idem, *The Forest of Symbols* (Ithaca: Cornell University Press, 1967), pp. 50-51.
6. Victor Turner, *The Ritual Process: Structure and Antistructure* (Chicago: Aldine, 1969); Victor Turner and Edith Turner, *Image and Pilgrimage in Christian Culture* (New York: Columbia University Press, 1978); Victor Turner, *Process, Performance and Pilgrimage: A Study in Comparative Symbology* (New Delhi: Concept Publishing Company, 1979); idem, *From Ritual to Theatre: The Human Seriousness of Play* (New York: Performing Arts Journal Publications, 1982).
7. Idem, *Dramas, Fields and Metaphors*, p. 13.
8. Quoted in Turner, *Schism and Continuity*, p. xvii.

9. Turner, *Dramas, Fields and Metaphors*, pp. 78-79.
10. Idem, *From Ritual to Theatre*, p. 69.
11. Idem, *Dramas, Fields and Metaphors*, p. 17.
12. Idem, *From Ritual to Theatre*, p. 92.
13. Idem, *Process, Performance and Pilgrimage*, p. 149.
14. Idem, *The Forest of Symbols*, p. 19.
15. Ibid., p. 20.
16. Idem, *Dramas, Fields and Metaphors*, p. 164.
17. Idem, "Religion in Current Cultural Anthropology," *Concilium* 136 (1980), pp. 70-71.
18. Arnold van Gennep, *Les Rites de Passage* (Paris: E. Nourry, 1908), p. 13.
19. Turner, *Process, Performance and Pilgrimage*, p. 17.
20. Idem, *Forest of Symbols*, p. 99.
21. Victor Turner and Edith Turner, *Image and Pilgrimage*, p. 250.
22. Turner, *Dramas, Fields and Metaphors*, p. 20.
23. Ibid., p. 274.
24. Turner, *Ritual Process*, p. 132.
25. Victor Turner, "Symbolic Studies," *Annual Review of Anthropology* (1975), eds. B. Siegal et al..
26. Idem, *Forest of Symbols*, p. 20.
27. Ibid., p. 30 et seq..
28. Ibid., p. 19.
29. Idem, *Ritual Process*, pp. 37-40.
30. Idem, "Religion in Current Cultural Anthropology", p. 69.
31. Idem, *Forest of Symbols*, p. 36.
32. Ibid., p. 30.
33. Ibid., p. 33.
34. Ibid., p. 36.
35. Turner, *From Ritual to Theatre*, p. 18.
36. Idem, *Process, Performance and Pilgrimage*, p. 92.
37. Dario Zadra, Foreword to *Il Processo Rituale: Struttura e Antistruttura* by Victor Turner (Brescia: Morcelliana, 1972), p. 26.
38. Turner, *From Ritual to Theatre*, pp. 76-78; 82-83.
39. Dario Zadra, "Symbol and Sakrament," *Christlicher Glaube in moderner Gesellschaft. Enzyklopädische Bibliothek*, eds. Franz Böckle, Franz-Xaver Kaufmann, Karl Rahner, Bernhard Welte, Robert Scherer, (Freiburg im Br.: Herder, 1982), vol. 28, pp. 88-122; idem, "Symbolic Time: The Christian Liturgical Year", University of Rome Lectures 1981-1982, *Sociologia* (1983); idem, "Sacraments and Mental Transformation," University of Chicago, 1982. (Mimeographed.); idem, "Sacramenti e Tempo," *Problemi e Prospettive di Teologia Dogmatica*, ed. Karl Neufeld (Brescia: Queriniana, 1983).
40. The periodical distribution of ritual and the 'qualitative' character of calendrical time has been noted in archaic, primitive and traditional forms of religion by Henri Hubert and Marcel Mauss, "La Représentation du Temps dans la Religions et la Magie," *Mélanges d'Histoire des Religions* (Paris: Alcan, 1922), pp. 189-229.

CHAPTER V

Women's Stories, Women's Symbols: A Critique of Victor Turner's Theory of Liminality[1]

Caroline Walker Bynum

Having been asked to consider the usefulness of Victor Turner's "processual symbolic analysis" or "social drama approach" to my work as a historian of the religion of the western European Middle Ages, I should begin by saying what I do *not* intend to do.[2] First, I do not intend to address the general relationship of history and anthropology as academic disciplines or methods. Much has, of course, been written on this topic. Traditional historians are fond of the cliché that anthropology seeks to delineate general laws, history to describe particular events. But the more venturesome in both fields have sought a marriage of the two disciplines. The anthropologist Evans-Pritchard repeatedly argued that good history *is* good anthropology and vice versa, and dubbed eminent medieval historians such as Marc Bloch and F. W. Maitland the best of anthropologists.[3] The British historian Keith Thomas wrote recently that in the history departments of the 1980s the last vestiges of the innovations of the 60s may lie in the use of certain insights from cultural anthropology.[4] I cannot, on the basis of study of a single figure, launch a new theory of the relationship of the disciplines. But my sympathies have always lain with those in each camp who make use of the other. And it seems clear to me that Victor Turner's own sense of what he is up to, taken very broadly, is appealing to any historian of religion. Turner's notion of the fundamental units of social reality as dramas builds temporality and change into all analysis;[5] Turner's sense of dominant symbols as multivocal requires that symbols and ritual be understood in their social context;[6] Turner's emphasis on the "orectic" (sensory) pole of meaning enables students of religion to talk of emotional, psychological and spiritual elements which psycho-history has tried, woefully unsuccessfully, I fear, to introduce into historical analysis.[7] Therefore, in concluding that certain of Turner's theories seriously misrepresent the complexity of religious experience, I shall *not* be suggesting that anthropology and history are incompatible. Rather I shall be arguing both that some of Turner's generalizations violate the subtlety of his own methodological commitments and that Turner's theory of religion is inadequate because it is based implicitly on the Christianity of a particular class, gender, and historical period.

Second, I do not intend to provide a critique of Turner's own application of his theory to the European Middle Ages, particularly in his well-known essays on Thomas Becket and Francis of Assisi.[8] It would be easy to show that, compared to the richness of Turner's analysis of Ndembu ritual, his sense of twelfth and thirteenth-century symbols is thin. "Poverty" to Francis, the *imitatio Christi* or *via crucis* to Becket, become in Turner's own hands almost "signs" rather than "symbols"; they lose much of the multivocality they unquestionably have in their own historical context. For all Turner's effort to use a social drama analysis, his history of the Franciscan order sounds remarkably like the history of the institutionalization and, therefore, corruption of a dream which was the standard interpretation of Francis until recently;[9] his discussion of Becket does not advance much beyond the picture of radical conversion from one ideal to another which has always been seen as the crux of the matter – in legend and literature as well as in the work of historians.[10] It is not surprising that Turner uses Turner's model best when he knows the society under study most deeply. And indeed one is struck by the fact that even in his most recent writings, the Ndembu examples are the most powerful – the clearest, most precise, most analytical and cogent – whereas the modern examples are often tossed in without the care or the elaboration necessary to make the analysis convincing.[11] But for me to suggest simply that Turner could sometimes do a Turnerian analysis better than he does would contribute nothing to a study of Turner's model.

What I want to do, therefore, is to apply to my own research in the later Middle Ages Turner's notion of social drama as underlying both narrative and ritual. I want to focus especially on two aspects of Turner's notion of social drama, namely his understanding of "dominant symbols" (particularly as elaborated in the *Forest of Symbols* [1967]) and his notion of the central place in what he calls "liminality" of images of status reversal or status elevation (particularly as elaborated in *The Ritual Process* [1969] and in subsequent works).[12] I understand Turner to be arguing at his most general (and he is frequently quite general) that human experience, at least a great part of the time, occurs in units Turner calls "social dramas" (a subset of what he calls "processual units") – that is, that it takes a four-stage form: breach between social elements, crisis, adjustment or redress, and finally either reintegration of the group or person or "element" into the social structure or recognition of irreparable breach.[13] This social drama, to Turner, underlies both narrative – that is, the way we tell our important stories – and ritual – that is, the way we behave when we perform or enact certain formal, prescribed patterns that not only express but also move us into and elaborate our shared values. It is in the third stage that we find what Turner calls, borrowing the idea from van Gennep, "liminality" – a moment of suspension of normal rules and roles, a crossing of boundaries and violating of norms, which enables us to understand those norms, even (or perhaps especially) where they conflict, and move on either to incorporate or to reject them.[14] In the specific form of social drama called ritual, we find that rituals of life-crisis (i.e. change in life status, for example puberty or election as chief) often use images of inversion in the liminal stage (for example, the initiate becomes a "fool" or a "woman"); calendrical rituals (i.e. those that celebrate the recurring pattern of the year, for example harvest rituals) often use images of status elevation (for example, children wear masks of adults or of monsters at Halloween). Especially central in the liminal stage of ritual are what Turner calls "dominant symbols"—symbols which "condense" and "unify" into a moment disparate *significata* and bring together two poles of meaning: normative and emotional. A dominant symbol (for example, the Ndembu milk tree) can, therefore, only be understood in the context in which it is experienced. There it has meaning that includes as much the sensory, natural and physiological facts to which it refers (for example, milk, food, nurture, nursing, breasts, etc.) as the disparate social values for which it may stand (for example—in the case of the milk tree—both tribal custom and matriliny, on the one hand, and, on the other, conflict between mother and daughter, men and women).[15] From such fine and multitextured analysis of symbol and story, Turner sometimes moves on—quite a bit less successfully, I feel—to general cultural critique, calling for the liminoid (that is, the liminal-like) in modern life and cautiously praising *communitas*, his term for that feeling of union with one's fellow human beings which in pre-industrial societies was released in the liminal phase of ritual.[16]

There are some obvious problems with applying Turner's writings to historical research, not least among them the fact that Turner does not have a complete and coherent theory to the extent that Geertz and Lévi-Strauss do. As I indicate above, all Turner's ideas involve in some way the insight that, in explaining human experience, one is explaining process or drama rather than structure, and that liminality or suspension of social and normative structures is a crucial moment in process. But the very fact that periods of liminality provide escape from roles and critiques of structures (in a functionalist sense of "structure") indicates that Turner has in certain ways never left the functionalist anthropology in which he was trained. And Turner himself, however quick he may have been to provide commentary on the modern world, has said repeatedly that for the industrialized world "liminality" is only a metaphor.[17] It is, therefore, not certain either how far Turner's insights fit together into a system or how many of Turner's own insights Turner himself thinks applicable to the European Middle Ages, a society between "primitive" and industrialized. I do not, however, want either to create a single "Turner theory" or to criticize such a theory by doing an exegesis of Turner. Others can do that better than I—among them Turner himself. Rather I want to apply what clearly *are* some of Turner's insights—his notion of narrative, his notion of dominant symbol, his notion of imagery of reversal and elevation—to my work on later medieval piety. Since Turner himself has extrapolated from analysis of ritual in "primitive" societies to more general theories about symbols and stories, I feel free to test his ideas against the religious texts which are the major source for historians of the Middle Ages. I want to show how certain of Turner's ideas, especially his sensitive and subtle notion of dominant symbols, enables me to describe aspects of European religiosity for which scholars have long needed terms.

But I also want to argue that those places where Turner's notions fail to describe what I find in my research fit into a pattern and that that pattern suggests a fundamental limitation in the Turnerian idea of liminality, at least in the extended or metaphorical sense of the later Turner writings.

In evaluating Turner's social drama model and his theory of symbol, I want to concentrate on a major form of medieval narrative, the saint's life, and on a major Christian ritual or dominant symbol, the eucharist. I chose these initially because they seem to be the most obvious illustrations of Turner's ideas. Although many historians of religion and literature have pointed out that saints' lives as a genre are *not* chronologically or linearly arranged—the goal of the biographer being to depict the saint as static model—conversion *is* often the climax of the story which lies behind and generates the literary life.[18] And the eucharist is not only obviously a dominant symbol, condensing, unifying and polarizing meaning; it is also the central symbol in a clearly processual ritual, one which recapitulates what is certainly a social drama—the crucifixion—and one in which the moment of reception of sacred food was frequently accompanied by the extreme liminality of ecstasy or possession. Moreover, although the eucharist is not in any simple sense either a calendrical or a life-crisis ritual, the imagery of this liminal moment is obviously imagery of reversal: omnipotent God becomes dying man; the receiving Christian gains eternal life by eating and becoming the moment of death.[19] But when I have explored more closely the relationship of Turner's models to these medieval stories and symbols, a curious fact has emerged. Turner's ideas describe the stories and symbols of men better than those of women. Women's stories insofar as they can be discerned behind the tales told by male biographers are in fact less processual than men's; they don't have turning points. And when women recount their own lives, the themes are less climax, conversion, reintegration and triumph, the liminality of reversal or elevation, than continuity. Moreover, women's images and symbols—which, according to Turner's model, should reflect either inversion (for example, poverty) insofar as women are superior (for example, from the aristocracy) or elevation (for example, maleness, military prowess) insofar as women *qua* women are inferior—do not quite do either. They rather continue or enhance in image (for example, bride, sick person) what the woman's ordinary experience is, so that one either has to see the woman's religious stance as permanently liminal or as never quite becoming so.

These observations suggest to me that Turner's theory of religion may be based more than he is aware on the particular form of Christianity (with its strong emphasis on world denial and inversion of images) that has characterized elites in the western tradition—educated elites, aristocratic elites, and male elites. We will, however, understand this only if we use the category of gender very carefully. For my examination of Turner in no way implies that he fails to look at women either in his theory or in his fieldwork (where surely his analysis of women's rituals has been extensive and subtle).[20] In many places he suggests that women are liminal or that women, as marginals, generate *communitas*.[21]

What I am suggesting is exactly that Turner looks *at* women; he stands with the dominant group (males) and sees women (both as symbol and as fact) as liminal to men. In this he is quite correct, of course, and the insight is a powerful one. But it is not the whole story. The historian or anthropologist needs to stand *with* women as well.[22] And when Turner attempts to stand with the inferior, he assumes symmetry—that is, he assumes that the inferior are exactly the reverse of the superior. If the superior in society generate images of lowliness in liminality, the inferior will generate images of power. To use Turner's own example, ghetto teen-agers in Chicago have first and second vice-presidents in their street gangs.[23] My research indicates that such things are very rare and that the images generated by the inferior are usually not reversals or elevations at all. Thus liminality itself—as fully elaborated by Turner—may be less a universal moment of meaning needed by human beings as they move through social dramas than an escape for those who bear the burdens and reap the benefits of a high place in the social structure. As recent liberation theologians have pointed out, it is the powerful who express imitation of Christ as (voluntary) poverty, (voluntary) nudity, and (voluntary) weakness. But the involuntary poor usually express their *imitatio Christi* not as wealth and exploitation but as struggle.[24]

Let me now turn to the later Middle Ages to illustrate the strengths and limitations of Turner's notion of liminality. First, then, the stories and symbols of men.

Male lives from the twelfth to the fifteenth centuries—both as lived and as told—may be nicely explicated as social dramas. As one would expect for religious *virtuosi*, charismatic figures, saints, the liminal phase usually issues in breach with previous role and previous group—i.e., in conversion. Images of reversal and inversion are dominant in the converted life, particularly at moments of transition. If we take as an example one of the most famous of all medieval biographies, Bonaventure's life of Francis, we find that the story is not only told as a series of successful crises, breaches with former status and life, but that Francis, the wealthy merchant's son, adopts images not just of poverty but also of nudity, weakness and femaleness at key moments. At the two most decisive breaches of a life filled with crisis—i.e., when he renounces his earthly father and when he dies—Francis takes off all his clothes.[25] These two moments are each accompanied by adoption of disease and suffering (in the first case, dwelling among lepers; in the second, the union with the crucifix in stigmata).[26] And the moment of conversion is a moment of womanly fertility: Bonaventure tells us that Francis took off his clothes and his shoes, renounced his father, threw away his money, prayed to Mary, and like her gave birth to his first conceived child (his first disciple).[27] When the pope first rejects and later accepts Francis, Francis tells the story of a poor woman (by implication himself) who bears children of the Holy Spirit;[28] three women meet Francis and address *him* as "Lady Poverty";[29] Bonaventure suggests that ministers are fathers and preachers but Francis, who insisted on remaining layman rather than cleric, is a mother, laboring for her children by example–that is, by suffering birth pangs.[30] Francis is described as cradling all creation–from a rabbit to the baby Jesus–in his arms as a mother.[31] But Francis's renunciation of his earthly father is decisive; real change occurs. And, in Bonaventure's prose, the Francis who returns from being crucified in the stigmata is now a "knight," a captain of Christ's army, sealed (for all his lay status) by the seal of Christ the High Priest.[32] In death Francis is described as founder and leader, model and exemplar, and father of his friars.[33] The life is a drama. The story told of it is a drama. From the liminality of weakness, nudity and womanliness comes the leader and model who changes the religious life of the thirteenth century.

Not only are male lives social dramas; men themselves use images of reversal to express liminality. And chief among these images is woman–as fact and as symbol. As Simone Roisin has shown, recourse to and comfort by the Virgin is a more common theme in the visions of men than in those of women.[34] Men frequently describe not only themselves but even Christ and God as female and, as I have argued elsewhere, such descriptions are frequently part of their anxiety over administrative responsibilities. Abbots and novice masters in the throes of self-doubt about their leadership talk of themselves and their God as tender and maternal.[35] "Woman" was clearly outside medieval European notions of social structure, as Georges Duby repeatedly emphasizes in his study of the "three orders" of society;[36] and male writers clearly saw the image of the "female" (virgin, bride or mother) as an image for the male self when it escaped those three orders. In a very common metaphor, the monk Guerric of Igny wrote of the advancing soul as the "mother of Christ."[37] Bernard of Clairvaux not only elaborated the notion of the soul as bride and of the religious leader as mother but even suggested that monks, who fled the world, were women, whereas bishops, who led the world, were men.[38] To Bonaventure, not only the soul but also the illumined mind is bride, daughter, friend, sister and member of Christ.[39] Monks and friars, whose status as set-apart was what Turner calls institutionalized liminality, also spoke of themselves as "fools," "acrobats," and "children"–all images of reversal–and even in their clothing adopted the child's hood as a distinctive feature.[40] In a particularly vivid fourteenth-century example, Richard Rolle underlined his conversion and his rejection of family by fashioning hermit's clothing for himself out of two of his sister's dresses.[41]

To the well-known fact that men described themselves as women in moments or statuses of liminality, we can add the less commonly observed fact that men had recourse to actual women as liminal. Hildegard of Bingen, Birgitta of Sweden, Catherine of Siena and Joan of Arc are only the most obvious examples of women whose visions, attained while they were in a state of radical apartness (underlined by virginity or illness or low social status), were *for men* a means of escape from and reintegration into status and power.[42] Two important biographers of the early thirteenth century, Thomas of Cantimpré and Jacques de Vitry, created, through a number of lives, the image of the holy woman as critique of, reproach to, and solution for male pride, ambition and irreligiosity.[43] The biographers of two Franciscan tertiaries, Angela of Foligno and Margaret of Cortona, see these women as "mothers" who have only "sons"—i.e., the local friars for whom they provide healing, visions, advice, rebuke and comfort.[44] John Coakley in his study of fifteenth-century saints' lives points out that, in sharp contrast to male saints who often hold power and office in the world, all women saints from this period are known through the eyes of their male confessors and are depicted by these confessors as models of interiorized spirituality.[45] The woman is thus, to the man, a retreat from the world into inner, often mystical repose. What she says (and her rhetoric is sometimes strident) and what she is, is a criticism of male power and an alternative to it. Contact with her is, for the male, an escape from the world; after recourse to her he returns to that world girded with information and consolation. The male biographers of Christina of Markyate in the twelfth century, Juliana of Cornillon in the thirteenth and Angela of Foligno in the fourteenth century stress explicitly that God chose to act through the weak vessel, the woman, as a condemnation of male religious failure, so that the last becomes first, the first last.[46] Victor Turner himself expresses this sense of woman as liminal for man in his recent work on pilgrimage when he refers repeatedly to the Virgin as expressing the affectional, emotional side of human character, holding up to society that escape from and evaluation of status and wealth which those who possess power apparently need in order to survive psychologically.[47]

Moreover, in the Middle Ages as today, men tended to assume that reversal was symmetrical. In other words, men writing about women assumed that women went through sharp crises and conversions and that their liminal moments were accompanied by gender reversal (in this case, of course, elevation). The twelfth-century biographer of Christina of Markyate tells a highly dramatic story of Christina escaping from marriage disguised as a man.[48] And from the patristic period (even more than from the later Middle Ages) there survive a host of stories of women disguising themselves as men in order to flee the world and join monasteries.[49] The lives of such early thirteenth-century saints as Margaret of Ypres or Mary of Oignies—although noticeably lacking in any images of gender reversal—are, as told by their male biographers, tales of high romance. Margaret avoided an earthly suitor by "marrying" Christ, and Mary, married young, more or less escaped marriage through extraordinary self-torture and starvation. It is only by reading between the lines that we realize that circumstances and social norms denied to Mary the mendicant poverty she really wanted as *imitatio Christi* or that Margaret sought in an unresolved pattern to become dependent on one male after another (uncle, lover, Dominican spiritual adviser, the other clergy of Ypres, finally Christ).[50] The stories are not exactly social dramas with crises, liminality, reintegration, although the male biographers shape them into the traditional medieval narrative form of situation, rupture, resolution.[51] Moreover, the male dress adopted in fact by such women as Joan of Arc, Margery Kempe, Dorothy of Montau and Christina of Markyate was less a religious symbol than a social mechanism. Joan of Arc wore it in order to be a warrior; Margery Kempe and Dorothy of Montau in order to go more safely on pilgrimage; Christina of Markyate in order to escape husband and family.[52] Although a powerful and sometimes threatening image to the *men* who encountered it, so much so that they perhaps saw female cross-dressing where none existed,[53] to women it was a means to change roles. In the later Middle Ages, it is male biographers who describe women as "virile" when they make religious progress. To men, women reverse images and "become men" in renouncing the world.[54] But medieval women do not describe themselves as men as a way of asserting either humility or spiritual prowess. Women either describe themselves as truly androgynous (that is, they use male and female images without a strong sense of a given set of personality characteristics going with the one or the other gender) or as female (bride, lover, mother). If we look at the relatively few women whose own writings survive, Gertrude of Helfta and the Flemish mystic Hadewijch are examples of the former; Mechtild of Magdeburg and Beatrice of Nazareth examples of the latter.[55]

The complex and powerful imagery in the writings by and about Catherine of Siena also illustrate this point. When Catherine's male biographer, Raymond of Capua, worried about the validity of her ecstatic experiences, he received from God a vision in which Catherine's face fused into or became a bearded male face, which Raymond understood to be Christ. Thus, the man needed the woman's visionary ability authenticated either by seeing her as male or by seeing a male Christ acting through her. But Raymond reported that God told Catherine herself that she need not adopt male disguise, as she had desired to do when she was a child; God, "who has created both sexes and all sorts of men," who can "create an angel as easily as an ant," would send her to preach and teach *as a woman* in order to shame immoral men. The woman in her own vision remains woman and the male dress once wished for (not, however, as image but as mechanism of actual role change) is not necessary.[56] In her *Dialogue*, Catherine's own images for herself are female; her Christ is androgynous—bridegroom but also mother.[57]

So, when we take our stand with male story tellers, whether their tales be of women or of men, we find social dramas everywhere, with liminal moments expressed in images of gender reversal. But when we stand with women and look at how their stories and their symbols really work, we find something different. The life of Beatrice of Ornacieux, for example, written by another Carthusian nun is an entirely static picture of extreme self-mortification and eucharistic frenzy.[58] There are dramatic elements certainly. At one moment Beatrice, locked in by her caretaker because she has made herself ill by extreme asceticism during Lent, passes through the locked door by putting a picture of the Virgin out through a little window.[59] But there is no conversion, no breach and reintegration. Beatrice's own self-image in her visions and her biographer's images for her are female. Like dozens of other thirteenth-century women, Beatrice repeatedly receives the Christ child at the eucharist and cradles him as a mother; her central images for her encounters with Christ in ecstasy are eating and illness or suffering.[60] To an astonishing extent, hers is a life in which "nothing happens," at least if we expect to find a social drama.

Moreover, if we turn to what is one of the most fascinating of all medieval texts, the autobiography of the English woman Margery Kempe, written in the early fifteenth century, we find constant change and excitement but no completed social drama. There are dozens of occasions on which, we might say, Margery strains desperately for liminality, strains for transition in status, for conversion, for escape from her normal role as "married woman" into the role, two hundred years old at least, of the *mulier sancta*. As the book opens, her depression about her failed business venture into brewing and her guilt about sex and food culminate in a vision in which Christ seems to substitute for her husband as her true lover, the eucharist to substitute for fleshly meat as her true food.[61] But the vision does not result in a conversion to chastity and abstinence. Margery must obey her husband, who, annoyed by her asceticism, says he will insist on the marriage debt unless she gives up her fasting. Margery then reports a conversation with Christ in which Christ says that she may give up the less important practice, fasting, in order to gain chastity. There is thus the amusing suggestion that Christ and Margery together have tricked the male, who has the power to grant to—and withhold from—the woman her own conversion.[62] Such manipulating and maneuvering then is the pattern of Margery's life. Wandering on pilgrimage, she must take her husband along or find another male protector; desiring weekly communion, she must get permission from her bishop and her confessor.[63] When Christ comes to tell her she is pregnant, he comforts her: "I love wives also, and especially those wives who would live chaste if they might."[64] And once her husband permits her to live in chastity (although for long years she cannot escape the responsibility of caring for him physically), Christ admonishes her: "Daughter, if thou knewest how many wives there are in this world that would love me and serve me right well and duly if they might be free from their husbands as thou art from thine, thou wouldst see that thou wert right much beholden unto me."[65] The message is almost: "be grateful for the little liminality permitted to you." In her own vivid prose, Margery sees herself as mother to the baby Jesus and bride to the human Christ, carrying such images to heights of literalism by actually feeling Jesus's toes in her hands in bed and weeping profusely at the sight of any male baby.[66] In her own eyes, Margery achieves spiritual growth not by reversing what she is but by being more fully herself with Christ. It is not possible to see Margery's dominant symbols—virginity (which is also its opposite, sexuality) and eucharist (which is also its opposite, fasting)—as moving her through a crisis, redressing or consolidating a breach or a conflict of norms. This is because Margery, for all her fervor, her courage, her piety, her mystical gifts and her brilliant imagination, cannot write her own script.

Such constriction is what we find in women's stories generally, even when they are told by men. Juliana of Cornillon received a vision of the new liturgical feast of *Corpus Christi* and was ordered by Christ to have it established in the church. For twenty years she did nothing. She finally dared to approach a powerful male and, with his help, the observance made limited headway; but her further efforts to support monastic as well as liturgical reform led to her exile, and she wandered indecisively from religious house to religious house until her death. Dorothy of Montau, a fourteenth-century precursor of Margery Kempe, took her husband and her daughter along on pilgrimage. Although used by her confessor as propaganda for eucharistic devotion, she had to fight that same confessor in her lifetime for access to the eucharist and, when dying, was denied the final reception she craved. Even the life of Christina of Markyate, so skillfully organized by medieval narrative convention into a series of exciting crises, is, when one reads between the lines, a story of very *un*decisive change. Christina hangs from nails behind tapestries and leaps from windows to avoid her husband's advances; but it is years before she can legally escape the marriage and then only because her husband desires to marry someone else.[67] Umiltà of Faenza (or (Florence) was able to adopt chastity only when doctors persuaded her husband that he must practice continence to preserve his health.[68] When Clare of Assisi's sister Agnes tried to flee her family, she was beaten half to death by her kinsmen; and the author of the nuns' book of Unterlinden tells a similar but even more gruesome story.[69] Although Clare herself did manage to renounce her noble family, shedding her jewels and her hair, she was never able to live the full mendicant life she so desired. Her story is a complex one, but it seems that, fleeing family and a possible husband only to accept the leadership of brother Francis, she was led by Francis's rejection to accept enclosure, which she did not originally want. It was only two days before her death that her rule with its insistence on poverty was confirmed.[70] Indeed, in a recent quantitative study of saints' lives from 1000 to 1700, Weinstein and Bell have demonstrated that, in general, women's saintly vocations grew slowly through childhood and into adolescence; a disproportionate percentage of women saints were certain of their commitment to virginity before age seven. Despite the fact that both chastity and marital status were more central themes in women's lives than in men's, male saints were far more likely to undergo abrupt adolescent conversions, involving renunciation of wealth, power, marriage, and sexuality.[71]

The point I am making here is an obvious one. Women could not take off all their clothes and walk away from their fathers or husbands, as did Francis. Simple social facts meant that most women's dramas were incomplete. And there may be psychological reasons for women's images as well as social ones. Ramanujan, who has found a similar pattern in the lives of female Indian saints, has argued, using Nancy Chodorow's psychological research, that women are in general less likely to use images of gender reversal or to experience life-decisions as sharp ruptures because women, raised by women, mature into a continuous self whereas boys, also raised by women, *must* undergo one basic reversal (i.e.. from wanting to "be" their mothers to acceptance of being fathers).[72]

If we turn from women's stories to women's symbols, we find that certain aspects of Turner's approach are extremely helpful. Although western Christianity had few women's rituals, certain key Christian rituals and symbols were especially important in women's spirituality in the later Middle Ages. One of these was the eucharist. And if one applies to late medieval eucharistic devotion Turner's notion of "dominant symbol," much that was before neglected or obscure becomes clear. Turner's idea of symbols as polysemic or multivocal, as including in some real sense the physiological and natural processes to which they refer as well as normative and social structural abstractions, provides a welcome escape from the way in which the eucharist and its related devotions have usually been treated by liturgists, historians of theology, and literary historians.

Such historians have frequently assumed that a devotion or an experience is "explained" once its literary ancestors or theological content are found: thus Dorothy of Montau's quite physical pregnancy (swelling) with Christ before receiving the eucharist is explained by the Biblical metaphor of the good soul as Christ's mother (Mark 3.35); Margery Kempe's cuddling with Christ in bed is simply a case of an uneducated woman's taking literally metaphors from the Song of Songs.[73] Turner's sense of ritual as process or drama moves us beyond this old-style history of theology or literature with its search for sources toward the new "history of spirituality"—where "spirituality" really means "lived religion"—which has been proposed recently by scholars like André Vauchez and Lester Little.[74]

When we turn to the eucharist in particular, Turner's notion of symbol as involving in some deep way a "likeness" between the orectic (the sensory) and the abstract or normative poles of meaning redirects our attention to the fact that the communion was *food*. People were eating God. The eucharist, albeit a recapitulation of Christ's execution, was not therefore a symbol of death but of life, birth, and nursing. As I have argued elsewhere, it stood for Christ's humanness and therefore for ours.[75] By eating it and, in that eating, fusing with Christ's hideous physical suffering, the Christian not so much *escaped* as *became* the human. By "saturating," as Turner puts it, the fact of eating, the eucharist itself summed up the asceticism (denial of the body, especially through fasting) and the anti-dualism (joy in creation and in physicality), which were part of medieval Catholicism. Not merely a mechanism of social control, a way of requiring yearly confession and therefore submission to the supervision of local clergy, the eucharist was itself both intensely feared and intensely desired. As symbol, it encapsulated two themes in late medieval devotion: an audacious sense of the closeness of the divine (Christians ate Jesus!) and a deep fear of the awfulness of God (if one ate without being worthy, one ate one's own destruction!). Moreover processual analysis helps us to see that the liturgy surrounding the eucharist was a drama. Thus we understand that when, in the thirteenth century, elevation of the host came to replace either consecration or reception of the elements as the climax of the ritual, the entire meaning was changed. God came to be taken in through the eyes rather than the mouth; he was thus taken in most fully where ecstatic, out-of-the-body experiences added a deeper level of "seeing" to bodily seeing.[76]

But if Turner's notion of dominant symbol is useful in deepening any historian's understanding of this central Christian ritual, certain problems arise in seeing *women's* relationship to the eucharist in particular as processual. Turner's model would predict that, for women (excluded in theory from church office because of social and ontological inferiority), the eucharist would express status elevation.[77] To some extent, this is what we find. A not infrequent women's vision at the moment of reception of eucharist is the vision of self as priest.[78] Gertrude of Helfta, Angela of Foligno, and Lukardis of Oberweimar, among others, receive from Christ in the eucharist the power to preach, teach and criticize, to hear confessions and pronounce absolution, to administer the eucharist to others.[79] But the woman, released into another role in vision and image, never of course became a priest. And such visions, exactly as Turner's model would predict, serve as much to integrate the woman ecstatic into basic Christian structures as to liberate her from them when they fail her. In some visions, recipient is elevated above celebrant, as when the host flies away from the corrupt priest into the mouth of the deserving nun or when Christ himself brings the cup to a woman who has been forbidden to receive it exactly because of her ecstatic possession.[80] But the very fact that the majority of visions which project women into power through reversed images in fact come in the context of the eucharist ultimately only integrates the woman more fully into clerically controlled structures. In order to have visions, she must attend the liturgy, controlled by exactly that clergy which her visions might seem to criticize.

There are thus elements of status elevation ritual in women's images. But the more thoroughly one explores women's experience the more unimportant images of reversal appear to be. Indeed, unlike teen-age gangs with second vice-presidents or Indian untouchables who mimic high caste structures,[81] women's religious life in the later Middle Ages is strikingly without structure. The beguines, the only movement created by women for women before the modern period, were a puzzle to contemporary male chroniclers, who sought (as modern historians have continued to do) a specific founder for the movement and a specific legal status or rule or form of life characteristic of it.[82] But that which characterized the beguines (women who simply lived chastely and unostentatiously in their own houses or in groups, praying and working with their hands) was exactly *lack* of leaders, rules, detailed prescriptions for the routine of the day or for self-regulation, *lack* of any over-arching governmental structures. Moreover, many of the women saints of the later Middle Ages whose lives we know in detail cannot be located within any specific religious status. Although male orders fought to define themselves and each other in sometimes very uncharitable polemic,[83] women floated from institution to institution. Later claimed by the various orders as Premonstratensians, Cistercians, or Franciscans, a strikingly large number of the women saints of the thirteenth and fourteenth centuries cannot really be seen as affiliated closely with any religious house or possessing any clear status. They were simply women in the world (in their fathers', uncles' or husbands' houses), being religious.[84] Historians have repeatedly argued that women's failure to create or to join orders was owing to male oppression. In their different ways, Grundmann, Greven, Southern, and Bolton all suggest that women were quasi-religious because male orders and supervisors would not take them on or because the church was not prepared to allow women to create their own structures.[85] It may be, however, that women's rather "structureless" religion simply continued their ordinary lives (whose ultimate status they usually did not control), just as the economic activity of "holy women"—weaving, embroidery, care of the sick and small children—continued women's ordinary work. Recent research indicates that in some instances, women who could have chosen the more formal life of the convent chose the quasi-religious status instead. The loosely organized beguines were a desired alternative.[86] In any case, if women's communities (convents or beguinages) were institutionalized liminality in Turner's sense, that liminality was imaged as continuity with, not as reversal of, the women's ordinary experience.

Of course, if one starts by assuming Turner's notion of "antistructure," one may describe this "structureless" aspect of woman's religious life by Turner's term *communitas*. But Turner's *communitas* is the antithesis to structure: the source for it, the release from it, the critique of it. What I am describing here is not something which "breaks into society through the interstices of structure" but something both simpler and more central: a normal aspect of women's lives.[87] If one looks *with* women rather than *at* women, women's lives are not liminal *to* women—but neither, except in a very partial way, are male roles or male experiences.[88]

Medieval women, like men, chose to speak of themselves as brides, mothers, and sisters of Christ. But to women this was an accepting and continuing of what they were; to men, it was reversal. Indeed all women's central images turn out to be continuities. Equally important, for women, in eucharist and in ecstasy, were images of eating and images of illness—and both eating and illness were fundamentally expressions of the woman's physicality. Told by the theological and exegetical tradition that they represented the material, the physical, the appetitive and lustful whereas men represented soul or mind, women elaborated images of self that underlined natural processes. And in these images, the woman's physical "humanness" was "saved," given meaning by joining with the human-divine Christ. Illness, self-induced or God-given, was identification with the crucifixion; eating was consuming and being consumed by the human body that was also God. We should not be misled by modern notions of illness or of brides as images of passivity. When the woman saw herself as bride or lover, the image was deeply active and fully sensual; when the woman sought illness as fact and as metaphor, it was a fully active fusing with the death agonies of Christ. Although each of these women's symbols is complex in ways I cannot elaborate here, none is in any obvious sense either elevation or reversal.[89]

Moreover, those women mystics like Margaret Porete (burned in 1310 for the "Free Spirit" heresy—i.e., antinomianism), who seem from the standpoint of the culture as a whole an extreme case of liminality or antistructure, are really not in their own context liminal at all.[90] It is true that Margaret (like Eckhart, whom Turner loves to cite) recommends by-passing all "works," all practices and disciplines, rules and formulae, to escape to an ultimate freedom, a sort of God beyond God.[91] But one questions whether, for women, such quietism and structurelessness (which in Margaret's case is intended to be permanent!) is a moment of oneness with humankind achieved as an escape from the weight of social structure and human responsibility. Is it not rather a reflection in image of the woman's own experience of the irrelevance of structure, of continuing striving without resolution, of going beyond only by becoming what one is most deeply?

My work on late medieval religiosity thus indicates that Turner's notion of liminality, in the expanded, "metaphorical" sense which he has used for non-primitive societies, is applicable only to men. Only men's stories are full social dramas; only men's symbols are full reversals. Women are fully liminal only to men. I do not think the problem lies in the fact that later medieval Europe is a society which presented far greater variety of roles and possibility of choice than the society of the Ndembu, for which Turner first began to formulate his processual anthropology. If this were so, I would not find both his specific and his general insights so useful for understanding male stories. Bonaventure's view of Francis and Jacques de Vitry's view of Mary of Oignies seem well described and deeply penetrated when scrutinized through the lens of "liminality." The problem seems rather to be that the dichotomy of structure and chaos, from which liminality or *communitas* is a release, is a special issue for elites, for those who in a special sense *are* the structures. A model which focuses on this need for release as *the* ultimate socio-psychological need may best fit the experience of elites. Indeed in the western tradition, such a model may, however unwittingly, arise from a particular form of Christianity which has been that of the elites. The model of Jesus as poor, naked, defenseless, suffering, tender and womanly—which was particularly popular in the later Middle Ages—was an idea which especially appealed to the lower aristocracy and the new urban, merchant class.[92] As Herbert Grundmann pointed out many years ago, the Marxists were wrong to see medieval notions of the "poor of Christ" as the revolt of either the economically disadvantaged or of women; voluntary poverty *can* be a religious response *only* to those with some wealth to renounce.[93] But, as recent liberation theology reminds us, the "suffering servant" can be a more polysemic image than most Christians are aware. There are options beyond a claim to victory and kingship on the part of the oppressed, a release into poverty and suffering on the part of the advantaged.[94] To medieval women, at any rate, Christ on the cross was not victory or humility but "humanity." And in eating and loving that "humanness" one became more fully oneself. What women's images and stories expressed most fundamentally was neither reversal nor elevation but continuity.

I would object to any effort to make my description of women's images at a particular moment in the western tradition either universalist or prescriptive. A good deal of what seems to me irresponsible theologizing about women has been done recently, based on a superficial understanding of the history of Christianity; and certain claims about women's need for female symbols or for affectivity or for the unstructured are among the most empty and ill-informed.[95] Indeed they may succumb to something of the same stereotype of "the female" that is built into Turner's notion of women as liminal *for men*. But my description of how actual women's stories and symbols function in the later Middle Ages does raise doubts about Turner's notion of liminality as universalist and prescriptive. Perhaps, after all, "social drama" and van Gennep's concept of liminality are less generalizable than Turner supposed and speak less fully to the complexity of human experience.

These doubts, however, throw us back exactly to the implications of the very best of the work of the early Victor Turner. Insofar as I am arguing that we must, at least some of the time, stand *with* those whom we study, Turner has already said it. If symbols are, in fact, multivocal, condensing and lived, we will understand them only when we look *with* as well as over and beyond the participants who use them, feeling as well as knowing their dramas in their own context. My critique of Turner's theory of liminality is thus one he might have given himself.

Notes and References

1. Since I am writing here for an audience of non-medievalists, I have cited modern translations of medieval texts wherever possible. I have also tried to use examples that will be familiar, or at least accessible, to non-specialists through secondary literature. It is obviously not possible in an article of this sort to deal with the technical problems of recensions, authenticity, authorship, etc., associated with medieval texts. I would like to thank Peter Brown, Charles Keyes and Guenther Roth for arguing with me extensively about Victor Turner.
2. The term "processual symbolic analysis" was coined by Charles Keyes to describe the theory of symbol held by both Victor Turner and Clifford Geertz; see Keyes, "Notes on the Language of Processual Symbolic Analysis," unpublished paper, 1976. It has been adopted by Turner in *Process, Performance and Pilgrimage: A Study in Comparative Symbology*, New Delhi, 1979, pp. 143-154, which is reprinted in Victor and Edith Turner, *Image and Pilgrimage in Christian Culture: Anthropological Perspectives*, New York, 1978, pp. 243-255. A recent statement which stresses the centrality of social dramas in Turner's perspective is Victor Turner, "Social Dramas and Stories About Them," *On Narrative*, ed. W. J. T. Mitchell, Chicago, 1981, pp. 137-164.
3. E. E. Evans-Pritchard, *Essays in Social Anthropology*, London, 1962, pp. 13-65.
4. Keith Thomas, "The Ferment of Fashion," *Times Literary Supplement*, April 30, 1982, p. 479.
5. See, for example, *Dramas, Fields and Metaphors: Symbolic Action in Human Society*, Ithaca, 1974, pp. 33-34; *Image and Pilgrimage*, pp. 249-51; and "Social Dramas and Stories About Them."

6. See, for example, *The Forest of Symbols: Aspects of Ndembu Ritual*, Ithaca, 1967, chapters 1 and 2; *The Ritual Process: Structure and Anti-Structure*, Chicago, 1969, p. 41; and *Dramas, Fields*, pp. 50 and 55.

7. See *Forest*, chapters 1 and 2; and *Image and Pilgrimage*, pp. 245-49.

8. On Becket, see "Religious Paradigms and Political Action: Thomas Becket at the Council of Northampton," *Dramas, Fields*, pp. 60-97. On Francis, see "Communitas: Model and Process," *Ritual Process*, pp. 131-165 and passim.

9. New interpretations of Francis, not available to Turner, would make his ideal more complex than simply poverty. See, for example, E. Randolph Daniel, *The Franciscan Concept of Mission in the High Middle Ages*, Lexington, 1975; Barbara H. Rosenwein and Lester K. Little, "Social Meaning in the Monastic and Mendicant Spiritualities," *Past and Present* 63 (1974), pp. 4-32; and Lester K. Little, *Religious Poverty and the Profit Economy in Medieval Europe*, Ithaca, 1978.

10. The novel aspect of Turner's analysis seems to me not his notion of the root paradigm of the cross or martyrdom or *imitatio Christi*, an understanding of which seems to have been implicit in all analyses of Becket, but the importance Turner places on Becket's incorporating the model into himself at the votive mass on October 13; see *Dramas, Fields*, pp. 84-85.

11. In "Social Dramas and Stories," Turner writes (p. 147): "I have found that among the Ndembu, for example, prolonged social dramas always revealed the related sets of oppositions that give Ndembu social structure its tensile character: matriliny versus virilocality; the ambitious individual versus the wider interlinking of matrilineal kin; the elementary family versus the uterine sibling group (children of one mother); the forwardness of youth versus the domineering elders; status-seeking versus responsibility; sorcerism (*wuloji*)—that is, hostile feelings, grudges, and intrigues—versus friendly respect and generosity toward others. In the Iranian crisis the divisions and coalitions of interests have become publicly visible, some of which are surprising and revelatory. Crisis constitutes many levels in all cultures." One is struck here by the lack of precision with which the modern analogy is used.

12. On dominant symbols, see also *Dramas, Fields* and *Image and Pilgrimage*, pp. 243-255. On status reversal or elevation, see especially "Humility and Hierarchy: the Liminality of Status Elevation and Reversal," *Ritual Process*, pp. 166-203.

13. For the four phases of social drama, see "Social Dramas and Stories," p. 145. The model of rites of passage from which Turner derives his notion of social drama has three phases: separation, margin or limen, and reaggregation (see *Image and Pilgrimage*, p. 249); and he frequently seems to assume three phases in social drama. See *Forest*, chapter 4.

14. See Arnold van Gennep, *The Rites of Passage*, 1908; reprint, London, 1960.

15. See *Forest*, chapters 2 and 3.

16. See especially *Process, Performance and Pilgrimage*.

17. For example, *Process, Performance, and Pilgrimage*, p. 23.

18. See Hippolyte Delehaye, *The Legends of the Saints: An Introduction to Hagiography*, tr. Crawford, London, 1907; Simone Roisin, *L'hagiographie cistercienne dans le diocèse de Liège au XIIIe siècle*, Louvain, 1947; Charles Williams Jones, *Saints' Lives and Chronicles in Early England*, Ithaca, 1947; Baudoin de Gaiffier, "Hagiographie et historiographie: quelques aspects du problème," *La storiografia altomedievale*, Settimane di Studio del Centro italiano de Studi sull'alto medioevo, 17, Spoleto, 1970, vol. 1, pp. 139-166.

19. On the eucharist generally, see Joseph A. Jungmann, *The Mass of the Roman Rite: Its Origins and Development*, tr. Brunner, 2 vols., New York, 1955; F. Baix and C. Lambot. *Le dévotion à L'eucharistie et le VIIe centenaire de la Féte-Dieu*, Namur, n.d.,; and n. 76 below.

20. See, for example, *Forest*, and *The Drums of Affliction: A Study of Religious Processes Among the Ndembu of Zambia*, Oxford, 1968.

21. For example, *Process, Performance and Pilgrimage*, pp. 104-105; *Ritual Process*, pp. 99-105.

22. I am aware that this is a very complicated issue, for it is difficult to sort out how a sub-group relates to the dominant culture; and we cannot *assume* that women will *not* agree with stereotypes of them generated by dominant males. The point is discussed well in Judith Shapiro, "Anthropology and the Study of Gender," *Soundings*, 64. 4 (1981), pp. 446-465. To "stand with" does not, of course, mean simply to take the view of informants. Turner himself discusses the problems with such an approach, which, he says, makes symbols merely "signs." See *Forest*, pp. 25-27, and "Symbolic Studies," *Annual Review of Anthropology* 4 (1975), pp. 145-161. What we see when we "stand with" a subculture will no more be simply what its members tell us than what we see when we stand with the dominant culture will be.

23. *Ritual Process*, pp. 192-193.

24. Gustave Gutiérrez, *A Theology of Liberation: History, Politics and Salvation*, tr. by Inda and Eagleson, Maryknoll, New York, 1973, especially chapter 3, pp. 287-306.

25. Bonaventure, The Life of St. Francis, in *Bonaventure: The Soul's Journey into God . . .*, tr. Cousins, New York, 1978, pp. 193-194 and 317. On Francis, see also n. 9 above. For many other examples of male lives characterized by crisis and abrupt conversion, see Donald Weinstein and Rudolph M. Bell, *Saints and Society: The Two Worlds of Western Christendom, 1000-1700*, Chicago, 1982, pp. 50-79 and 109-115.

26. Bonaventure, Life of Francis, pp. 195 and 303-307.

27. Ibid., pp. 199-200.

28. Ibid., pp. 204-206.

29. Ibid., p. 243.

30. Ibid., pp. 251-252.

31. Ibid., pp. 257 and 278.

32. Ibid., pp. 311-313.

33. Ibid., p. 321.

34. Roisin, *L'hagiographie*, pp. 108, 111-113 and passim.

35. Bynum, *Jesus as Mother: Studies in the Spirituality of the High Middle Ages*, Berkeley, 1982, pp. 110-169.

36. Georges Duby, *The Three Orders: Feudal Society Imagined*, tr. Goldhammer, Chicago, 1980, pp. 89, 95, 131-133, 145 and 209.

37. On Guerric, see *Jesus as Mother*, pp. 120-122 and passim.

38. Bernard of Clairvaux, sermon 12 on the Song of Songs, *The Works of Bernard of Clairvaux*, vol. 2: *On the Song of Songs*, vol. 1, tr. Walsh, Kalamazoo, 1976, pp. 77-85. And see *Jesus as Mother*, pp. 115-118 and 127-128.

39. Bonaventure, The Soul's Journey into God, in *Bonaventure . . .*, p. 93.

40. For example, Bernard of Clairvaux, *The Letters of St. Bernard of Clairvaux*, tr. B. S. James, London, 1953, letter 90, p. 135. On clothing, see *RB: 1980: The Rule of St. Benedict*, ed. Timothy Fry, et al., Collegeville, Minnesota, 1981, pp. 261-263. In the modern world, of course, male religious clothing is a "reversed image" in another sense: monks and priests "wear skirts." On monasticism as institutionalized liminality, see *Ritual Process*, p. 107.

41. See the *Legenda* or Office of Rolle in Richard Rolle, *The Fire of Love or Melody of Love and The Mending of Life . . . translated by Richard Misyn*, ed. and done into modern English by F. Cowper, London, 1914, p. xlvi.

42. For this argument see *Jesus as Mother*, pp. 257-262, and Bynum, "Women Mystics and Eucharistic Devotion in the Thirteenth Century," *Women's Studies*, 1984, to appear.

43. On Jacques and Thomas, see Ernest W. McDonnell, *The Beguines and Beghards in Medieval Culture with Special Emphasis on the Belgian Scene*, 1954, reprint, New York, 1969, pp. 20-40 and passim; and Brenda M. Bolton, "*Vitae Matrum*: A Further Aspect of the *Frauenfrage*," in *Medieval Women*, ed. D. Baker, Studies in Church History: Subsidia 1, Oxford, 1978, pp. 253-273.

44. *The Book of Divine Consolation of the Blessed Angela of Foligno*, tr. Steegmann, reprint, New York, 1966; the Life of Margaret of Cortona, *Acta sanctorum*, February, vol. 3, ed. Bollandus and Henschius, Paris and Rome, 1865, pp. 302-363.

45. "The Female Saint as Hagiographical Type in the Late Middle Ages," unpublished paper delivered at American Historical Association meeting, December, 1981. See also John Coakley, "The Representation of Sanctity in Late Medieval Hagiography: Evidence from *Lives* of Saints of the Dominican Order," Ph.D. dissertation, Harvard, 1980; and *Jesus as Mother*, chapter 5.

46. *The Life of Christina of Markyate*, tr. C. H. Talbot, Oxford, 1959; the Life of Juliana of Cornillon, *Acta sanctorum*, April, vol. 1, Paris and Rome, 1866, pp. 434-475; *The Book of Divine Consolation of Angela of Foligno*.

47. *Image and Pilgrimage*, pp. 161 and 236. See also *Process, Performance and Pilgrimage*, pp. 104-106; and *Ritual Process*, pp. 105, 183 and 200.

48. *The Life of Christina of Markyate*.

49. See John Anson, "The Female Transvestite in Early Monasticism," *Viator* 5 (1974), pp. 1-32. (See also Vern Bullough, "Transvestites in the Middle Ages," *American Journal of Sociology* 79 [1974], pp. 1381-1394.) Caesarius of Heisterbach tells a few such stories from the late twelfth

century, but they are imitated from patristic examples: Caesarius of Heisterbach, *The Dialogue on Miracles*, tr. Scott and Bland, New York, 1929, vol. 1, pp. 51-59. One of the problems with the emphasis that Marina Warner places on Joan of Arc's transvestism in her recent book is her failure to give other late medieval examples of women cross-dressing: see Marina Warner, *Joan of Arc: The Image of Female Heroism*, New York, 1981. For two examples, see Michael Goodich, "Contours of Female Piety in Later Medieval Hagiography," *Church History* 50 (1981), p. 25. Delehaye, *The Legends of the Saints*, pp. 197-206, traces many of the later stories back to a single prototype.

50. The Life of Margaret of Ypres in appendix to G. Meersseman, "Les frères prêcheurs et le mouvement dévot en Flandre au XIIIe siècle," *Archivum Fratrum Praedicatorum* 18 (1948), pp. 106-130; the Life of Mary of Oignies by Jacques de Vitry, *Acta sanctorum*, June, vol. 5, Paris and Rome, 1867, pp. 547-572. On Mary's inability to adopt complete mendicant poverty, see Bolton, "*Vitae Matrum*," pp. 257-59. For another parallel story, see Thomas of Cantimpré's Life of Lutgard of Aywières or of St. Trond, *Acta sanctorum*, June, vol. 4, Paris and Rome, 1867, pp. 189-210.

51. On medieval narrative technique see William J. Brandt, *The Shape of Medieval History: Studies in Modes of Perception*, New Haven, 1966.

52. On Joan, see Warner, *Joan of Arc*. On Dorothy of Montau (or of Prussia), see Stephen P. Bensch, "A Cult of the Maternal: Dorothea of Prussia (1347-94)," unpublished paper; Richard Kieckhefer, "Dorothy of Montau: Housewife and Mystic," unpublished paper; and Ute Stargardt, "The Influence of Dorothea von Montau on the Mysticism of Margery Kempe," Ph.D. dissertation, The University of Tennessee, 1981. Margery's life is available in a modern English translation: *The Book of Margery Kempe*, tr. W. Butler-Bowdon, New York, 1944. On Christina, see *The Life of Christina of Markyate*, and Christopher J. Holdsworth, "Christina of Markyate," *Medieval Women*, pp. 185-204.

53. Anson, "Female Transvestite," argues convincingly that these stories, like the later legend of Pope Joan, were the result of psychological projection. One of the major charges against Joan of Arc, who was accused of heresy (with overtones of witchcraft as well), was cross-dressing; see Warner, *Joan of Arc*.

54. See, for example, the biographies of Christina of Markyate and Juliana of Cornillon cited above.

55. Gertrude of Helfta, *Oeuvres spirituelles*, vols. 1-3, Sources chrétiennes, Série des textes monastiques d'Occident, Paris, 1967-68; *Hadewijch: The Complete Works*, tr. Hart, Paulist Press, New York, 1980; Mechtild of Magdeburg, *The Revelations . . . or the Flowing Light of the Godhead*, tr. Menzies, London, 1953; Beatrice of Nazareth (or Tienen), *Vita Beatricis: De Autobiografie van de Z. Beatrijs van Tienen O. Cist. 1200-1268*, Antwerp, 1964. On Gertrude and Mechtild of Magdeburg, see *Jesus as Mother*, chapter 5. Hadewijch, who uses intensely erotic language to describe her relationship to God, frequently casts herself in the role of a knight seeking his lady. On androgynous imagery in women's visions, see Elizabeth Petroff, *Consolation of the Blessed*, Alta Gaia Society, New York, 1979, pp. 66-78.

56. Raymond of Capua, Life of Catherine of Siena, *Acta Sanctorum*, April, vol. 3, Paris and Rome, 1866, pp. 892 and 884. I have been unable to consult the English tr. by George Lamb, *The Life of St. Catherine of Siena*, London, 1960.

57. Catherine of Siena, *The Dialogue*, tr. Suzanne Noffke, Paulist Press, New York, 1980.

58. Marguerite of Oingt, Life of Beatrice of Ornacieux, *Les oeuvres de Marguerite d'Oingt*, ed. Duraffour, Gardette and Durdilly, Paris, 1965, pp. 104-137.

59. Ibid., pp. 136-137.

60. Ibid., p. 105 (she pierces her hands with nails to achieve stigmata); p. 117 (she sees Christ as a little child at every elevation of the host); p. 122 (the host swells in her mouth until she almost chokes, and after this she can eat no earthly food). For other lives of women by women, one can consult the several nuns' books from the early fourteenth century.

61. *The Book of Margery Kempe*, p. 10. It is interesting that the anchorite who advises her here describes Christ as mother and tells her to suck his breast; but Margery herself never uses reversed imagery. Her Christ is always male and she is always female; see, for example, pp. 22-23 and 76-77.

62. Ibid., p. 17.

63. On her need for male protection, see ibid., pp. 25, 28, 32, 98-100. Margery was quite bold about opposing authority figures. This may have been owing in part to her father's status

(see Anthony Goodman, "The Piety of John Brunham's Daughter, of Lynn," *Medieval Women*, pp. 347-358), although to say this is not to detract from Margery's personal courage and insouciance.

64. Ibid., p. 39.
65. Ibid., p. 192.
66. Ibid., pp. 76 and 190; ibid., pp. 74-75 and 81.
67. For the texts discussed here see nn. 46 and 52 above. I should emphasize that later medieval women's lives include peasants as well as aristocrats, lay women as well as nuns and quasi-religious.
68. See Petroff, *Consolation of the Blessed*, p. 123; for other examples of circumstances constraining women's decisions, see ibid., p. 42. Weinstein and Bell, *Saints and Society*, pp. 88-97, give a number of examples of saintly women who are unable to determine their marital status and therefore the course of their lives.
69. *The Legend and Writings of Saint Clare of Assisi* (based on German work by E. Grau), St. Bonaventure, New York, 1953, pp. 35-37; Jeanne Ancelet-Hustache, ed., "Les *Vitae Sororum* d'Unterlinden: édition critique . . .," *Archives d'histoire doctrinale et littéraire du moyen âge* 5 (1930), pp. 374-375.
70. See *Legend of Saint Clare* and Rosalind B. Brooke and Christopher N. L. Brooke, "St. Clare," *Medieval Women*, pp. 275-287. For other women's lives in translation, see Petroff, *Consolation of the Blessed*.
71. Weinstein and Bell, *Saints and Society*, part I, especially pp. 34, 48, 71, 97, 108, 121 and 135.
72. A. K. Ramanujan, "On Women Saints," in *The Divine Consort: Rādhā and the Goddesses of India*, ed. Hawley and Wulff, Berkeley, 1982, pp. 316-324. Nancy Chodorow, *The Reproduction of Mothering: Psychoanalysis and the Sociology of Gender*, Berkeley, 1978. Ramanujan says about the Indian situation: "The males take on female personae . . . Before God all men are women. But no female saint, however she may defy male-oriented relational attitudes, takes on a male persona. It is as if, being already female, she has no need to change anything to turn toward God" (p. 324). See n. 89 below.
73. Examples of excellent scholarship in this vein, which nonetheless result in pejorative assessments of figures like Dorothy, Margery, Marguerite of Oingt, etc., are Edmund Colledge and James Walsh, eds., *A Book of Showings to the Anchoress Julian of Norwich*, 2 vols., Toronto, 1978, introduction; and Wolfgang Riehle, *The Middle English Mystics*, tr. Standring, London, 1981.
74. André Vauchez, *Le spiritualité du moyen âge occidental VIIIe - XIIe siècles*, Paris, 1975; Little, *Religious Poverty*.
75. On the eucharist, see Bynum, "Women Mystics and Eucharistic Devotion," *Women Studies*, 1984, to appear.
76. See Jungmann, *Mass*, vol. 2, pp. 120-122 and 206ff.; Peter Browe, *Die Verehrung der Eucharistie im Mittelalter*, Munich, 1933; and Edouard Dumoutet, *Corpus Domini: Aux sources de la piété eucharistique médiévale*, Paris, 1942.
77. On women as inferior, according to scientific and theological theory, see Vern Bullough, "Medieval Medical and Scientific Views of Women," *Viator* 4 (1973), pp. 487-493; Eleanor McLaughlin, "Equality of Souls, Inequality of Sexes; Women in Medieval Theology," *Religion and Sexism*, ed. Ruether, New York, 1974, pp. 213-266; Marie-Thérèse d'Alverny, "Comment les théologiens et les philosophes voient la femme?" *La femme dans les civilisations des Xe - XIIIe siècles, Cahiers de civilisation médiévale* 20 (1977), pp. 105-129.
78. Mechtild of Hackeborn has a vision of herself distributing the chalice; see *Revelationes Gertrudianae ac Mechtildianae* 2: *Sanctae Mechtildis virginis ordinis sancti Benedicti Liber specialis gratiae*, ed. the monks of Solesmes, Paris, 1877, pp. 7-10. More common is the vision in which Christ is priest to the woman recipient; see Peter Browe, *Die Eucharistischen Wunder des Mittelalters*, Breslau, 1938, pp. 20-30. On Mechtild of Hackeborn and Gertrude (cited in n. 79 below), see *Jesus as Mother*, chapter 5.
79. Gertrude of Helfta, *Relevationes Gertrudianae ac Mechtildianae* 1: *Sanctae Gertrudis . . . Legatus divinae Pietatis . . .*, ed. the monks of Solesmes, Paris, 1875, pp. 392-395, and *Oeuvres spirituelles*, vol. 2, pp. 196-198; Angela of Foligno, *Book of Divine Consolation*, p. 223; the Life of Lukardis of Oberweimar, in *Analecta Bollandiana* 18 (Brussels, 1899), p. 337. See also the Life of Ida of Louvain, *Acta sanctorum*, April, vol. 2, Paris and Rome, 1865, p. 183.
80. For these examples, see the case of the Viennese beguine, Agnes Blannbekin, discussed by Browe, *Die Eucharistischen Wunder*, p. 34, and by McDonnell, *Beguines*, pp. 314-317;

and the Life of Ida of Léau, *Acta Sanctorum*, October, vol. 13, Paris, 1883, pp. 113-114.

81. See Michael Moffatt, *An Untouchable Community in South India: Structure and Consensus*, Princeton, 1979, for data which support Turner's idea of reversal.

82. On the beguines see the works cited in n. 85 below. In the south of Europe groups like the Humiliati and the mendicant tertiaries paralleled the beguines, who were a Low-Country and Rhineland movement.

83. See *Jesus as Mother*, introduction and chapter 3.

84. Brenda Bolton makes this point in *"Vitae Matrum,"* p. 260. And note the number of female saints designated "lay" in Vauchez's list: André Vauchez, *La Sainteté en Occident aux derniers siècles du moyen âge d'après les procès de canonisation et les documents hagiographiques*. Bibliothèque des écoles françaises d'Athènes et de Rome, 241, Rome, 1981, pp. 656-676; see also pp. 315-18.

85. Joseph Greven, *Die Anfänge der Beginen: ein Beitrag zur Geschichte der Volksfrömmigkeit und des Ordenswesens im Hochmittelalter*, Münster in Westphalia, 1912; Herbert Grundmann, *Religiöse Bewegungen im Mittelalter*, 1935, reprint, Hildesheim, 1961; R. W. Southern, *Western Society and the Church in the Middle Ages*, Harmondsworth, England, 1970, pp. 318-331; Brenda Bolton, *"Mulieres Sanctae," Studies in Church History*, 10: *Sanctity and Secularity*, ed. D. Baker (1973), pp. 77-95, and *"Vitae Matrum."*

86. Frederick Stein, "The Religious Women of Cologne: 1120-1320," Ph.D. dissertation, Yale, 1977. The interpretation which blames male resistance to the religious needs of women must also be modified in light of John B. Freed, "Urban Life and the 'Cura Monialium' in Thirteenth-Century Germany," *Viator* 3 (1972), pp. 311-327.

87. The quotation is from Turner, *Image and Pilgrimage*, p. 251.

88. The point I raise here parallels the criticism that has been made of certain interpretations of women's symbols that come out of the structuralist camp. For example, the much discussed essay by Sherry Ortner ("Is Female to Male as Nature is to Culture?" *Women, Culture and Society*, ed. Rosaldo and Lamphere, Stanford, 1974, pp. 67-87), which argues that women are universally imaged as "nature" to the image of man as "culture," has been criticized for, among other things, viewing culture monolithically as the dominant culture. See Eleanor Leacock and June Nash, "Ideologies of Sex: Archetypes and Stereotypes," *Issues in Cross-Cultural Research*, New York Academy of Sciences, vol. 285, New York, 1977, pp. 618-645; and C. P. MacCormack and M. Strathern, eds., *Nature, Culture and Gender*, Cambridge, England, 1980, especially p. 17.

89. For an example of fusion with Christ through eroticism, see Hadewijch, *Complete Works*; for fusion through eating, see the Life of Ida of Louvain, *Acta Sanctorum*, April, vol. 2, Paris and Rome, 1865, pp. 156-189; for fusion through illness, see the life of Alice of Schaerbeek, *Acta Sanctorum*, June, vol. 2, Paris and Rome, 1867, pp. 471-477, and Julian of Norwich, *Showings*, tr. Colledge and Walsh, Paulist Press, New York, 1978. See also Ernst Benz, *Die Vision: Erfahrungsformen und Bilderwelt*, Stuttgart, 1969, pp. 17-34. Ramanujan's formulation of differences in Indian lives of men and women (see n. 72 above) cannot be completely applied to the medieval tradition exactly because the passivity he implies in women's images does not accurately describe the intensely dynamic aspect of erotic and ascetic images in the west.

90. *The Mirror of Simple Souls*, long known to scholars but discovered only in this century to be Margaret's "heretical" treatise, has been printed in Romana Guarnieri, "Il movimento del Libero Spirito . . II. Il 'Miroir des simples âmes' di Margherita Porete," *Archivio italiano per la storia della pietà*, vol. 4, Rome, 1965, pp. 513-635. On the work, see Robert E. Lerner, *The Heresy of the Free Spirit in the Later Middle Ages*, Berkeley, 1972, pp. 72-76 and 200-208.

91. Such mysticism is one of Turner's favorite examples of "metaphorical liminality." See *Process, Performance and Pilgrimage*, p. 125, where he claims that mysticism is interiorized ritual liminality, ritual liminality is exteriorized mysticism.

92. See Little, *Religious Poverty*, and Bynum, *Jesus as Mother*, p. 183. Turner is, of course, aware that reversal is more central in some religions than in others; see *Ritual Process*, p. 189. But his paradigm of Christianity seems late medieval, even Franciscan, rather than early modern or antique. In a rather obvious sense, the Reformation was a rejection of elaborate images of reversal — not just of carnival, monks and friars, but of the general notion of world denial as well.

93. Grundmann, *Religiöse Bewegungen*. On late medieval religiosity as upper class — and especially on conversion as an upper-class phenomenon — see Weinstein and Bell, *Saints and Society*, chapter 7, especially p. 216.

94. See above n. 24.

95. This writing has been surveyed recently by Rosemary Ruether, "The Feminist Critique in Religious Studies," *Soundings* 64.4 (1981), pp. 388-402; and Mark Silk, "Is God a Feminist?" *New York Times Book Review*, April 11, 1982.

CHAPTER VI

Space and Transformation in Human Experience

Robert L. Moore

I. Introduction

In recent decades studies in the interface between psychology and religion have become an increasingly important arena of discourse in the academic study of religion. New perspectives in both psychological and theological disciplines have provided an impetus not only for innovative approaches in the psychological study of religion, but for significant metatheoretical reflection on the religious significance of psychotherapeutic theory and practice. The present essay is based upon the assumption that studies in psychology and religion can enter an exciting new phase by drawing upon the resources now available from the discipline of cultural anthropology in general and from the work of anthropologist Victor Turner in particular. While certainly some creative appropriation of anthropological theories and methods has been forthcoming in the field of religion and psychological studies, a critical mass of research using such resources has yet to be generated. One of the purposes of this volume is to encourage specialists in the field to take a fresh look at the possible implications of current anthropological theory for the task of reframing the questions central to their particular research areas.

In this chapter I will offer an assessment of Turner's contribution to our understanding of the relationship between space and transformative process in human experience. That this topic in particular has not received more attention from specialists in the field of religion and psychological studies may seem extremely puzzling to those who lack familiarity with the development of studies in this field over the past few decades.[1] A brief reflection on the models and resources which have been dominant in past attempts to discern the relationship between religion and psychotherapy is necessary at this point. By the early 1950s interest in the mutual significance of religion and psychotherapy was growing rapidly. Two classics appeared at this time which have proven to be extraordinarily influential in the establishment of the subsequent methodological assumptions and dominant models of inquiry in the field. The first was David Roberts' *Psychotherapy and a Christian View of Man*, which appeared in 1950.[2] The second was Albert Outler's 1954 monograph, *Psychotherapy and the Christian Message*.[3] The authors were both brilliant young

Protestant Christian theologians whose social location was in a major Protestant Christian center of theological studies during the height of the influence of theological neo-orthodoxy and existentialism.

While we occasionally give lip-service to the perspectives of the sociology of knowledge, researchers in this field have given inadequate attention to the impact of the social location of these and other "fathers" of the field. In fact, the field has been and continues to be dominated by the culture of Protestantism and by the categories, issues, and assumptions which are generated by it. A perusal of the literature of the past thirty years reveals that the religious dialogue partner with the secular therapies has almost always been Protestant Christianity. Certainly one of the major reasons for this has been the influence of the rise of the pastoral counseling movement in the United States. Again, this movement was founded by and continues to be dominated by Protestant Christians.[4] These practitioners of the newly created professional speciality of pastoral counseling of course had an investment in showing the ways in which dynamic psychotherapy, whether Freudian or Rogerian, could be viewed as an expression of or medium for grace, divine acceptance, atonement and the like.[5] Insights into the nature of psychopathology were brought forward as ways of deepening and extending the understanding of Christian views of human nature in general and of sin in particular.[6]

The academic and training programs which focused on pastoral theology or pastoral psychology had, then, an extremely narrow view of what constituted the religious pole in any ongoing dialogue between religion and psychotherapy. Of course an important factor was the intellectual milieu in which these developments were occurring. Theological neo-orthodoxy, dominant at the time in the most influential centers of theological education, provided the foundation for the cultural attitudes which characterized the field. The interest in the relationship between religion and psychotherapy, then, developed in an era in which the psychology of religion of an earlier period seemed discredited in theological circles. The tradition of Schleiermacher with its careful attention to the nature of religion and the importance of cultural hermeneutics in the theological enterprise was out of favor. The study of the history and phenomenology of religions and attention to the perspectives of cultural anthropology were not deemed to be of importance either for the task of Christian theology or for preparation for the ministry. The anti-religious and ultimately anti-cultural attitudes which characterized the theological education of this time carried over into the studies of religion and psychotherapy which were carried out during this period. The designation of the field variously as pastoral theology or theology and personality was an acknowledgement of the ill-fortune of phenomenological emphases during this period. Even in the old centers of theological liberalism (Boston, Iliff, etc.) where the designation pastoral psychology was in vogue, the subtle cultural and religious hermeneutics of the Schleiermacher tradition were nowhere to be found. Less emphasis on theology in these centers was not balanced by significantly more substantial studies in religion and culture, but was accompanied by a less critical and comparative devotion to the current vogues in developmental and clinical psychology.

Why, then, has the field not generated more studies that give attention to non-Protestant or non-Christian religious structures? Why has it failed to engage the disciplines of cultural anthropology and the history of religions in a more substantial and fruitful way? Why has so little attention, for example, been given to the importance of understanding the psychology of ritual processes as well as the ritual processes implicit in much psychotherapeutic practice?

The answer to these queries is a quite simple one: studies in religion and psychotherapy have been heavily influenced by a myopic hyper-Protestant stance in matters of religion and culture which has not yet been overcome. We will know that this Protestant methodological hegemony in the field has ended when the history and phenomenology of religions and its cognate disciplines begin to receive *at least* as much emphasis as studies in Christian systematic theology and theological ethics. A number of correctives for the field would result from such a shift in resources utilized. First, a comparative perspective would replace the narrowly Christian focus which has characterized the vast majority of previous studies. Not only would this guarantee that other traditions receive the attention they merit, but the subtle issues of cultural hermeneutics which underlie every aspect of inquiry in the field would be highlighted. Secondly, many important religious structures previously neglected because of a relative lack of interest in phenomenological analysis would be examined for the insight which they could yield into transformative processes in both religion and psychotherapy. I have in mind here, for example, such important religious structures as pilgrimage, initiation, sacrifice, and blessing.

Finally, I am convinced that the most important next agenda in the psychology of religion in general and in studies in religion and psychotherapy in particular is to devote much more of our effort to understanding not only the psychology of ritual processes, but also the ritual processes fundamental to psychotherapeutic practice. There is no better example of the negative impact of Protestant cultural biases on the field than the manner in which the psychosocial role of ritual has been typically either neglected or viewed as somehow regressive. We are currently at the beginning of an exciting new era in ritual studies which is forcing us to reexamine our most fundamental assumptions about ritual processes in human life.[7] Inquiry in religion and psychological studies will be one of the fields which will benefit most from this new focus on the importance of ritual process.

Victor Turner, of course, is one of the most important theorists responsible for the current renewal of interest in ritual. In the following discussion I will argue that his work enables us to think in a fresh way about the nature and dynamics of the human experience of space as it is manifest in psychosocial transformative processes. The balance of this essay, I believe, will provide an example of the genre of reflection which I have called for in this introduction.

II. ELIADE ON SPACE AND TRANSFORMATION

In any discussion of the importance of the concept of sacred space in understanding religion in general and ritual process in particular the seminal work of Mircea Eliade on this topic must be a key reference point. Many of Eliade's most fundamental insights into the nature and dynamics of human religious life are based on his assumptions about the *heterogeneity of space* in human experience.[8] In the following reflections I will examine these assumptions and show how they are extended by the work of Turner.

For Eliade, the human experience of the world is divided into two fundamentally different modalities. In his influential monograph, *The Sacred and the Profane*, he characterized the differences between the human experience of sacred space and time and profane space and time.[9] In profane space and time there is no fixed point or center from which one can gain orientation. There is no contact with the really real, with the power which alone can renew life and through which regeneration can occur. Profane space is a formless expanse, homogeneous in its fundamental unreality. It is a space essentially devoid of creativity. Rather than persons and things being created or renewed in profane space, it is in fact the locus of the deterioration of the cosmos as ordinary temporal duration, profane time, runs its course.

Homo religiosus, however, has periodic contact with a totally different kind of space:

> For religious man, space is not homogeneous; he experiences interruptions, breaks in it; some parts of space are qualitatively different from others. "Draw not nigh hither," says the Lord to Moses; "put off thy shoes from off thy feet, for the place whereon thou standest is holy ground" (Exodus, 3, 5). There is, then, a sacred space, and hence a strong, significant space; there are other spaces that are not sacred and so are without structure or consistency, amorphous. Nor is this all. For religious man, this spatial nonhomogeneity finds expression in the experience of an opposition between space that is sacred — the only *real* and *real-ly* existing space — and all other space, the formless expanse surrounding it.[10]

It is this break in ordinary profane space which allows the world to be regenerated. Because of this break a center for orientation, a fixed point grounded in absolute reality is revealed. The sacred has manifested itself in a *hierophany*, and this irruption of the sacred "results in detaching a territory from the surrounding cosmic milieu and making it qualitatively different."[11] Discussing Jacob's dream at Beth-el Eliade elaborates:

> The symbolism implicit in the expression "gate of heaven" is rich and complex; the theophany that occurs in a place consecrates it by the very fact that it makes it open above — that is, in communication with heaven, the paradoxical point of passage from one mode of being to another . . . Often there is no need for a theophany or hierophany properly speaking; some *sign* suffices to indicate the sacredness of a place . . . When no sign manifests itself, it is

provoked . . . This amounts to an evocation of sacred forms or figures for the immediate purpose of establishing an *orientation* in the homogeneity of space. A *sign* is asked, to put an end to the tension and anxiety caused by relativity and disorientation – in short, to reveal an absolute point of support.[12]

Once the sacred breaks into the profane realm and sacred space is constituted, an irrevocable change has occurred. The sacredness of the place will continue even through major changes in the dominant religious tradition of the area. The hierophany continues to repeat itself in that place.

In this way the place becomes an inexhaustible source of power and sacredness and enables man, simply be entering it, to have a share in the power, to hold communion with the sacredness. This elementary notion of the place's becoming, by means of a hierophany, a permanent "center" of the sacred, governs and explains a whole collection of systems often complex and detailed. But however diverse and variously elaborated these sacred spaces may be, they all present one trait in common: there is always a clearly marked space which makes it possible (though under very varied forms) to communicate with the sacred.[13]

Though sacred space cannot be generated by a simple act of will on the part of human beings, they do have important responsibilities in the consecration of the space and in the stewardship of its boundaries. Whether the space was directly generated by a hierophanic event or the result of the application of traditional techniques for the provoking of a sign, the creation of an enclosure, a clear boundary between the two realms, was always important. "The enclosure, wall, or circle of stones surrounding a sacred place – these are among the most ancient of known forms of man-made sanctuary. They existed as early as the early Indus civilization."[14]

The importance of the establishment and maintenance of the boundaries of a sacred space can hardly be overemphasized. Not only does the boundary serve notice that entry into a radically different mode of human existence is near, but the recognition of and proper respect for the boundary is the *sine qua non* for a proper relationship to sacred space and the primary condition for being benefited and not harmed by contact with it.

The enclosure does not only imply and indeed signify the continued presence of a kratophany or hierophany within its bounds; it also serves the purpose of preserving profane man from the danger to which he would expose himself by entering it without due care. The sacred is always dangerous to anyone who comes into contact with it unprepared, without having gone through the "gestures of approach" that every religious act demands . . . Hence the innumerable rites and prescriptions (bare feet, and so on) relative to entering the temple, of which we have plentiful evidence among the Semites and other Mediterranean peoples. The ritual importance of the thresholds of temple and house is due to this same separating function of limits, though it may have taken on varying interpretations and values over the course of time.[15]

The recognition of and respect for the boundary, then, is the most fundamental affirmation in praxis of the reality and importance of the heterogeneity of space in human life. This relationship between boundary and space is one of the key elements in understanding the relationship between space and transformation in both religion and psychotherapy, and we will return to this repeatedly as we examine different theorists. At this point it will suffice to note that for Eliade, archaic *homo religiosus* understood clearly that for him sacred space was the indispensable locus of all of the paradigmatic transformations fundamental to human existence. Without it there would be no access to the powers of creativity and renewal, no access to the primordial patterns which are the source of all correct order, no access to a transhistorical center which can give orientation and structure in a time of deterioration and impending chaos.

For Eliade, not only is sacred space linked to the myriad transformations of archaic experience of cosmos and culture, more specifically it is closely linked to *phases of transition* in that experience. Certainly, while one can argue that all religious transformation involves transition of a sort, the relationship between space, transformation and transition stand out most clearly when one examines Eliade's treatment of rituals of initiation.

> Broadly speaking, the initiation ceremony comprises the following phases: first, the preparation of the "sacred ground," where the men will remain in isolation during the festival; second, the separation of the novices from their mothers and, in general, from all women; third, their segregation in the bush, or in a special isolated camp, where they will be instructed in the religious traditions of the tribe; fourth, certain operations performed on the novices, usually circumcision, the extraction of a tooth, or subincision, but sometimes scarring or pulling out the hair. Throughout the period of the initiation, the novices must behave in a special way; they undergo a number of ordeals, and are subjected to various dietary taboos and prohibitions. Each element of this complex initiatory scenario has a religious meaning.[16]

As in other rituals for renewing the cosmos, initiation rituals include a reenactment of the cosmogony. Here, the individual's return to origins offers the initiand himself an opportunity for regeneration. In the symbolism of initiation the sacred space which is the locus of initiation is often identified with the place of the individual's origin, the womb.

> First and foremost, there is the well-known symbolism of initiation rituals implying a *regressus ad uterum* . . . We will limit ourselves here to some brief indications. From the archaic stages of culture the initiation of adolescents includes a series of rites whose symbolism is crystal clear: through them, the novice is first transformed into an embryo and then is reborn. Initiation is equivalent to a second birth. It is through the agency of initiation that the adolescent becomes both a socially responsible and culturally awakened being. The return to the womb is signified either by the neophyte's seclusion in a hut, or by his being symbolically swallowed by a monster, or by his being symbolically swallowed by a monster, or by his entering a sacred spot identified with the uterus of Mother Earth.[17]

In rituals of initiation, then, the relationship between space and transformation stands out in bold relief. Because of the heterogeneity of space, the initiand has an opportunity to undergo a return to origins, a *regressus ad uterum*, to touch once again the creative powers and to be reborn into a new mode of existence. "The basic idea is that, to attain to a higher mode of existence, gestation and birth must be repeated; but they are repeated ritually, symbolically."[18] The context of this symbolic action is always sacred space, and according to

Eliade one of the primary tasks of archaic technicians of the sacred was to be able to locate and utilize effectively the properties of this extraordinary transformative milieu. For archaic society the importance of this ability to help initiands enter and leave this transformative space effectively can hardly be exaggerated.

> From a certain point of view it could almost be said that, for the primitive world, it is through initiation that men attain the status of human beings; before initiation, they do not yet fully share in the human condition precisely because they do not yet have access to the religious life. This is why initiation represents a decisive experience for any individual who is a member of a premodern society; it is a fundamental existential experience because through it a man becomes able to assume his mode of being in its entirety.[19]

On the basis of the above discussion it is easy to see why Eliade views human existence under the conditions of modern industrial culture to be so radically impoverished. In his view, the fall into modernity brought an end to the availability of transformative access to sacred space. Space in modernity is homogeneous and therefore relative.

> No *true* orientation is now possible, for the fixed point no longer enjoys a unique ontological status; it appears and disappears in accordance with the needs of the day. Properly speaking, there is no longer any world, there are only fragments of a shattered universe, an amorphous mass consisting of an infinite number of more or less neutral places in which man moves, governed and driven by the obligations of an existence incorporated into an industrial society.[20]

For Eliade, the only traces left in modern life of the truly religious experience of nonhomogeneous space consist of mere vestiges which cannot offer a milieu of fundamental transformation.

> Yet this experience of profane space still includes values that to some extent recall the nonhomogeneity peculiar to the religious experience of space. There are, for example, privileged spaces, qualitatively different from all others − a man's birthplace, or the scenes of his first love, or certain places in the first foreign city he visited in youth. Even for the most frankly nonreligious man, all these places still retain an exceptional, a unique quality; they are the "holy places" of his private universe, as if it were in such spots that he received the revelation of a reality *other* than that in which he participates through his ordinary daily life.[21]

Still, it is clear that for Eliade, the experience of space in modern industrial society is fundamentally characterized by homogeneity. Certainly, he is correct in his assumption that human transformative experience requires heterogeneity in the experience of space. But his assumption that such heterogeneity is *never* available in modernity has undoubtedly been a key factor in limiting the impact of his thought on attempts to understand contemporary cultural and personality processes. It is here that the work of Victor Turner has made its greatest contribution to our understanding of the human experience of space. Turner has shown that *even under the conditions of modern industrial culture the human experience of space is anything but homogeneous.* Let us now turn to an examination of the impact of Turner's work on our understanding of the relationship between space and transformative process.

III. TURNER ON SPACE AND TRANSFORMATION

Like Eliade, Turner has devoted much of his research to the task of understanding the nature and significance of the heterogeneous forms of space which may be discerned in human experience. Indeed, while reflections on the relationship between space and transformation constitute an important component in Eliade's approach to human religious process in archaic culture, in Turner's work the issue is more central and receives a more sustained focus. Deeply influenced by his intellectual progenitor Arnold van Gennep, Turner has based many of his insights on van Gennep's pioneering monograph, *The Rites of Passage.*[22] Van Gennep, of course, was a pioneer in describing the ways in which time and space are altered during a psychosocial transition. His distinguishing of the three phases in a rite of passage, *separation, transition,* and *incorporation,* was fundamental for the development of Turner's understanding of ritual process. *Separation* was the phase in a ritual which served to draw a clear distinction between sacred space and time and profane or ordinary space and time. During this part of the ritual a cultural realm is created which is clearly out of ordinary space and time and which is to be the locus of the activities of the intervening phase of *transition.* This phase was called "margin" or "limen" ("threshold" in Latin) by van Gennep. During this middle phase the ritual subjects pass through a period of ambiguity in which they are stripped of the statuses and attributes which were characteristic of their previous state, undergo ordeals, and receive instruction from ritual elders. The final phase van Gennep called "reaggregation" or "incorporation." Here ritual actions returned the subjects to ordinary space and time prepared for the new demands of a different cultural location.

Turner's great contribution to our understanding of the relationship between space and transformation has been his extensive elaboration of the significance of the "cultural realm" of the middle transitional phase of *liminality.* For Turner it is the presence of liminality which clearly distinguishes ritual from ceremony. "Ceremony *indicates,* ritual *transforms,* and transformation occurs most radically in the ritual 'pupation' of liminal seclusion − at least in life-crisis rituals."[23] Turner goes on to characterize the cultural significance of this special space.

> Ritual's liminal phase, then, approximates to the "subjunctive mood" of sociocultural action. It is, quintessentially, a time and place lodged between all times and spaces defined and governed in any specific biocultural ecosystem (A. Vayda, J. Bennet, and the like) by the rules of law, politics and religion, and by economic necessity. Here the cognitive schemata that give sense and order to everyday life no longer apply, but are, as it were, suspended − in ritual symbolism perhaps even shown as destroyed or dissolved. Gods and goddesses of destruction are adored primarily because they personify an essential phase in an irreversible transformative process. All further growth requires the immolation of that which was fundamental to an earlier

state — "lest one good custom should corrupt the world."[24]

Turner emphasizes that while this "liminal space-time 'pod' " can sometimes be dangerous to the *liminar* or ritual subject, it is important that we see that much more than destruction of the previous life-world is taking place in liminality.

> Nevertheless, the danger of the liminal phase conceded, and respected by hedging it around by ritual interdictions and taboos, it is also held in most cultures to be regenerative, as I mentioned earlier. For in liminality what is mundanely bound in sociostructural form may be unbound and rebound . . . New meanings and symbols may be introduced — or new ways of portraying or embellishing old models for living, and so of renewing interest in them. Ritual liminality, therefore, contains the potentiality for cultural innovation, as well as the means of effecting structural transformations within a relatively stable sociocultural system.[25]

While many parallels can be drawn between Turner's views and those of van Gennep and Eliade, it is not difficult to discern the extent to which he has surpassed them in the subtlety of his understanding of the relationship between the heterogeneity of space and psychocultural processes. By focusing his attention in both field work and theoretical reflection on the differences between ordinary and transformative social space, he has been able to offer us a far more adequate "mapping" of the geography of the existential space of human lived experience. Turner has been quite conscious of the extent to which he has accepted the enormous task of helping us formulate a geography of human space — and not just that, as in van Gennep and Eliade, of premodern cultures.

> I am frankly in the exploratory phase just now, I hope to make more precise these crude, almost medieval maps I have been unrolling of the obscure liminal and liminoid regions which lie around our comfortable village of the sociologically known, proven, tried and tested. Both "liminal" and "liminoid" mean studying symbols in social action, in praxis, not entirely at a safe remove from the full human condition. It means studying all domains of expressive culture, not the high culture alone nor the popular culture alone, the literate or the non-literate, the Great or the Little Tradition, the urban or the rural. Comparative symbology must learn how to "embrace multitudes" and generate sound intellectual progeny from that embrace. It must study *total* social phenomena.[26]

Turner's distinction between liminal and liminoid phenomena has itself grown out of his willingness to examine complex modern societies as well as tribal and early agrarian ones. For Turner, liminal phenomena are more characteristic of transitions in tribal societies. They tend to be collective and to be related to biological, calendrical, and other socio-structural rhythms as well

as to social crises resulting either from internal adjustments or external adapta-
tions. They characteristically appear at the natural breaks and disjunctions in
the ongoing flow of natural and social processes. Usually integrated into the
total social process of the culture in question, liminal phenomena usually are
organized around symbols which have a common intellectual and emotional
meaning for all of the members of the group. The symbols and behaviors reflect
the history of the group over time and in order to represent the negativity and
subjunctivity of the group, often are in the form of reversals, negations,
disguises, inversions, and so on. For example, under the conditions of *structure*
in a preliminal or postliminal status system social space permits distinctions of
rank, clothing, sex, and degrees of autonomy. In liminal space, on the contrary, such distinctions are minimized. Turner has shown that where liminality
is fully developed and unfragmented, the properties of liminality form a
relatively consistent set of binary oppositions to the properties of life in structure, of course expressed in the dominant symbolic forms of the group.[27]

Liminoid phenomena, more characteristic of complex modern societies, are
usually individual products though they may have widespread effect on the
society. Not cyclical in nature, they develop independently of the central
political and economic processes of the culture. Marginal to the dominant
cultural institutions, they are more fragmentary, plural, and experimental in
character than liminal states. Associated with leisure time and therefore with
play, liminoid phenomena are more idiosyncratic and are usually generated by
individuals or groups who are competing for recognition. Liminoid
phenomena, Turner suggests, can be seen as representing the "dismembering of
the liminal" for in them "various components that are joined in liminal situations split off to pursue separate destinies as specialized genres – for example,
theater, ballet, film, the novel, poetry, music, and art, both popular and
classical in every case, and pilgrimage."[28]

In seeking to develop a more nuanced approach to the differences in expressive culture between societies before and after the Industrial Revolution,
Turner has emphasized the importance of this distinction between liminal and
liminoid. He has gone so far as to suggest that the use of the term "liminality"
properly belongs only in interpretations of tribal systems. "When used of processes, phenomena, and persons in large-scale complex societies, its use must in
the main be metaphorical."[29] But elsewhere, he moves away from this stark
contrast and affirms that in "modern societies both types coexit in a sort of
cultural pluralism. But the liminal – found in the activities of churches, sects,
and movements, in the initiation rites of clubs, fraternities, masonic orders and
other secret societies, etc. – is no longer society-wide."[30]

Here we confront the major limitation of Turner's theory in relation to issues
of space and transformation. By limiting, or appearing to limit, the application
of the category of liminality to tribal systems Turner has led us away from the
question of whether or not there may be forms of liminality manifest in modern
culture which – though different from those in tribal culture – are far more

liminal than liminoid. That Turner vacillates a bit on this issue is a testament to his characteristic openness and willingness to view his system as an open one. Still, the stark way in which the liminal/liminoid distinction has come to be viewed as paralleling premodern/modern or tribal/industrial in contemporary appropriations of his work is an unfortunate reification of an important theoretical contribution.

Certainly, both liminal and liminoid space have clearly distinguishing characteristics. His mapping of these differences is a major part of his contribution to our understanding of the heterogeneity of space in human social life. Turner has not, however, given enough attention to the importance of the relationship between boundary and space in his reflections. Rather than basing distinctions between liminal and liminoid on the totality and comprehensiveness of ritual involvement in the social system, I suggest *that this judgement should be made on the basis of how the boundaries that delimit the space are constituted and maintained or "stewarded."* The issue should not be drawn as whether the practice is "society-wide" or not; it should be focused on *the nature and permeability of the boundaries of the space involved* and on *the relative importance of the leadership of ritual elders or "technicians of the sacred" in making judgements as to the appropriate utilization of the space.*

Ritual leadership, then, is *the* key variable which Turner has not highlighted in his distinctions between liminal and liminoid space. The central point may be phrased simply as follows: while liminal space *requires* ritual leadership, liminoid space does not. A ritual leader *may* be present in liminoid space, but *must* be present for liminal space to exist. Liminality can occur at or near the center in tribal society not just because the social processes are relatively "simple," integrated, or totalistic—but because of the *availability* of knowledgeable ritual elders who understand how transformative space is located, consecrated, and stewarded. In modern culture knowledgeable ritual leadership is so lacking that a quest for transformative space together with a lack of ritually created boundaries usually leads to the boundaries provided by the socially marginal or by actual movement through natural or sacred geography. Liminoid space is, then, not so much constituted by boundaries as it is *on the boundary*. This is, of course, one reason for the association of leisure with seashore and mountains and for the popularity of deserts as a location for liminoid phenomena. In the case of sacred geography, the space of pilgrimage shrines is usually liminoid precisely because the structure of pilgrimage does not require ritual leadership to exist.

The point can be made in another way: one can participate in liminoid space without there being present in any social actor conscious intentionality as to the psychocultural purposes of the activities involved. Liminal space cannot properly be said to exist without the existence of such conscious intentionality on the part of its stewards. The unstewarded boundaries of liminoid space are permeable and hence cannot sustain or "hold" the intensity of transformative process characteristic of liminal states. It is a commonplace among ritual specialists that transformative processes in liminal states go awry when the leaders do not prevent such permeability of boundaries from developing. Turner's interest in the promise of some forms of theatre as a postmodern recovery of cultural transformative modes should be seen in this context: knowledgeable directors can function as ritual elders and dramatic forms may be able to create a "liminal space-time 'pod' " where human beings may experience transformation.[31]

It is indeed the presence of observable liminal "pods" in contemporary culture which necessitate the above amendments to Turner's understanding of transformative space. I have for some time been analyzing the special forms of space which appear in contemporary psychotherapy in the light of Turner's theories. I have become convinced that much of the phenomena observable in a wide range of therapies cannot adequately be designated as liminoid, but rather should be viewed as a contemporary expression of liminal space. Let us turn now for some evidence for this sort of space from contemporary psychotherapeutic theory and practice.

IV. SPACE AND TRANSOFMRATION IN CONTEMPORARY PSYCHOTHERAPY

Reflection on ritual processes and psychotherapy to date has been dominated by the tendency to view pre-industrial tribal healing rituals as "primitive psychotherapy."[32] Since ritual process is characteristically not valued by the culture of modernity, little effort has been made to understand the ritual processes involved in contemporary psychotherapeutic practice. The time has come for us to recognize that contemporary psychotherapy provides a narrow spectrum of our population with important ritual leadership in times of crisis. In a recent survey of ritual dimensions in psychotherapy I sought to draw attention to some of the ways in which these therapies offer individuals an opportunity to engage in what Turner has called *transformative performances*.[33]

In the course of my research and reflection on this topic I realized that most genres of contemporary therapy manifest within their process ritualized *submission, containment,* and *enactment*.[34] In order to facilitate a needed deconstruction of the old personality structure of the individual, the individual is offered an opportunity temporarily to surrender autonomy, to submit to a total process which has an autonomy of its own and which can enable the individual to maintain needed orientation and structure during this time of deconstruction. Built into the therapeutic process is the creation of a relatively safe psychosocial space in which this deconstruction and surrender of autonomy can occur. It is in this ritually constructed therapeutic space that the enactment, both playful and painful, of innovative new behaviors and styles of thinking can be tested experimentally before returning to the world of *structure* and its merciless demands for adaptive effectiveness.[35] While many other ritual dimensions in therapy exist and merit careful research, it is this creation of the therapeutic container or "vessel" which is most salient to our discussion of space and transformation.[36]

We should be clear here that few clinicians would see their construction and stewardship of the therapeutic space as a ritual process in Turner's terms. Ritual process has characteristically received such a negative evaluation in modernity that when a psychotherapist is told that he is providing ritual leadership, the remark is often taken as an insult! A similar lack of awareness exists among many therapists with regard to the actual nature and dynamics of the special space which is constituted in the interpersonal field of the therapeutic milieu. This is not to say that the therapist lacks a "conscious intentionality" directed toward the creation of a therapeutic space and the maintenance of its boundaries. Yet often these concerns are understood in the language of professionalism, including the emphasis on the professional *contract* between therapist and client and other concerns of professional ethics which are viewed as a means of protecting the client from unprofessional behavior on the part of the therapist.[37] There is usually also an awareness of the need to put limits on the kinds of expectations which the client may have of the therapist. The therapeutic contract is usually the means of spelling out these limits and expectations in an attempt to avoid inappropriate behaviors on the part of either therapist or client.

Only recently, however, has there been focused and sustained attention to the nature of the therapeutic environment as a special space created by the therapeutic contract and other agreements and behaviors of both therapist and client. Current attention to issues relating to space and transformation in depth psychology suggests that a revolution may be beginning in our awareness of the importance of the heterogeneity of space in the therapeutic environment. Nowhere is this increase in interest in the nature and dynamics of space more pronounced than in contemporary Freudian and Jungian psychoanalytic theory and practice. Psychoanalyst Simon Grolnick recently characterized this new emphasis in psychoanalysis:

> At this writing, psychoanalysts are beginning to realize that given the contemporary patient, the psychoanalytic situation evokes far more than an interpretation of unconscious conflict. It is more than simply a place to deal with the analyst's or therapist's role as an oedipal-level transference figure. We are finding that the dramatic illusionary nature of analytic interplay and the manifestations of the transference must take place within a facilitating environment, a facilitating analytic *setting*, to provide a fertile ambience for the ultimate building, or rebuilding, of the self, and its capacity to create a richness of symbolic meaning. The more traditional function of psychoanalytic treatment, the interpretation of hidden or repressed meanings from the unconscious and the past, can proceed concurrently and dialectically. Without *both* processes, there is danger of substituting dead, affectless and nonsynthesizing symbols (intellectualized new understandings or reconstructions) for the often incapacitating "sick" or "neurotic" symbols (symptoms) developed by the patient.[38]

The healing process of innovative and creative symbolization in psychoanalytic process, then, has begun to be viewed as being dependent upon the presence of a very special therapeutic space *which may or may not be mani-*

fest at any given time in the process of analysis or therapy.[39] Many contemporary analysts are addressing these issues in their clinical work and research.[40] Two of the most influential currently are Freudian analyst Robert Langs and Jungian analyst William Goodheart.[41] Let us turn now to an examination of the deepened insight into the heterogeneity of space in analysis shared by these theorists.

First, both Langs and Goodheart emphasize that the securing of a stable *frame* or boundary for the therapeutic space is more than just an expression of professional ethics. For them, it is the *sine qua non* which must be present for the facilitation of any *truly* transformative therapeutic space. It is the establishment and maintenance of the frame which makes possible the evocation of the kind of interpersonal field which can allow the unconscious materials to manifest without unnecessarily terrorizing the analysand. This containment, in short, does not guarantee that a transformative field will be constituted – but its absence will either inhibit the emergence of materials from the deeper levels of the unconscious or make such an emergence more dangerous for both analyst and analysand.[42]

Secondly, both emphasize that several types of space may be discerned through close observation of the therapeutic interaction.[43] If the analyst does not pay close attention to the maintenance and stewardship of the boundary or frame, the space – while it could certainly not be called ordinary – does not become a truly transformative field. If the frame is broken and the boundary becomes too permeable, then analyst and analysand unconsciously collude in avoiding the truths about themselves which might become manifest if the boundaries were maintained.[44] In effect, the intensity and depth of the process are truncated. From a Turnerian perspective, this would suggest that lack of attention to the frame constitutes an interpersonal field which is liminoid in nature. We have noted above that the mere presence of a ritual leader does not in itself guarantee the constitution of liminal space. Here we can see that those interpreters of psychotherapy that consider it to be liminoid in nature are at least partially correct.[45] *Psychotherapy in our culture is always at least liminoid.* However, by adhering to Turner's criteria for understanding the nature of liminality and by neglecting, with Turner, the critical importance of the relationship between boundary and space, these interpreters do not grasp the fact that liminal space can be – and often is – manifest in the therapeutic environment.[46]

We should be clear here that neither in tribal culture nor in contemporary psychoanalysis is the ritual leader the *master* or *controller* of transformative space. Such space, ritual leaders have always understood, cannot be commanded – it can only be invoked.[47] The leader can facilitate the right conditions by avoiding the kinds of behavior which clearly destroy the possibility of its appearance. Even the most knowledgeable tribal elder or analyst, nevertheless, cannot generate it or sustain it *on demand.* Here again in Langs and Goodheart we see the critical emphasis on the creation and stewardship of the boundary without which there is no possibility of a secured, truly transformative space.

We noted above that individuals, when sensing the need for a liminal space, will seek out boundary and containment wherever they can. If knowledgeable ritual elders are not present to invoke liminal space and lead them through it, then they gravitate to the liminoid and try to find containment or generate it on their own.[48] Both Langs and Goodheart note that analysands always are aware at an unconscious level of failures of the analyst in stewarding the boundary of the therapeutic space. Close observation of the analysand's materials, they believe, reveals that the analysand is constantly commenting on whether the boundary is being maintained in an appropriate manner.[49] The unconscious psyche, we might say, is aware of the radical difference between the liminoid and the liminal. Albeit in an unconscious manner, the individual notes that the therapeutic space is merely liminoid and gives the analyst clues about how the process is failing and what is needed to repair the boundaries and thereby to invoke the liminal space that is needed for transformation.

This turn to a new sensitivity to the heterogeneity of space in psychoanalysis has had the unexpected effect of making Jung's own understanding of the analytical relationship seem much less esoteric and incomprehensible. Jung of course viewed the alchemical vessel or *vas* as a parallel to the appropriate therapeutic relationship. In his words, the *"vas bene clausum* (well-sealed vessel) is a precautionary rule in alchemy very frequently mentioned, and is the equivalent of the magic circle. In both cases the idea is to protect what is within from the intrusion and admixture of what is without, as well as to prevent it from escaping."[50] In a manner anticipating this recent turn in psychoanalytic theory, Jung emphasized that the transference was more than just the compulsive repetition of old object relationships in the present—for him it was a transformative container.[51] Only recently, with the new attention to the heterogeneity of space in analysis, has the importance of Jung's references to the significance of the study of alchemy in understanding transference begun to be positively reassessed.[52]

The importance of these developments in psychoanalysis should not be lost on specialists in the study of religion and psychology. Without doubt we are entering an exciting new era in understanding the *dynamic internal* relationships between religious and psychotherapeutic processes—an era in which we can get beyond the formalistic theological genres which have dominated the field to date. Among Turner's contributions to this new era is the manner in which his theory has helped us to realize that the heterogeneity of space is not a reality which is limited to the world of archaic *homo religiosus*. Contemporary human beings, too, experience space as heterogenous. Using his insight to look freshly at contemporary culture, we have been enabled to see that, contrary to prevailing interpretations of Turner's theory, transformative liminal space does indeed exist in modern industrial culture. Modernity's fall into homogenous space was not as complete as Eliade has believed. If I am correct in my conclusions with regard to the heterogeneity of space in contemporary culture, then we must place on our agendas a wide-ranging rethinking of the nature of the relationship between *homo religiosus*, sacred space, and ritual leadership. I anticipate that we will soon come to a fresh appreciation of the role of the ritual leader as the steward of the thresholds and boundaries of transformative space in *all* human cultures – past, present, and future.

Notes and References

1. See the extensive annotated bibliography on recent research in the field in Donald Capps, Lewis Rambo, and Paul Ransohoff, eds., *Psychology of Religion: A Guide to Information Sources* (Detroit: Gale Research, 1976).

2. David E. Roberts, *Psychotherapy and a Christian View of Man* (New York: Charles Scribner's Sons, 1950).

3. Albert C. Outler, *Psychotherapy and the Christian Message* (New York: Harper & Brothers, 1954).

4. While evangelical Christians and Roman Catholics are currently very deeply involved in research and writing in the relationship between theology and psychology, they are relative latecomers to the field. The dominant organization of clinicians in the field of religion and psychotherapy continues to be the American Association of Pastoral Counselors. The A.A.P.C. was organized by mainline Protestants and its membership continues to be constituted primarily by representatives of the major Protestant denominations.

5. See, for example, Don S. Browning, *Atonement and Psychotherapy* (Philadelphia: The Westminster Press, 1966), and Thomas C. Oden, *Kerygma and Counseling* (Philadelphia: The Westminster Press, 1966). Also instructive is Oden's *Contemporary Theology and Psychotherapy* (Philadelphia: The Westminster Press, 1967).

6. Since these writings were generally done by theologians whose knowledge of psychodynamics came primarily from the reading of theoretical treatises on the basic dynamics of psychopathology, the resulting correlations between sin and psychopathology were usually abstract and unrelated to clinical observation. Little attempt was made to pursue careful reflection on discrete syndromes from a religious or theological perspective.

7. See the symposium "Ritual in Human Adaptation" edited by Robert L. Moore, Ralph W. Burhoe, and Philip J. Hefner in *Zygon: Journal of Religion and Science* 18 (September 1983): 209-325.

8. Few concepts in Eliade's work are as important as that of the *heterogeneity of space* in relation to human ritual and religious experience. It is therefore strange that so little attention has been given to elaborating the many implications of this characteristic of the human experience of space.

9. Mircea Eliade, *The Sacred and the Profane: The Nature of Religion* (New York: Harper and Row, 1961).

10. Ibid., 20.

11. Ibid., 26.

12. Ibid., 26-28.

13. Mircea Eliade, *Patterns in Comparative Religions* (New York: Sheed and Ward, 1958), 367-369.

14. Ibid., 369-371.

15. Ibid.

16. Mircea Eliade, *Rites and Symbols of Initiation: The Mysteries of Birth and Rebirth* (New York: Harper and Row, 1958), 4-5.

17. Mircea Eliade, *Myth and Reality* (New York: Harper and Row, 1963), 79-82.

18. Ibid.

19. Eliade, *Rites*, 3.

20. Eliade, *Sacred and the Profane*, 23-24.

21. Ibid., 24.

22. Arnold van Gennep, *The Rites of Passage* (Chicago: The University of Chicago Press, 1960).

23. Victor Turner, *From Ritual to Theatre* (New York: Performing Arts Journal Publications, 1982), 80-81.

24. Ibid., 84.

25. Ibid., 84-85.
26. Ibid., 55.
27. Victor Turner, *The Ritual Process: Structure and Anti-Structure* (Ithaca: Cornell University Press, 1969), 106.
28. Victor and Edith Turner, *Image and Pilgrimage in Christian Culture* (New York: Columbia University Press, 1978), 253.
29. Victor Turner, *Process, Performance and Pilgrimage: A Study in Comparative Symbology* (New Delhi: Concept Publishing Company, 1979), 23.
30. Ibid., 54.
31. Turner, *Ritual to Theatre*, 86, 120.
32. Jerome D. Frank, *Persuasion and Healing: A Comparative Study of Psychotherapy* (New York: Schocken Books, 1963).
33. Robert L. Moore, "Contemporary Psychotherapy as Ritual Process: An Initial Reconnaissance," *Zygon 18* (September 1983): 283-294.
34. Ibid., 292-293.
35. I am using the word *structure* in Turner's technical sense. See the definition of the term in *Image and Pilgrimage*, 252.
36. For an interesting recent discussion of ritual elements in psychotherapy see Onno van der Hart, *Rituals in Psychotherapy: Transition and Continuity* (New York: Irvington Publishers, 1983).
37. See the discussion of the rise of professionalism in Burton J. Bledstein, *The Culture of Professionalism* (New York: W. W. Norton, 1976). Professionalism in modern industrial culture carries many unacknowledged ritual functions in secular forms.
38. Simon A. Grolnick and Leonard Barkin, eds., *Between Reality and Fantasy: Transitional Objects and Phenomena* (New York: Jason Aronson, 1978), 538.
39. There is an increasing realization in psychoanalysis that technical virtuosity on the part of the analyst does not in itself assure that healing will result in the analysand. A healing interpersonal field can be facilitated by certain behaviors of the analyst. It cannot, however, be guaranteed—even by the most competent analysts.
40. The influence of D. W. Winnicott has been a key factor in this new attention to therapeutic space. See Madeleine Davis and David Wallbridge, *Boundary & Space: An Introduction to the Work of D. W. Winnicott* (New York: Brunner/Mazel, 1981).
41. See William B. Goodheart, "Theory of Analytical Interaction," *San Francisco Jung Institute Library Journal 1/4* (1980): 2-39; See also Robert Langs, *The Bipersonal Field* (New York: Jason Aronson, 1976), and *Technique in Transition* (New York: Jason Aronson, 1978).
42. See Alexander McCurdy III, "Establishing and Maintaining the Analytical Structure" in Murray Stein, ed., *Jungian Analysis* (LaSalle: Open Court, 1982), 47-67.
43. See Goodheart's "Theory of Analytical Interaction" for a careful discussion of the heterogeneity of space in the analytical setting.
44. Langs has referred to such unconscious collusion of analyst and analysand as "lie therapy."
45. See Volney P. Gay, "Ritual and Self-Esteem in Victor Turner and Heinz Kohut," *Zygon 18* (September 1983): 271-282.
46. It should be clear here that I am not suggesting that psychotherapy is the *only* locus of liminal experience in modern industrial culture. See, for example, J. Gordon Melton and Robert L. Moore, *The Cult Experience: Responding to the New Religious Pluralism* (New York: The Pilgrim Press, 1982), 47-64.
47. It is a mistake, for example, to conclude that the rigorous attention to detail characteristic of ritual elders reflects a sense of mastery of sacred space. On the contrary, such care is an indication of the ritual leader's awareness of the fragility of regenerative space and the ease with which it can be spoiled.
48. The attraction of geographical boundaries such as seashores to those in transition states is a striking example of this intuitive quest for the boundary. Finding a natural boundary is, of course, relatively simple. Locating an appropriate transformative container, however, is much more difficult.
49. Goodheart, "Theory of Analytic Interaction," 28-32.
50. C. G. Jung, *Psychology and Alchemy. Collected Works*, Vol. 12. 2nd ed., rev. (Princeton: Princeton University Press, 1968), 167.
51. See the discussion of the transference in C. G. Jung, *The Practice of Psychotherapy. Collected Works*, Vol. 16 (New York: Pantheon Books, 1954).

52. Jung's views of the transference as resembling an alchemical process in a sealed vessel have often been dismissed as vague, mystical, and without any practical significance. There is now an increasing realization that Jung's emphasis on the transference as a transformative space was in fact one of his most creative contributions.

Part Three

Lévi-Strauss and Beyond

Chapter VII

Lévi-Strauss, Mythologic and South American Religions[1]

Lawrence E. Sullivan

I never had, and still do not have, the perception of feeling my personal identity. I appear to myself as the place where something is going on, but there is no 'I' no 'me.' Each of us is a kind of crossroads where things happen. The crossroads is purely passive: something happens there. A different thing, equally valid, happens elsewhere. There is no choice, it is just a matter of chance. Claude Lévi-Strauss, *Myth and Meaning*, p. 4.

Claude Lévi-Strauss is a powerful mind impelled by uncommon energy. Motivated to know better the thought of peoples in native America, Africa, Australia, Oceania, and folk Europe, he is convinced of the authenticity and validity of the thought of all those whose ideas have been alienated from a "history" which is too narrowly construed. He has a love and fascination with myth and is captivated by its imagery, its vitality, and its clarity. He senses its power to penetrate reality. Writing with great sympathy about the predicament of the modern intellectual, he feels deeply that same alienation and con-templates the vision of realities painted by artists of alienation.

"THE ADVENTURES OF A SEVERED HEAD"[2]

Claude Lévi-Strauss has immense impact on all the sciences of culture and, in particular, on the study of religions. It is, therefore, surprising that one cannot accuse him of constructing a theory of religion. Religion, as a category of any kind—whether as "cultural system," "set of distinctive features," and so on—lies unexamined in his studies of culture. He neither examines religion as a con-stitutive "elementary structure" of the mind (as he does the avunculate) nor im-plies a new interpretation of religion in any substantive terms.[3] One would argue only from absence to contend that Lévi-Strauss has an original idea of religion. His true focus is the *esprit humain* which, as he conceives it, in no way resembles the *homo religiosus* familiar to any circles in history of religions in theories as different as those of Max Müller, Rudolph Otto, R. Pettazzoni, and Mircea Eliade. The *esprit humain* speaks. The meaning of its own messages is not entirely to be trusted. Like a disembodied head, an objective mind without a subject, the *esprit humain* possesses no direct sense experience which can reliably legitimate what it says. Its experience is reported in its own speech.

For Lévi-Strauss, the *esprit humain* is, above all else, *homo linguisticus*; collec-tively, a thinker in words, a speaker of words, a teller of tales, a musician, even a poet. Human language is a set of codes which exists as a subset of larger communicative systems found throughout all levels of natural history: visual codes, musical codes, codes of space and motion, genetic codes, chemical codes of the nervous system, chemical codes of inorganic structures, codes of color, anatomy, and smell among animals, and so on. The Talking Head of Descartes[4] comes to speak in the world of Darwin.[5] *Homo linguisticus* is also a *homo economicus* because human nature, as a subset of natural history, expresses its distinctive features, its code, by arranging relations. This entails control over the many realms of natural history. In such a way, air, bone, and muscle "alienated" from "nature" become "resources" for the breath, teeth, and tongue used in phonetic codes. In a similar way, the wild forest becomes the cleared space of a residence, and heavenly bodies become a "resource" used in measuring precise time periods. Furthermore, alienated from the orders of natural history by the power of communicative systems, they become not only resources of use-value but also of "meaning" on another level. The use of phonetics yields "meaningful" strings of words in speech. The cleared residence space, when assigned in a system of "meaning," may be construed as a "mother's brother's village" in a network of generalized exchange. Astronomic periodicities become markers—"meaningful" zodiacal coordinates of the agricultural cycle of tasks and rites. For Lévi-Strauss this movement from natural history to "meaning" proceeds away from elementary deep structures toward surface features. This accounts for his choice of non-hermeneutical modes of analysis. Such a dialectical relationship with the sign-systems of natural history entails the establishment of symbolic means for their control as "culture."[6] In Lévi-Strauss's view, it is Marx who introduces the Talking Head of Descartes to the creatures of the world of Darwin and makes clear the way they are related to one another. Nevertheless, these essential economic relations always remain a species of the generic rules of the larger linguistic universe.[7]

Homo linguisticus may also be a *homo psychologicus*, if psychology be a kind of epistemology. By repeating its code in varying expressions and permutations, the *esprit humain* comes to perceive its own epistemics; becomes conscious of its own thought processes which, once embedded and hidden, now come to light through repeated use and exhibition. Descending the ladder, the orders of relations, of Darwin and Marx into the deep structures of its own mind, the Talking Head of Descartes meets Sigmund Freud.[8] Where Freud revealed the unconscious order of Unreason, Lévi-Strauss discloses the rational order of the Unconscious unconnected with a subject and even the extreme rationality of its process of self-discovery. Although Lévi-Strauss investigates the *esprit humain* from so many points of view,[9] it is fruitless to ask why he does not include the religious dimension of experience. Since he has so many other important things to say, why persist in looking in the very place where he intends to shed so little light? More illuminating are those areas of his interest common also to historians of religion. The most remarkable of these is the world of myth.

This article examines key ideas developed by Lévi-Strauss's study of culture in order to elucidate aspects of his theory of myth. An estimation of his work is offered from two points of view: the strength and coherence of his theoretical claims, and an evaluation of his mammoth interpretation of myth on its merits as an investigation of South American religious thought.

A THEORY OF MYTH

This section systematically exposes Lévi-Strauss's theory of myth by considering it under several headings: what myth is (the nature of its meaning, its source), the process of its degeneration, the proper approach to its study, and the intended goal of its investigation. Precisely these vital areas are the ones addressed by historians of religions in their considerations of myth. Given the economy of space in this article, which precludes explicit comparison between Lévi-Strauss and other specific theorists, it is hoped that such an analysis implies and makes possible further evaluation.

I. What is Myth?

Myth is that aspect of thought which "lies between but shares aspects of images (which are concrete) and concepts (which have power of reference)."[10] Unlike science, a different mode of thought, myth is unable to detach itself from concrete events.[11] It is imbedded in them. Like science and all logical systems of thought, it refers to concepts. However myth lives a disturbing, tense, and dual existence because the concepts to which it refers remain unconscious. Caught in the impossible position of referring to concepts which are unconscious with images of concrete events and experience, myth "never tires of ordering and reordering in its search to find them a meaning."[12] It is for this reason that myths are repeated and internally repetitious. Myth is systematic, but its systems remain preconscious. What it presents on the conscious level is a series of semantic functions which remain partial, fragmentary, or subjective.[13] To this extent, it is not much different than the other message systems of social organization and art which Lévi-Strauss has analyzed.[14] The difference is that myth points to the elementary structures of the unconscious itself. For this reason above others, mythic thought is a closed logical system.[15] It acquires depth only when it sacrifices its redundancy.[16] The content of myth, ironically, is its rigorous form.[17] The heart of myth is "completely empty"[18] – a formal construction.

In keeping with his Kantian-Cartesian heritage, Lévi-Strauss views all thought as a thin bridge, epistemologically unsafe, spun of logical threads and suspended between the conceptual inner mind and a concrete outer reality known only in image. Given the existence of this fundamental chasm, it is no wonder that he believes that myth deals with unresolvable oppositions which are the symbolic consequences of this fundamental chasm: nature/culture;

existence/nonexistence; life/death; one/many. The peculiar destiny of myth is to overcome its internal and constitutive contradiction: to build a bridge of "meaning" between its own contradictory elements of concrete image and unconscious concept. In its attempt to do so, of course, myth can only perpetuate its own existence and inherent dilemma. The mythic process is an expression of the inextricable contradiction of human existence. The paradox of the human condition and its depiction *par excellence* in myth is a view not entirely strange to the history of religions. However, Lévi-Strauss's dismal assessment of mythic and human destiny has not been accepted as justifiable from the evidence.

Lévi-Strauss holds that mythic language is a unificative one. Such a view, variously conceived, is also found in the history of religions. At the most fundamental level, like all collective representation, myth unites the elementary structures of the mind and the natural world beyond the mind. (Let us not speak yet of the cost of such a union in terms of alienation and generation of "meaning".) This primordial thrust to unify the inside of the mind with the outside of the mind further impels mythic language to integrate other cognitive categories symbolizing all the realms of the natural order by manipulating the codes generated in perceiving them. For example, the Kalina describe phases of the moon by enumerating different animals. The moon is viewed as a hunter who kills, roasts, consumes, and digests different sized game. His rising is said to be influenced by the size of his quarry and eventual meal—from rat through tapir. In this way, the unificative power of mythic language (the thought-mode myth) draws the codes of the phases of the moon and periods of time into relation with codes drawn from the observations of the animal kingdom, the systematized and distinctive symbolic features of human hunting, the symbolic conceptions of the food cycle, and so on. Notice, however, that we have never strayed far from the inner mind. It is human thought which has the power to perceive realities as ordered codes and, by mentally manipulating and rearranging these symbolic systems, bring "realities" into "meaningful" coincidence.[19]

It is not difficult to see, then, that any one logical opposition is capable of a high degree of complexity where a single symbol (e.g., the moon) can express the "total sum of the successive values that a relationship can take along a semantic axis before being reversed into its opposite along the other axis."[20] In a hasty reading, Lévi-Strauss describes the unificative properties of mythic language in tones which sound similar to Mircea Eliade's theory of the "transconsciousness of the symbol,"[21] Carl Jung's notions of Pleroma, Paul Mus' "rupture of planes," or any of a number of theories hovering around a concept of *coincidentia oppositorum* from Anselm and Cusanus to Jakob Böhme. However, for Lévi-Strauss the complexity of symbols is due to their arbitrary quality as signs whose meanings may only be determined by their locus in a set of formal relations. Symbolic complexity and semantic values are not so much susceptible to a hermeneutics of meaning as to the logical analysis of communicative systems theory. Lévi-Strauss's intention is not to enter into a relationship with the text—not to wade into the hermeneutic circle—but to "stand far enough back" so that "a mythic field which appeared extraordinarily rich and complex when subjected to a close and detailed study will, seen from a distance, seem *completely empty*."[22] For, in the end, the binary oppositions and operations are of a logical order only and may "cancel each other out"[23] without adversely affecting one's understanding of reality. Oddly enough, it is this emptiness which accounts for the richness of "meaning" which a logical opposition may carry; e.g., "the opposition between sun and moon, provided it remains an opposition, can take on any meaning."[24] At the same time, it presages the estranged existence of "meaning" in the world of arbitrary signs: a misplaced concreteness, a reified content in a world of empty conceptual form.

Lévi-Strauss comes to the study of myth with a history of ideas and research. He has a certain priority of concerns when he sets out to ascertain the nature of myth.[25] He is interested in myth as a communicative system, which is to say, a mode of thought. This is his first concern. He studies variants of myths in multiple expression because the "thought" he speaks of is to be observed, above all, in collective representations.[26] Concrete behavior is to be examined only at a remove, as it appears in the images of the mind. From such images and collective representations in myth one can hope to see the universal processes of thought which somewhat desperately try to disclose themselves to themselves. By examining the objective processes of thought, far from raw events, the deepest and most elementary structures of communicative systems may be brought to light. These are the generative, formal, and empty contradictions exhibited in the process of mythic thinking.[27] The "content" and "shared meaning" of myths are not of great concern to Lévi-Strauss. They are surface features examined only to pierce through them to the uncoded systems of formal relations below.

Let us point out the relationship between two uses of the word "meaning" in Lévi-Strauss's treatment of myth. The first is the "shared meaning" exhibited in the text on the level of surface features and common sense; the second is the "deeper meaning" found in the deep structure of linguistic relations. Although shared meaning is an arbitrary assignment of value, it is never spontaneous or creative. Value and common sense are the fruit of a merely phantom freedom. In reality, they spring from the "obligation we feel to grant a meaning"[28] to surface features. In dealing with spontaneity and creativity of this kind, Lévi-Strauss feels he "can at least demonstrate the necessity of this freedom."[29] At its deepest level "meaning" consists of formal relations of empty categories. The obligation to assign "shared meaning" stems from the formal structure of meaning at its deepest levels. At the deeper level, "to speak of rules and to speak of meaning is the same thing."[30]

Lévi-Strauss is prepared to answer the pressing and related question about the nature of truth in myth. In his view, the images and codes brought together in the mind through myth demonstrate that "we live in several worlds, each truer than the one it encloses, and itself false in relation to the one which en-compasses it."[31] The obligation felt to grant meaning to surface features and to deny it to deep structures disguises the contradictions inherent in the coex-istence of worlds of action and thought. "Truth lies in a progressive dilating of the meaning, but in reverse order, up to the point at which it explodes."[32] Shared meaning and truth cannot live in the same house without tearing each other into pieces or partial semantic functions. Shared meanings serve best as signposts marking the trail of relations to the land of true contradiction. Along the way, meaning signifies so many things that, finally, its own contrary truth is disclosed: it means no thing. It is empty. Where meaning explodes, truth reigns. Truth lies where meaning is buried.[33]

One is struck by the ironic stance into which Lévi-Strauss leads himself.[34] The irony is not without precedent in the history of religions. Over a century ago, the meanings of myth were deemed the fruit of a "disease of language" by the school of nature mythology. The judgement rendered on Max Müller, the leader of the nature mythology school, carries eerie parallel applications when considered in relation to the work of Lévi-Strauss. "Müller's work is then an in-tegrative effort, but an unfortunate one, for when he was done with mythology it was stripped of belief, separated from religion, and divested of narrative, poetic, and imaginative interest . . . [H]is exclusive reliance on language, which even he at last distrusted, narrowed his work disastrously and he was left crying up the study of mythology while he trivialized myth itself."[35] It is remarkable that both scholars delivered themselves to their position through the vehicle of a Kantism manquée.[36]

2. Wringing the Water Out of Myth

It is not unusual for important theories about myth to include some con-sideration of its partial appearance in legend, folk tale, and fiction. From the point of view of the integrity of myth such a process represents a disintegration or fall. The aspect of a mythic theory which deals with its degeneration into other narrative forms stems from the theoretical judgement made about the nature of myth itself. A general theory of myth and the corollary of its degeneration are usually connected and mutually illuminating dimensions. This is true as well for Lévi-Strauss's mythologic. It is the elemental thought-form—the basic category of logico-opposition accounting for myth's dynamism—which foreshadows its ultimate dissolution into themes and fragments. The ontogeny of language from *real* contradiction of thought, through *symbolic* oppositions, to *imaginary* expressions of mythic language is recapitulated in the phylogeny of narrative species from myth, through legend and epic, to episodic fiction.[37] The formal processes of language which con-tinually carry thought back and forth across the three structural levels of the real, the symbolic, and the imaginary are the very same ones which continually conduct narrative expression through those three levels of structure manifest as myth, epic, and fiction. The processes of thought transform elementary structures of the mind by building symbolic bridges between contradictions. These symbolic bridges become in turn the focus of the same unceasing formal processes and are recycled as images which, in their turn, become the object (or victim) of processes which reorder their relations in the attempt to give them meaning.

In Lévi-Strauss's view, during the move from myth to fiction, these transformations become increasingly feeble because "structural content is diminished."[38] It is appropriate to speak of this passage from myth to fiction as "a fall" since, for Lévi-Strauss, the movement is unilinear and the origin left behind is irretrievable.

> Now something irreversible occurs as the same narrative substance is being subjected to this series of operations: like laundry being twisted and retwisted by the washerwoman to wring out the water, the mythic substance allows its internal principles of organization to seep away. Its structural content is diminished.[39]

The decline of myth shows itself in two important ways. First, the codes which previously functioned in a highly visible fashion become latent. Codes are drawn from the orders of natural history as perceived in image in human thought. The orders of natural history, in dialectic relationship with the perceiving mind, present themselves as marked systems of signs. In his studies of myth Lévi-Strauss has outlined many such codes: anatomical, astronomical, sociological, and so on. Lévi-Strauss implies that a successive and progressive withdrawal from the immediate symbolic perceptions of nature entails, or at least accompanies, the demise of the clarity of such codes as found in myth.[40] One would have to ask whether Lévi-Strauss does not subscribe to a latent Romanticism which holds that mythic thought is a form of thinking peculiar to humans whose perceptions of nature are more "participatory."

Secondly, the oppositional structures of elementary thought give way to seriality. In this instance, the redundant character of myth which repeats and reorders oppositions passes into an episodic reduplication of the same pattern. Eventually, the process of reduplication comes to replace entirely the generative template of contradiction. Rather than repeating the unconscious and fundamental opposition in myriad symbolic expression, seriality rehearses the same pattern in monotonously similar episodes. "Being itself no more than the form of a form, it echoes the last murmur of expiring structure. The myth, having nothing more to say, or very little, can only continue by dint of self-repetition."[41]

Contrary to Lévi-Strauss's optimistic appreciation of the possibilities of science which may develop from myth (the science of the concrete), Lévi-Strauss holds a dim and pessimistic view concerning the prospects of poetic and narrative creativity spurred by myth. We may say that for Lévi-Strauss the modern novel is a "disease of myth." The novel, as compared with myth, is reduced to telling its own story, "saying not only that it was born from the exhaustion of myth, but also that it is nothing more than an exhausting pursuit of structure, always lagging behind an evolutionary process that it keeps the closest watch on, without being able to rediscover, either within or without, the secret of forgotton freshness . . ."[42]

For Lévi-Strauss, there is no return to creative power of the beginnings. The degenerative process of myth is irreversible. It becomes the occasion for his apocalyptic of human creativity and the universe.[43] All of this brooding on the degeneracy of myth and the hopelessness of the quest to recover the freshness of its original structure has a bearing on his view of the significance of myth. For him, the "shared meanings" and the content of surface features of many heroic myths tell the pathetic story of myth's own reduced destiny. The fall of the hero signifies the fall of mythic form itself. "It is, then, as if the myth's message reflected the dialectical process that had produced it, and which is an irreversible decline from structure to repetition."[44]

Lévi-Strauss relates the degeneration of mythic paradigms into serials to a process of imitation which gradually distorts the nature of the source and to a subservience to very short forms of periodicity. It is true that in myth brief periodicities were recognized. However, they occasioned no fragmentation of myth since the periods spoken of arose from the nature of what was signified (e.g., the daily visibility and apparent movement of the moon). Instead, the harmful forms of temporality to which Lévi-Strauss attributes the demise of myth stem from the rhythms of a more complicated economic order. In serial fiction, short periodicity "is imposed from without as a practical requirement of the signifier (e.g., the daily appearance and circulation of newspapers)."[45] In the case of myth, there exist formal constraints *to signify* short periodicities; in the case of serial fiction, on the other hand, there exist formal constraints *to be signified* by short periodic forms. Here is an instance where Lévi-Strauss's theory of human creativity relies heavily on an historical economic evolutionism.

3. The Study of Myth

The study of myth appears to be, for Lévi-Strauss, an exercise in location. If we may judge from the predominantly spatial metaphors used to describe its operation, mythologic is a kind of geometry. The mythologician attempts to discover the postulates and corollaries which have generated the imaginary bridgework of myth. Once uncovered, these operational principles are applied *in reverse order* to dismantle superstructural imagery and return the attention of the mind to its true focus: its own internal chasm of contradiction, incomplete and unbridged. He reverses the processes of imagination[46] (which order and reorder images) by locating and then relocating imaginary beings on either bank of the canyon of the mind.[47] In order to move them "back into their relevant mythic paradigms,"[48] they must first be removed from the locus of their apparent "reality" where they are suspended, for example, in zoological or zodiacal codes.[49] Above the firm ground of their mythic paradigms of elementary and unconscious contradiction they remain impossible to interpret.[50] Whereas for historians of religions the search for the original situation of myth may lead to a spiritual or existential experience (whether that be studied historically or phenomenologically) for Lévi-Strauss it is a search back through inversions and tables of transformations to tight, logico-linguistic dichotomies. For him, myths are *collages* whose cut-and-pasted images must be removed from the context of their appearance[51] and become once again bundles of opposed relations.

In the end, Lévi-Strauss totally dismantles the multidimensional bridges of shared meaning suspended across the levels of language. He reduces the spun webs of complex topologies which he finds in myth to a *single line* (or a series of them related as a permutation table) passing between the two points of a dialectically related elementary contradiction. The unificative propensities of mythic thought which shuffle together different coded orders into increasingly complex relations must be undone in order to explain and understand myth's formal meaning. In keeping with his locative view of logical relations, Lévi-Strauss imagines mythemes as "spread out over hyperspace" until the investigator defines them "in terms of a limited number of oppositions such as *male* or *female*, *near* or *distant*" and arranges them "in a closed set."[52] With admirable consistency of geometric metaphor, Lévi-Strauss thinks of himself as a place.[53] Disturbingly, however, he confesses that such a perception offers him neither a grasp of his own identity nor a sense of his existence. Although we must accept his perceptions of himself as a datum of some sort, must we also conclude that the myths of South America are making the same sort of statement? Are they only a more elaborate way of stating his own dilemma, or might they include, albeit in the cultural terms of native South America, attempts at its resolution?

One begins by comparing many variants of myths and isolating their distinctive features or mythemes. K. L. O. Burridge correctly identifies these units as, essentially, *words*. We must add that it is not the words themselves or their meanings which are compared but their changing *location* in the map of comparative logical relations. Thus, for example, honey in tropical South America is comparable to berries in North America and the berries bear a logico-functional equivalence to insects.[54] This equivalence is possible because each one of these words, in their respective mythic setting, inhabits the same location. They share the same "borderline quality, being situated at the point of intersection of nature and culture."[55] Although there be an overriding metaphor of a landscape in movement through space, it is possible to conclude with Burridge that mythemes are essentially key *words*, for in this case the words "nature" and "culture" define the spatial field (once again, basically a single line formed by the intersection of two planes) where the structurally equivalent words "honey," "berries," and "insect" reside.

In the third volume of the *Mythologiques*, Lévi-Strauss pushes his locative model beyond the geometric sphere of epistemology into the realm of ethics and morality. Throughout this work, he develops the idea of "right relations," of proper distance between categories. Logical arrangements of proper space and proper time pass into a consideration of propriety expressed in polite manners, hygiene, and morality. In many myths, such ethical concerns lie latent in deep structural relations. For example, Lévi-Strauss associates with the loss of a constituent category of human thought the distortions in a series of oppositions in frog-myths which portray unacceptable social behaviors.[56] By the end of the volume, however, Lévi-Strauss makes explicit this implied morality of proper distance. He does so by using the words "inside" and "outside" to characterize the locations in space of symbolic moral forces. We have seen already how important this pair of words is in his own definition of human knowledge and existence. Here he uses them to compare his own culture to those from which he takes his mythic corpus.

> . . . as regards moral training, we continue to respect the traditional model: more often than not, we behave as if our aim were to control disorder and violence coming from within, whereas, in matters of hygiene, we are anxious to protect weakness, also internal in origin, and an as yet uncertain balance, against aggression from without. Nothing could be more diametrically opposed to the philosophy of education that we have encountered in M425-428 and in other myths, where the human female wards learn, at one and the same time, how to use domestic utensils, how to cook, and how to control their physiological functions; to prove their feminine virtues, they must show their skill in housekeeping, menstruate regularly, and give birth punctually at the appointed time.[57]

He concludes:

> whereas we think of good manners as a way of protecting the internal purity of the subject against the external impurity of beings and things, in savage societies, they are a means of protecting the purity of beings and things against the impurity of the subject.[58]

Given the need to compare variants of a myth, what are the outer limits of comparison? What constitutes a variant? On what grounds may one circumscribe the broad borders of comparison? Here are questions which have brought much agony to the fields of anthropology and history of religions.[59] Due to the once-regnant fad of historicism, the problem was often most acute when comparison was made between cultures not immediately proximate historically or geographically.

Of course, Lévi-Strauss is always and everywhere undergirded by his convictions about the universal and objective processes of human thought. However, this idea, philosophically underdeveloped in his writings even though spoken of at great length, does not account for the particular selections of myths he makes for comparison. In fact, when the moment comes, and in spite of the deeper issues of "psychic unity of humankind" involved, it appears to be expedience which motivates his choice of specific comparative material. This in itself is not alarming. Even the uncovering of important facts in field work is often serendipitous: a mixture of the ethnographer's talents and interests, an informant's knowledge, the friends one makes, the time and place of the investigation, and a host of other uncontrollable variables. Nevertheless, it is important to keep clear the basis of comparison chosen by any particular investigator.

In the case of Lévi-Strauss, we may allude to the example of his decision to include North and South American myths of the clinging-woman in his solution of the "rolling head" myths found in South America.

> . . . by extending the paradigm to North America—which, as we have just seen, will be inevitable in any case—I can present the problem of the clinging-woman in much simpler terms, and provide a solution that can be quickly verified without reference to myths so numerous that their analysis would require a separate volume.[60]

The "inevitable" ground he alludes to but does not develop here is the need to make a closed permutation table of the transformations of all distinctive mythemes (words) at work in the myth under investigation. More importantly, however, is the justification that comparison affords an economy of motion. He skirts the need to refer to an inordinate number of myths of the "rolling head" by turning to the ostensibly different myths about the "clinging-woman" which emit a structurally similar signal. Comparison is a shortcut in illustrating the set of transformations which demonstrate the closed set.[61]

Once Lévi-Strauss has compared North and South American myths, he finds it possible, on the basis of the equivalences he discovers in the locations of key images in the myths, to consolidate into one paradigm those myths which appeared at first to belong to two distinct groups. For instance, this is his procedure when he draws together "those [myths] with a clinging-woman as heroine and those in which the character is a frog-woman. The two groups of myth transmit the same message, which in each instance concerns a clinging-woman, although the attribute may be literal in one case and figurative in the other."[62] Here he has rolled by the "head" myths, past the "clinging-woman" myths to another structurally similar set of myths about a frog-woman. Having isolated the single "message" of this body of myths, he proceeds to consolidate related themes; in this instance, the frog's lover, the man with the long penis, and the creator of fish. Confident of the basic signal communicated in all these myths, he can interpret "new" themes as embellishments and restatements of it. The man with the long penis and the clinging-woman are correlated, opposed, and symmetrical in quality because "he can reach a mistress from a distance, and she can only be a wife by sticking to her husband's back."[63] Most striking in Lévi-Strauss's use of comparison is his drive to reduce multiplicities to the single categories with which he wishes to deal; to shrink the "hyperspace" of mythic symbolism into a series of "crossroads" which all signal "one message."

> In short, myths which appeared heterogeneous in content and geographical origin, can all be reduced to a single message, of which they effect transformation along two axes, one stylistic and the other lexicological. Some are expressed literally, others figuratively. And the vocabulary they use relates to three separate categories: the real, the symbolic, and the imaginary.[64]

Strangely enough, Lévi-Strauss, the man who loves and lauds science, has produced a procedure which may not be scientifically defensible or *useful*, in the strict sense of the word. His criteria for distinguishing mythemes, for establishing an equivalence between them, and for delineating the frontiers of their comparability are too subjective to be repeatable, predictable, or verifiable. On these grounds, from the perspective of science, his theory of myth risks falling into the category of over-determined theory because it admits no basis of falsifiability.[65] On the other hand, there is a large group of scholars unperturbed by Lévi-Strauss's claims for an orthomethodology. They base their hermeneutics of science on the critiques of Karl Popper, Imre Lakatos, Steven Toulmin, Ian Barbour. Ironically, for these humanists, interested in a hermeneutics which Lévi-Strauss deplores, his pondering of South American myths is *interesting* and *stimulating* as a procedure which sparks insight through subjective intuitions.[66]

4. The Goal of Mythologic

What, finally, is Lévi-Strauss looking for in his study of myth? What does he hope to learn? What is the point and promise of a science of mythologic? In his study of myth, Lévi-Strauss aims at nothing less than the exposure of all the operations of the mind at its deepest and most elementary level. In this way, the mythologician overcomes the gap between mind and experience and thereby solves problems which previously were deemed philosophical and historical. Myth offers the clearest illustration of the processes by which the mind relates to the orders of nature and the experience of it. Mythologic can unlock the character and *modus operandi* of that relationship (currently a philosophical or epistemological concern) and unlock as well all the possible forms which that relationship can take (an inquiry to which "retrieval" historians slavishly and hopelessly dedicate themselves).[67] If Lévi-Strauss can make a wide enough map of possible transformations of thought and perception, he not only can solve the problems of historical "retrieval" without doing history, but he can even predict the forms that future ideas will assume. The construction of such a comprehensive map of the transforms of elementary structures of the mind as it relates to nature is his goal.

> The mythological curve is thus completed so that, starting from any version, it is possible to discover all the others arranged in the "natural" order of the transformations which produce them. It must be furthermore noted that this complex curve—whose two outlines, if drawn in the planes of the two perpendicular axes, follow the imaginary surface of a sphere—defines a diffused semantic field in which *it would be possible, at any point inside the sphere, to locate the position of myths* already studied, or of other known, *or even potential myths.*[68]

It is Lévi-Strauss's conviction that with time, abundant data, and competence all mythic themes could be interpreted clearly enough to produce this great mythological curve if one included in structural analysis all the other dimensions found in myth: astronomy, anatomy, sociopolitical order, narrative style, syntax, vocabulary, and perhaps phonology. Lévi-Strauss confesses "the task would be beyond my competence."[69] Nonetheless, his faith in the abilities of mythologic science are as great as his belief that myth holds no mystery, in the analytical and Kantian sense of Rudolf Otto or the existential sense of Gabriel Marcel. For Lévi-Strauss, myth and the world which gives rise to it are not mysteries to be explored but problems to be solved, mystagogies to be explained.

5. Evaluation

It is pointless to rehearse the many criticisms brought against Lévi-Strauss's theory of myth and culture. They come from the fields of philosophy, linguistics, literary criticism, semiotics, theology, and especially anthropology and history of religions.[70] After mentioning in summary fashion some of the objections raised by scholars in this field, this section assays the more difficult task of accounting for Lévi-Strauss's enormous appeal among scholars of culture. Finally, his work as a mythologician of South American materials is evaluated alongside the work of other important investigators of religious life in that area. Lévi-Strauss's work must be judged ultimately by how well he illuminates the materials he has analyzed.

It is pointed out that Lévi-Strauss's theoretical base in the research of Troubetzkoy and Jakobsen is inadequate to the study of myth. In the first place, once beyond the level of phonological research, the overemphasis of only two tropes of language, metaphor and metonym, does not account for other important tropes which seem integral to mythic expression (e.g., irony).[71] The resultant primacy of axial relations (e.g., the "axis of selection" and the "axis of combination" on which Jakobsen bases his notion of "poetic function"[72]; or, alternately, the "syntagmatic" and "paradigmatic" axes of narrative[73]) and binary oppositions allows access only to those areas which precisely are *not* characteristic of myth *vis à vis* other linguistic forms. The tools are precisely the wrong ones to carry toward the investigation of myth.

In the second place, as Dell Hymes sternly warns, there is a very profound difference between the table of phonemes of a language and the symbolic systems of a society. Blurring these two orders of reality reduces structural analyses of symbolic and semantic systems to pure tautologies.[74] Even further, once these two levels are consolidated, the use of linguistic models in the study of symbolic meaning tempts one to a naturalistic explanation of the genesis of symbolic thinking. However, "the nature of explanation must change as radically as the newly appeared phenomenon differs from those which preceded and prepared for it."[75] Although Lévi-Strauss does not succumb to such a temptation in the study of the elementary structures of kinship and totemism, his location of the "real," and the "true" contradictions of thought in close proximity to the "natural" order does carry his study of myth too far in a naturalistic direction. The real is that which lies closest to the orders of nature.[76]

The ubiquitous and omnipotent model of binary oppositions, well suited to the computer analysis which Lévi-Strauss advocates, is vulnerable to the same kind of criticism which Goethe brought against Newton when the latter studied the "physics" of color by passing light through a prism. Are not the structures attributed to and analyzed as "colors of light" better described as functions of the instrument of analysis? If myths must be factored out for absorption into a computer's binary index systems, one should expect at best nothing other than more complicated algorithms of binary opposition in return. At question here is not the utility of the construct, but the generic and exhaustive claim that the nature of myth consists of nothing more than elementary binary contradictions. Such a claim would have more power if its application were limited to myths told to computers.

The argument that myth, like all language, is a closed system of signs within which any mytheme refers only to other structures of the system, "excludes the claim of hermeneutics to reach beyond the 'sense' — as the immanent content of the text — to its 'reference', i.e., to what it says *about* the world."[77] Such an argument rules out of bounds any consideration of the human situation of the text, the external world, the author who intended the text, and the listener who understands it. This aspect of Lévi-Strauss's theory has remained equally unacceptable to anthropology and history of religions.[78]

Because there is neither autonomous point of reference for mythic meaning nor even for the nature of its structural categories, there can be nothing which accounts for the nature of the disclosure (appearance, manifestation, or revelation) effected in its study. Instead, there is only a theory of endless repetition which has as its end either only the discovery of the process of repetition itself or intellectual exhaustion.[79] The repetition can never be granted the status of an anamnesis or entelechy. Nothing is retrieved or cogenerated in the process except the outline of the process itself.[80] As Terence S. Turner says, "Lévi-Strauss has, in his sense, no concept of 'deep structure' at all."[81]

The single most important concept which Lévi-Strauss uses to speak of the roots of myth is contradiction. His notion of it is not precise. It slips in and out of what might be called contraries, reciprocal and nonreciprocal oppositions, complementary and contrastive oppositions without regard for the distinctions between them. Investigators have pointed out that the oppositions found in myth cannot be reduced to one type and that a determination of their nature can only be made on the basis of an examination of the *semantic content* and referent of the two concepts in question, and these in their cultural *context*.[82] For instance, Mircea Eliade points out that religious systems in themselves have addressed the problem of bipartition and polarity, duality and alternation, antithetical dyads and *coincidentia oppositorum* with great creativity and have offered their own classical solutions to the problem. These systematizations of the nature of "contradiction" differ vastly from one another and from Lévi-Strauss's isomorphic solution. Eliade offers a long list of examples: the antagonism between two kinds of sacredness in Malekula, one male (ileo) and one female (igah). Though contradictory, neither one may be characterized as "profane." South American divine twins resolve universal bipartitions in very different and creative ways among the Kaingang, Cubeo, Apinaye, and Calinas. The solution of contradiction is never the same.

Eliade considers conceptions related to the theme of contradiction by examining polarity and complementarity among the Kogi, combat and reconciliation of Mänabush and the Medicine Hut societies of the Central Algonkian, the tension between High God and Culture Hero among the same groups who present three different solutions to the problem. Iroquois Dualism, which cultic ritual is compared to myth, distinguishes between antagonism and alternation in a way quite different than the complementary opposition of divine couples among the Pueblos. Eliade then compares these solutions to some others found in the religious expressions of South Asia (in ritual competitions, oratorical contests, myths of the Devas and Asuras, the relationship of Mitra-Varuna) as well as of East Asia (Yang and Yin). His point and conclusion is that

> the historian of religions is ultimately interested in finding out what a particular culture, or a group of cultures, has done with this immediate datum. A hermeneutics which pursues the comprehension of cultural creations hesitates before the temptations of reducing all the species of dyads and polarities to a single fundamental type reflecting certain unconscious logical activities.[83]

Not only are these dichotomies complicated multiple categories,[84] but they acquire "an amazing number of functions and values."[85]

THE BASIS OF LÉVI–STRAUSS'S APPEAL

Objections raised against any important theory seriously studied may comprise a long list. They are a function of the responsibility of scholars who hold one another accountable to mutually recognized concerns, criteria, and procedures of the academic community. However, the impact of a thinker often far exceeds the success warranted by the power and precision of his justifications. William James described this phenomenon as the "power of fashion in things scientific." There can be little doubt that Lévi-Strauss has captured the modern imagination. He impressed and provoked both the scholarly and popular thinking about myth and religion to a degree not appreciated by a recital of the criticisms levied against him. What constitutes his appeal?

E. Nelson Hayes and Tanya Hayes posed themselves this very question in *Claude Lévi-Strauss: The Anthropologist as Hero.*[86] They feel that his attraction is rooted in the disenchantment and alienation which is the lot of intellectuals in modern western society. Lévi-Strauss not only exhibits this same rejection of philosophical, historical, and humanistic bases of analysis, but he constructs an immense and complicated edifice of thought upon his apparent refusal to grant western intellectual history any place of privilege. The Hayes point out that his foundation stone is singularly modern—the programmed nature of the mind with a concomitant emphasis on thought form rather than content. However, the opinion that Lévi-Strauss is good company for the alienated mind does not adequately explain why his thought stands out above others who hold the same position.

Kenelm Burridge portrays Lévi-Strauss as a "pied piper" whose charism and persuasiveness beguile investigators into a less demanding confrontation with the realities of the text. By imposing a "spurious uniformity" on them, in which the materials appear to be ordered by the categories of a closed system, the task of the investigator is made to look easy—the possibilities are limited by the system itself. By ignoring the fact that order arises from the meeting of the researcher and the narrative, Lévi-Strauss "negates the whole task of discovering the different kind of forms within which the same sets of relations are organized or given coherence."[87] Burridge seems ultimately to suggest that the harsh sentence which Lévi-Strauss pronounces upon the human creativity exhibited in myth is, perversely, attractive to those unwilling to engage the plural expressions and meanings of myth.[88]

In fact, Lévi-Strauss's appeal seems to be existential. He captures the modern imagination because he smashes that which from the outside threatens its complacency and he binds together the fractured thought of the West which unsettles itself from within. He breaks up the integrity of mythic thought into manipulable units at the same time that he creates sweeping syntheses of those new waves of knowledge which batter the port of modern western experience: psychology, cybernetics, political economy, natural history, sociology, and linguistics. In his hands, linguistic structuralism integrates the scattered western disciplines and ideologies into a synthetic vision of the world even while it dismantles mythic thought.

On the one hand, wading into a bewildering world of South American myth which threatens to overwhelm an investigator with strangeness of expression and otherness of meaning, he reduces its complexities to utterly simple statements. The conclusions of his *Mythologiques* are reassuring (a kind of "Grammar of Assent" to one's own thought forms), for the complexity of exotic cultural expression, potentially so puzzling and disorienting,[89] dissolves before one's very eyes into terms which are exhaustively clear, demonstrable, and rational. Even more than that, these final categories are totally familiar ones. He effects his bid for intellectual stasis by rejecting history without appealing to anything beyond the historical. There is no call for a sense of trust in anything which is not visible.[90] There is present in his system and analysis no source of change, of spontaneous appearance, of the unexpected since everything may be accounted for. To this extent, his theory excites all the fascination of magical control. Its appeal is not only one of consolation in alienation and peace in stasis but of enchantment at the magical dissolution of complexity and disappearance of a mythic reality which had appeared strangely whole, valid, and powerful. What Lévi-Strauss does to myth is dazzling and entertaining. In his hands, structuralism is a myth-related magic which enthralls modern intellectuals without demanding from them any embarrassing naiveté or relaxation of their critical posture of control.

On the other hand, through the magic and power of South American myth, he knits together the quite separate strands and strategies of several western thinkers. Western intellectuals find the contradictions of their own intellectual heritage transformed, synthesized, and strengthened by the unificative power of myth. Scholars are attracted to Lévi-Strauss because he promises a powerful vision of unity of mind. Through the magic of myth, Lévi-Strauss claims to have put the humpty-dumpty of western thought together again.[91] Clearly, this is the "main attraction" of Lévi-Strauss in the West. Scholars are fascinated more by the way in which he effects a unity of their western disciplines and of the discursive thought forms in which they have a large stake than by the fate of South American myth at his hands. This magical synthesis is the basis of his enormous appeal outside the group of South Americanists—not so much how Kayapó relates to Bororo or Apinayé thought but how Marx relates to Freud and Roman Jakobsen.

THE STUDY OF SOUTH AMERICAN MYTHS AND RELIGIONS

As a South Americanist, Lévi-Strauss has kept alive, even revitalized, a tradition of the comprehensive and comparative study of myth. From this point of view, he joins the ranks of those few excellent researchers of native South America who investigated the key element of myth on a large comparative scale: Wilhelm Schmidt, Alfred Métraux, Raffaele Pettazzoni, Paul Ehrenreich, Robert Lehmann-Nitsche.[92] Lévi-Strauss is a salutary reminder of the immense value of myth in understanding a culture's thought, belief, and practice. The uniqueness of the mythical world of any culture is best brought into relief through broad comparison with others. Lévi-Strauss has helped place the center of gravity over myth and cosmological symbolism. He has redirected inquiry into religion away from an overemphasis on sociopolitical institutions studied without regard for their generative links to the mythic imagination. Because Lévi-Strauss establishes incontrovertibly that myth is articulate and important thinking, he obliges the researcher to consult this resource seriously. *Myth must be reckoned with* as a singularly important constituent of cultural thought.[93] That Lévi-Strauss makes this point more clearly and vociferously than other researchers is, ironically, a function of his treatment of myth to the exclusion of other forms of religious expression. The irony is that his too-exclusive insistence risks undermining the validity of his claim about the singular value of myth.

In regard to native South America, Lévi-Strauss reminds researchers who specialize in the study of one culture or, at most, a set of related cultures, that the concerns peculiar to one area are interrelated to symbolic structures in a much wider compass. The structures of the mythic imagination transcend local history and the closed cultural system. Myth cannot be reduced to a reflection of "life on the ground" without remainder. Such awareness of a larger scale need in no way detract from fine ethnographic study of particular peoples. Christine Hugh-Jones and Stephen Hugh-Jones provide an extraordinarily rich case in point. Stephen Hugh-Jones remarks in the preface of *The Palm and the Pleiades: Initiation and Cosmology in Northwest Amazonia* that he works within the wider framework of myth hypothesized by Lévi-Strauss. His research was aimed "to provide an empirical test for some of the grand generalizations that Lévi-Strauss had offered concerning the structure of South American Indian mythology and its relation to Indian thought and culture."[94] Christine Hugh-Jones acknowledges that her own close reading of Barasana culture is a "stage prior to comparison" on a larger scale. The acknowledged two-fold debt to Lévi-Strauss (the importance of myth and the sensitivity to comparison) in no way commits these investigators to his procedures or conclusions. In fact, their procedures more closely represent the history of concerns in British social anthropology than in French structuralism.

Striking, however, is the illumination they find in Lévi-Strauss's insistence on large comparative scale and the centrality of myth. "Without recourse to myth exegesis I would be quite unable to construct any model of the present-day situation, because I would be unable to 'see' it."[95] It is Christine Hugh-Jones' aim to present the interrelations of "secular" life and the domains of kinship, myth, and ritual. Stephen Hugh-Jones, studying the Yurupary rituals, is intrigued by Lévi-Strauss's demonstration of "an interrelation of several explanatory levels."[96] Lévi-Strauss's most important contribution makes itself felt in these works which are very different from his own. It is the awareness that the products of the mythic imagination, "many of which bear no apparent or superficial relationship to each other,"[97] are widely interrelated at the level of symbolic structure and meaning. ". . . Obscure when considered in isolation, [they] are clarified when related together as a set."[98] Barasana themselves informed Stephen Hugh-Jones that if he wished to comprehend their rituals, he should first understand their "myth" (bukura keti bukura: ancestors, ancients; keti: myth, stories, news, etc.). The term includes both formal narrative and exegetical glosses on particular symbols.[99]

This is precisely the insight Stephen Hugh-Jones adopts from Lévi-Strauss. The latter both claims "the right to make use of any manifestation of the mental or social activities (including ritual) of a given community that allows him to complete or explain their myths, and also emphasizes that myths can clarify the nature and existence of beliefs, customs, and institutions that appear incomprehensible at first sight."[100] Stephen Hugh-Jones provides an admirable and critical reapplication of Lévi-Strauss's principles. Neither of the Hugh-Jones shares Lévi-Strauss's priorities or preoccupation with universal mental structures. They are consummate ethnographers of a particular historical situation. However, they have seized upon a truth made clear in Lévi-Strauss: "that myths . . . are themselves only fully comprehensible in the light of other myths . . . Such an exercise involves the examination of something approaching the entire corpus of [Barasana] myths."[101]

Stephen Hugh-Jones points out that many of the mythic relationships isolated by Lévi-Strauss are confirmed in investigating the myths of the Barasana. Nevertheless, Hugh-Jones feels that deductive and large-scale comparative study of myth ought to be subservient to the facts of empirical inquiry into their context, especially as they relate to ritual.[102] He does not object to the comparative exercise itself but only to the status of its exclusive claims. Comparative study of myth is necessary and inevitable because of the fragmentary nature of our knowledge of cultures under study. Stephen Hugh-Jones is sharply critical of Lévi-Strauss's tendency to pass over *what* myths mean (their sense and referents) in favor of *how* they are organized internally.[103] ". . . He is left with a vast self-contained and self-enclosed system which relates to nothing but itself, a set of signifiers with no signifieds—'myths which operate in men's minds without their being aware of the fact.' "[104]

We find in the monographs of the Hugh-Jones a rich study of cosmic symbolism in Barasana myth, ritual, and public life. They carry off their investigation in the light of Lévi-Strauss's enormous comparison of myths in South America. In the process, they move beyond the shadows which Lévi-Strauss casts over religious meaning. Thanks to Lévi-Strauss they carry out their efforts confident in the validity and importance of Barasana mythic thought and conscious of its interrelatedness on a more than superficial level with the symbolic complexes of other cultures. They develop an anthropological judgement of myth which is more tractable and amenable to historians of religions: the *world of myth* exhibits an *integrity of meaning*, manifest in a whole mythic corpus, which cannot be grasped by isolating the equivalences between thematic fragments. Myth must be understood in its own terms and as a whole.

CONCLUSIONS

Is Lévi-Strauss's *Mythologiques* a place where history of religions and anthropology may meet? Lévi-Strauss himself may hope not. He not only contrives a highly personal and problematic definition of myth, but he prejudges the nature of *homo religiosus* and of history, placing them in frames objectionable to historians of religions. Paradoxically, by these very maneuvers he unites the ranks of anthropologists and historians of religions who wish to redress his exaggerations and redirect his priorities while at the same time make use of his stimulating techniques for comparison. There is a mutual dissatisfaction with his premises. In particular, both disciplines point to the need for a fuller understanding of myths in their context, their historical situation. In the case of Lévi-Strauss, that historical context is native South America. It is here that anthropology and history of religions can sow fruitful seed in the furrow turned over by Lévi-Strauss's *Mythologiques*.[105] The goal must be different than Lévi-Strauss's. It must be to *understand* the shared beliefs and meanings of peoples in their historical setting. History of religions and anthropology will be drawn into mutual illumination and collaboration not by debating the merits of Lévi-Strauss's linguisticism but by engaging themselves with the meaning of symbolic complexes as they have been and are understood by the peoples of South America.

There does appear to be an area of concern more to historians of religions than to anthropologists. Historians of religions certainly can agree with Lévi-Strauss when he says that *"structure itself is a primordial fact."*[106] In myth, as Lévi-Strauss asserts, structure may be primordial in such a way that the ultimate nature of reality "consists of structures which are undergoing transformation to produce other structures."[107] Historians of religions have long held that the primordial world described in myth is, in fact, a prestigious order of being which is transformed and replicated on multiple scales in order to justify the "reality" of everyday existence. Where one parts ways with Lévi-Strauss is in his assessment of the nature and origin of that structure as well as of the meaning associated with it. Lévi-Strauss chooses to ignore that this primordial structure, this *orientatio*, is *always meaningful* in the "surface" sense which he disvalues. Furthermore, in myth this meaning which is invariably associated with one primordial structure or another is always portrayed as rooted in the sacredness of a realm of being which transcends those structures in which it appears.[108] In the universal testimony of myth, *the sacred origin of meaning associated with structure is also a primordial fact.* In myths, the documents which serve as data for an historian of religions, the very possibility and appearance of primordial structure is bound up with the meanings derived from its sacred origins. Myth presents the primordial facts of structure, meaning, and sacredness as inseparable. To separate them as Lévi-Strauss does may provide him access to certain cognitive operations but it no longer wrestles with the wholeness—the *complex* of "facts"—of the primordial situation portrayed in myth. Lévi-Strauss opts to steer clear of this *integrity* of human experience confronted in myth in favor of only one of myth's dimensions, the logico-mathematical clarity which he so admirably highlights. However, the unity of human experience (which Lévi-Strauss recognizes when he speaks of the social, intellectual, anatomic, meteorological, spatial, temporal, economic, and political "codes") is, in the view of those telling myths, invariably constituted by an experience[109] of the sacred whose appearance is recounted in myth. It is this singularly important characteristic of myth which remains unengaged.[110] This special and troubling fact of the unificative religious experience in the face of the appearance of sacred realities in myth is not a theological one but an historical and ethnographic datum inviting interpretation.[111] By declining the invitation, Lévi-Strauss backs away from the most profound aspects of myth and leaves unexamined the religious motives and foundation for the societies he studies. It is for these reasons that we hesitate to endorse fully the evaluation Lévi-Strauss offers of his own investigations:

> In all these respects, far from abolishing meaning, my analysis of the myths of a handful of American tribes has extracted more meaning from them than is to be found in the platitudes and common places of those philosophers—with the exception of Plutarch—who have commented on mythology during the last 2,500 years.[112]

By highlighting the singular clarity and order of mythic thought, Lévi-Strauss has made an invaluable contribution to the study of myth. He not only establishes its articulateness and authenticity but shows *how* symbols may be arranged and discursively *displayed* in narrative. Although he has not taken into account those processes of the mythic imagination which *contemplate* this display in art, in symbolic action, in the reenactment of myth itself, and in mundane behavior, anthropologists and historians of religions may well profit from Lévi-Strauss's insistence on the central importance of myth, and his example of intense dedication to its comparative study.[113] In rerouting his program of study, they may also find themselves ever closer collaborators whose ethnological and historical interests are complementary. The knowledgeable interest in the connection of myth to its socio-cultural context and social processes, on the side of anthropology, redress Lévi-Strauss's too-detached study of universal and objective thought. The fuller appraisal of the multiple forms and meanings of religious experience in human history, from the side of history of religions, prevents stunted prejudgements of the nature of *l'esprit humain*. Together, their collaboration promises a deeper understanding of the possibilities of human experience, expression, and meaning, as well as of the roots of individual and cultural creativity. Such an enlarged grasp of the human mode of being in the world becomes a resource for taking our own place in it.

Notes and References

1 . This volume is a fitting context to extend thanks to Jean Comaroff, John Comaroff, Vincent Crapanzano, Raymond Fogelson, Paul Friedrich, Marshall Sahlins, David Schneider, Terence S. Turner, Victor W. Turner, and Valerio Valeri, under whose aegis I enjoyed the privilege of formal study in anthropology.

2 . Lévi-Strauss seems singularly fascinated by this widespread mythic image. Throughout his *Mythologiques*, the theme recurs again and again. See, for example, Lévi-Strauss, "Introduction to a Science of Mythology: 3." *The Origin of Table Manners*, New York: Harper and Row, 1978, p. 92.

3 . In *The Savage Mind* (Chicago: The University of Chicago Press, 1973), Lévi-Strauss tells us what he understands by the words *religion* and *magic*. These definitions can hardly be elevated to the status of a theory. Since they are not put to work in his studies, they are best considered notions about religion and magic and not operational definitions. ". . . although it can, in a sense, be said that religion consists in a *humanization of natural laws* and magic in a *naturalization of human actions* – the treatment of certain human actions *as if* they were an integral part of physical determinism – these are not alternatives or stages in an evolution. The anthropomorphism of nature (of which religion consists) and the physiomorphism of man (by which we defined magic) constitute two components which are always given, and vary only in proportion . . . The notion of a supernature exists only for a humanity which attributes supernatural powers to itself and in return ascribes the powers of its superhumanity to nature" (*The Savage Mind*, p. 221). Lévi-Strauss remains faithful to the theory of religion which he has inherited. Here, for example, Durkheim explains the ideas which Durkheim draws from Saint-Simon: "in point of fact the idea from which he [saint-Simon] takes his departure and which dominates his entire doctrine, is that *a social system is only the application of a system of ideas. Systems of religion*, . . . are nothing else than applications of a system of ideas, or if one prefers, it is the system of thought considered under different aspects." (Emile Durkheim, *Socialism* translated by C. Sattler. New York: Collier Books, 1962 [originally 1896], p. 127).

4 . Lévi-Strauss himself portrays his intellectual relationship to Descartes as theoretically complicated and nuanced (Lévi-Strauss, *The Savage Mind*, pp. 248-250). In this regard his critical appraisal of himself may be rather too gentle and, with respect to Descartes, rather too naive. In any case, Lévi-Strauss seems to have little patience with philosophers who, in his view, "disregarding their primary duty as thinkers, which is to explain what can be explained, and to reserve judgment for the time being on the rest, they are chiefly concerned to construct a refuge for the pathetic treasure of personal identity. And, as the two possibilities are mutually exclusive, they prefer a subject without rationality to rationality without a subject" (Lévi-Strauss, *Naked Man*, p. 686-7).

5 . "For nature appears more and more made up of structural properties undoubtedly richer although not different in kind from the structural codes in which the nervous system translates them, and from the structural properties elaborated by the understanding in order to go back, as much as it can do so, to the original structures of reality. It is not being mentalist or idealist to acknowledge that the mind is itself fact and product of this same world. Therefore, the mind, when trying to understand it, only applies operations which do not differ in kind from those going on in the natural world itself" (Lévi-Strauss, "Structuralism and Ecology," *Barnard Alumnae*, Spring 1972, pp. 13-14. Cited in Marshall Sahlins, *Culture and Practical Reason*, Chicago: The University of Chicago Press, 1976, p. 122).

6 . "What has been called 'the progress of consciousness' in philosophy and history corresponds to this process of interiorizing a pre-existent rationality which has two forms: one is immanent in the world and, were it not there, thought could never apprehend phenomena and science would be impossible; and, also included in the world, is objective thought, which operates in an autonomous and rational way, even before subjectivizing the surrounding rationality, and taming it into usefulness" (Lévi-Strauss, 1981:687).

7 . See, in this connection, the thoughtful appraisal of Marshall Sahlins, *Culture and Practical Reason*, especially pp. 1-126. Several commentators offer critical evaluations of Lévi-Strauss's stance. See Lucien Sebag, *Marxisme et structuralisme*, Paris: Payot, 1964; Michael Silverstein, "Shifters, linguistic categories, and cultural description," in *Meaning in Anthropology*, K. Basso and H. Selby (eds.), Albuquerque: University of New Mexico Press, 1976; Marvin Harris, *The Rise of Anthropological Theory: A History of Theories of Culture*, New York: Columbia University Press, 1968, esp. pp. 464-513; Victor W. Turner, *The Ritual Process*,

Chicago: The University of Chicago Press, 1969, pp. 1-43; Terence S. Turner, "The social structure of the Northern Kayapó," (manuscript, n.d.).

8 . A great deal is made of Lévi-Strauss's acknowledgement of Freud. However, we must agree with Paul Ricoeur that Lévi-Strauss's psychology is founded on "a Kantian rather than a Freudian unconscious, a combinative, categorizing, unconscious . . . A categorizing system unconnected with a thinking subject . . . homologous with nature; it may perhaps be nature . . ." Paul Ricoeur, "Symbole et temporalité," *Archivio di Filosofia*, Nos. 1-2 (Rome, 1963), pp. 9-10. We should mention that Lévi-Strauss affirms and applauds Ricoeur's judgement that his system is "a Kantism without a transcendental subject." Ricoeur's suggestion of the place of nature as the origin of categories providing sure knowledge finds affirmation in the final part of volume four of the *Mythologiques*: ". . . It may be that the attempt to decode the myths has a resemblance to the work of the biologist in deciphering the genetic code, but the biologist is studying *real objects* and he can check his hypotheses by their experimental consequences. We are doing the same thing as he is, the only difference being that social sciences worthy of the name are no more than the image-reflection of the natural sciences: a series of impalpable appearances manipulating ghost-like realities. Therefore, the social sciences can claim only a formal, not a substantial, homology with *the study of the physical world and living nature.* It is precisely when they try to come closer to the ideal of scientific knowledge that it becomes most obvious that they offer no more than a prefiguration, on the walls of the cave, of operations that will have to be validated later by other sciences, which will deal with the *real objects* of which we are examining the reflections." (Lévi-Strauss, 1981:643, emphasis added).

9 . Lévi-Strauss synthesizes different natural and social scientific perspectives in a highly idiosyncratic way. Kenelm Burridge contends that one source of the controversy which surrounds Lévi-Strauss is the way in which he adapts and distorts many theoretical positions. "All this is simply to emphasize that if Lévi-Strauss succeeds . . . [in being controversial] . . . [it is] because he is absolutely his contrary self. Not a Marxist, through Marx the bare bones of an ethnographic record are given coherence. Not wholly a Hegelian, at the level of total social fact, and in relation to articulate thought, a Hegelian treatment is demanded. Not a Darwinian, man in nature is his base." (Kenelm Burridge, "Lévi-Strauss and Myth," in Edmund Leach, ed., *The Structural Study of Myth and Totemism*, A. S. A. Monographs No. 5, New York: Tavistock Publications, 1967, pp. 91-119, p. 97).

10. Lawrence E. Sullivan, "History of religions: The shape of an art," in Mircea Eliade and David Tracy, eds., *What Is Religion?: An Enquiry for Christian Theology*, New York: The Seabury Press, 1980, pp. 78-85, p. 81.

11. Late in the second volume of the *Mythologiques*, Lévi-Strauss is forced to concede the inadequacy of his fundamental idea that myth is inextricably imbedded in the concrete. During his investigations in *From Honey to Ashes*, "a new aspect of mythic thought has been revealed" (. 472). Rather than a logic of tangible qualities (raw/cooked; fresh/rotten; dry/wet), mythic pairs refer to a logic of form (empty/full; internal/external; hollow/solid) – in short, "a body of common properties expressible in geometric terms and transformable one into another by means of operations which constitute a sort of algebra" (p. 472). As Lévi-Strauss himself points out, such a conclusion runs directly contrary to his earlier doctrine that myth, by definition, shared aspects of concrete images. This earlier character of myth was presented in vehement terms up until this point in his studies. Now he concludes, "We have reached a point where mythic thought transcends itself, and going beyond images retaining some relationship with concrete experience, operates in a world of concepts which have been released from any such obligations and combine with each other in free association: by this I mean that they combine not with reference to any external reality but according to the affinities or incompatibilities existing between them in the architecture of the mind." (Lévi-Strauss, *Honey to Ashes*, p. 473).

Lévi-Strauss confesses with admirable candor that it is the same mythic corpus which discloses this quite contrary nature of myth. The difference lies not in the materials themselves but in the eye of the investigator, "the observer adjusting his microscope" (Lévi-Strauss, *Honey to Ashes*, p. 474). However, he concludes in the same breath that this discovery of the radically opposite nature of myth requires from him no adjustment of his earlier view of myth but only "replaced one system of connections with another" (ibid).

This is clearly unacceptable on the grounds of internal evidence alone. It begs a reevaluation of the roles and relations assigned by him to "logic," "myth," "philosophy," and "science" as he had been presenting them. As it is, he sidesteps this whole question by alluding to the extraordinary complexity of historical conditions and external influences which preclude the possibility of isolating the inevitable causes of the development of one mode of thought into another. However, it is not the question of necessary conditions of transition from myth, to philosophy, to science which are at stake for us but a reassessment of their relative nature and status in something other than an evolutionary framework. For instance, what now may account for the repetitive structure of myth? Since Lévi-Strauss unaccountably and unfortunately allows this valuable insight into myth to slip away unincorporated into his further researches, we are left to present his original and unadjusted judgements about the nature of myth. With some regret we report that this important discovery, hard-won for Lévi-Strauss but known to historians of religions from the beginning of their investigations, does not represent a significant aspect of Lévi-Strauss's theory of myth. For this reason, important as it is, we have relegated it to a footnote since it makes no appreciable impact or alteration on his studies of mythologic.

12. Lévi-Strauss, *Structural Anthropology* (New York: Harper and Row, 1963), p. 22.
13. Lévi-Strauss, *Structural Anthropology*, pp. 47-48.
14. Ibid.
15. A judgment reaffirmed and defended in Lévi-Strauss, 1981:633.
16. Lévi-Strauss, *Origin*, p. 195.
17. Ibid.
18. Ibid.
19. This parallels the strategy of Emile Durkheim who claimed that the division of labor did not present individuals to one another but social functions (E. Durkheim, *The Division of Labor in Society*. Translated by G. Simpson, New York: Macmillan Publishing, 1933, p. 407).
20. Lévi-Strauss, *Origin of Table Manners*, p. 195.
21. Mircea Eliade, "Methodological Remarks on the Study of Religious Symbolism," in Mircea Eliade and Joseph M. Kitagawa, eds., *The History of Religions: Essays in Methodology*, Chicago: The University of Chicago Press, 1959, pp. 86-107; Lawrence E. Sullivan, "Mircea Eliade," *Religious Studies Review*, Vol. 9, No. 1 (January 1983): 13-22.
22. Lévi-Strauss, *Origin*, p. 195.
23. Ibid.
24. Ibid.
25. See Lévi-Strauss's own important statements in the "overture" to the first volume of his *Introduction to a Science of Mythology. The Raw and the Cooked*, New York: Harper and Row, 1975, pp. 1-31. K. O. L. Burridge has summarized these priorities in other words in "Lévi-Strauss and myth," p. 101.
26. "As he moves about within his mental and historical framework, man takes along with him all the positions he has already occupied, and all those he will occupy. He is everywhere at one and the same time; he is a crowd surging forward abreast, and constantly recapitulating the whole series of previous stages" (*Tristes Tropiques*, translated by John and Doreen Weightman, New York: Atheneum, 1974, p. 412).
27. "I believe that mythology, more than anything else, makes it possible to illustrate such objectified thought and to provide empirical proof of its reality" (Lévi-Strauss, *Raw and Cooked*, p. 11).
28. Lévi-Strauss, *Tristes Tropiques*, p. 412.
29. Lévi-Strauss, *Origin*, p. 128.
30. Lévi-Strauss, *Myth and Meaning*, New York: Schocken Books, 1979, p. 1.
31. Lévi-Strauss, *Tristes Tropiques*, p. 412.
32. Ibid.
33. In this connection Lévi-Strauss speaks warmly of "Buddhism," admiring its coherence and noting its strict parallelism to Marxism, at least as he reads the two doctrines. In Buddhism, "the complete denial of meaning is the end point in a succession of stages each one of which leads from a lesser to a greater meaning . . . Between the Marxist critique, which forces man from his initial bondage—by teaching him that the apparent meaning of his condition evaporates as soon as he agrees to see things in a wider context—and the Buddhist critique

which completes his liberation, there is neither opposition nor contradiction. Each is doing the same thing as the other, but on a different level." (Lévi-Strauss, *Tristes Tropiques*, p. 412). Primarily interested in the process of *formal relations* and not the shared meanings of the forms related, Lévi-Strauss isolates the critical dialectics, the formal process of "negating a negation" found in these two systems of thought. For an historian of religions, this tactic is costly and questionable because it ignores their radically different appraisals of human nature, history, the world, and reality. Aside from forfeiting the task of understanding these Weltanschauung, a costly manoeuvre for historians, it asks one to accept the world view of Lévi-Strauss along with his evaluation of the nature, purpose, and situation of the world of *l'esprit humain*. Whatever legitimate grounds could justify taking the meanings of Lévi-Strauss seriously ought also to be able to ground the study of the significant values of other world views with equal seriousness.

Lévi-Strauss is religiously unmusical. The closest he comes to a hermeneutic engagement with a religious system is when he speaks of affinities between Buddhism (as he understands it) and himself. "It was not a question of bowing down in front of idols or of adoring a supposed supernatural order, but only of paying homage to the decisive wisdom that a thinker or the society which created his legend, had evolved . . ." (Lévi-Strauss, *Tristes Tropiques*, p. 411). "As beliefs and superstitions dissolve when one thinks in terms of the real relationships between men, ethics gives way to history, fluid forms are replaced by structures and creation by nothingness" (Lévi-Strauss, *Tristes Tropiques*, p. 412). See also his closing paragraphs to *Naked Man*, 1981: 693-695 where the demise of the myth which *is* human history is described in the setting of the sun: the collapse, decay and vanishing of the universe, nature, and man. Lévi-Strauss admires this "religion of non-knowledge" because it exalts an ability to understand that truth takes the "form of a mutual exclusiveness of being and knowledge" and "through an additional act of boldness, it reduces the metaphysical problem to one of human behavior – a distinction it shares only with Marxism" (Lévi-Strauss, *Tristes Tropiques*, p. 411).

34. He is content to find himself in this position. Cf. Lévi-Strauss, *Raw and Cooked*, p. 11.
35. Burton Feldman and Robert D. Richardson, *The Rise of Modern Mythology: 1680-1860*, Bloomington: Indiana University Press, 1972, p. 482. An example of this trivialization may be found in the section where Lévi-Strauss speaks of beliefs surrounding the living and the dead as they are revealed in the mysteries of men's societies in tropical South America. "The natives are deluded by the logic of their system . . . when all is said and done, I cannot help feeling that the dazzling metaphysical dance I witnessed is little more than a sinister farce . . it is in vain that the Bororo crown their system with a fallacious impersonation of the dead: they have been no more successful than other societies in denying the truth that the image a society evolves of the relationship between the living and the dead is, in the final analysis, an attempt, on the level of religious thought, to conceal, embellish or justify the actual relationships which prevail among the living" (Lévi-Strauss, *Tristes Tropiques*, pp. 245-246).
36. Cf. Lévi-Strauss, *Raw and Cooked*, p. 11; Lévi-Strauss, *The Savage Mind*, especially chapters 1, 3, 5, 6, and 7. See also Friedrich Max Müller, translater, *Kant's Critique of Pure Reason*, second edition (New York: Macmillan and Co., 1886, pp. xxxiv-xxxviii); Friedrich Max Müller, *Natural Religion*, (London: Longmans, Green and Co., 1892, pp. 153-155); Friedrich Max Müller, *The Hibbert Lectures on Religion*, (London: Longmans, Green and Co., 1880, pp. 31-32 and 45-47).
37. Lévi-Strauss, *Origin*, p. 84.
38. Lévi-Strauss, *Origin*, p. 129.
39. Lévi-Strauss, *Origin*, p. 129.
40. Regarding his own science's proximity to perceptions of nature, "Structuralism, unlike the kind of philosophy which restricts the dialectic to human history and bans it from the natural order, readily admits that the ideas it formulates in psychological terms may be no more than fumbling approximations to organic or even physical truths." (Lévi-Strauss, *Naked Man*, p. 689).
41. Lévi-Strauss, *Origin*, p. 129.
42. The quotation is taken from Lévi-Strauss, *Origin*, p. 131; for his optimistic appraisal of science see Lévi-Strauss, *Myth and Meaning*, pp. 5-14.
43. Lévi-Strauss is often at his most eloquent and passionate when he describes the demise of being

into the reality of non-being, the "awareness of which inseparably accompanies the sense of being, since man has to live and struggle, think, believe and above all, preserve his courage, although he can never at any moment lose sight of the opposite certainty that he was not present on earth in former times, that he will not always be here in the future and that, with his inevitable disappearance from the surface of a planet which is itself doomed to die, his labours, his sorrows, his joys, his hopes and his works will be as if they never existed . . ." (Lévi-Strauss, *Naked Man*, p. 694-5).

44. Lévi-Strauss, *Origin*, p. 130.
45. Lévi-Strauss, *Origin*, p. 130.
46. In this way, Lévi-Strauss believes he is applying the lessons taught by Hegel, Marx, and the Buddha: negate the negation.
47. Lévi-Strauss, *Origin*, p. 128.
48. Ibid.
49. Ibid.
50. Ibid.
51. Ibid.
52. Lévi-Strauss, *Origin*, p. 105.
53. See the quotation cited at the head of this article.
54. Lévi-Strauss, *Origin*, pp. 67-68.
55. Lévi-Strauss, *Origin*, p. 66.
56. Lévi-Strauss, *Origin*, p. 79.
57. Lévi-Strauss, *Origin*, p. 500.
58. Lévi-Strauss, *Origin*, p. 504.
59. There are many bodies and walking wounded on this field of battle. We may simply mention the names of a distinguished few: Fred Eggan, Franz Boas, Georges Dumèzil, Wilhelm Schmidt, Benjamin Whorf, R. Pettazzoni, Mircea Eliade, Ananda K. Coomaraswamy, and so on. Attempts to solve the comparative problem have been founded on historical, linguistic, cultural-historical, morphological, and phenomenological grounds.
60. Lévi-Strauss, *Origin*, p. 56.
61. On the same grounds, apparently, Lévi-Strauss reaches into Bengali and Japanese myth to complete the circle of transformations of one set of mythic themes (Lévi-Strauss, *Origin*, p. 125).
62. Lévi-Strauss, *Origin*, p. 84.
63. Ibid.
64. Lévi-Strauss, *Origin*, p. 85.
65. "Internally, on his own ground, Lévi-Strauss's method is unassailable simply because it is self-justifying and self-explanatory" (K. Burridge, "Lévi-Strauss and Myth," p. 110).
66. "If we can so explain, for example, the codes in all our myths, all our stories, our entire culture as just that without remainder—codes with no messages—through methods of explaining with no understanding of rootedness in this effective history and its disclosure of some essential truth about existence, we seem to be in the presence of a new mode of explanation designed to alienate us still further from our actual experience of history, art, religion, thought and the event of understanding in each. Yet when these analyses are in the hands of a real master—a Lévi-Strauss, a Foucault, a Barthes—we instinctively recognize that these semiotic and structuralist explanations of codes, deep and surface structures, enrich our understanding of the text by developing that understanding further, by challenging our former complacent understanding, by compelling us to think again, by suggesting analogies that provoke our attention and expose our sloth." (David Tracy, *The Analogical Imagination: Christian Theology and the Culture of Pluralism*, New York: Crossroad, 1981, p. 117).
67. Lévi-Strauss confirmed his perception of the futility of history in his earlier studies of kinship. Previously, scholars had predicated their explanations of the avunculate on hopeless hypothetical histories of matrilineal and patrilineal systems. The solution was to view the avunculate as an elementary unit interior to an entire system of relations. Its appearance or disappearance owes nothing to the developmental or necessary causes of history. They are more a function of an entire system of relations, expressions of the structures of the human mind. It is not history which accounts for its presence or absence in a science of the concrete, but chance.

68. Lévi-Strauss, *Origin*, p. 104. Emphasis added.

69. Lévi-Strauss, *Origin*, p. 128.

70. See the "Finale" of *Naked Man* for Lévi-Strauss's own list of these objections together with his responses.

71. Paul Friedrich, "Poetic imagination and religious language," (manuscript, n.d.).

72. Roman Jakobsen, "Concluding statement: Linguistics and poetics," in T. A. Sebeok, ed., *Style in Language*, Cambridge, Mass.: MIT Press, p. 358.

73. Roman Jakobsen and Morris Halle, *Fundamentals of Language. Janua Linguarum*, s. n. I. Mouton, 1956, p. 82.

74. Dell Hymes, *Language in Culture and Society*, New York: Harper and Row, 1964, p. 43.

75. Hymes, *Language*, p. 51.

76. See footnotes 3, 5, and 7 on pages 2 and 3 above. It is, no doubt, on this basis that Marvin Harris views Lévi-Strauss as an extension and exaggeration of what Harris deems the best result of the French structural school: psychic communion with nature (Harris, *The Rise*, p. 489).

77. Paul Ricoeur, *The Rule of Metaphor: Multidisciplinary Studies of the Creation of Meaning in Language*, translated by Robert Czerny, Toronto: University of Toronto Press, 1979, p. 319. For a different reading of the nature of Lévi-Strauss's "system" see Marc Gaboriau, 1970 (1963), "Structural anthropology and history," in Michael Lane, ed., Structuralism: A Reader (London: Jonathan Cape, pp. 156-169).

78. Terence S. Turner, "Narrative structure and Mythopoesis: A critique and reformulation of structuralist concepts of myth, narrative and poetics," *Arethusa*, Volume 10, number 1, Spring 1977.

79. Lévi-Strauss, *Naked Man*.

80. Marshall Sahlins points out that Lévi-Strauss refuses to grant ontological status to Durkheim's separation of individual experience, social forms, and collective representations. Lévi-Strauss not only unites these and endows them with equal status, but insofar as the *perception* of them may be trusted, they are ontologically structured in the same way by the relational processes at work in the act of perceiving them. In this way, a psychologism which relates dialectically to the world becomes a sociology. Nevertheless, there is a kind of ontological argument underlying Lévi-Strauss's work. Ostensibly not interested in a philosophy of being, he initially makes claims about the operations of articulate thought which may be translated: "the way I think about the way I think, is the way (I think) I am." This appears to be a harmless and nongenerative tautology. However, the larger generalizations he makes about the systems of signs in the orders of nature do, in fact, betoken an ontological transcendence of the level of symbolic thought and perception to the level of being, for somehow he brings himself to judgments which may be translated: "the way I think about the way I am, is the way *everything is* (for, my mind being both alienated from and united to direct experience of the world by my thought processes, I have no other way of knowing)." The elementary structure of the mind which is responsible for the form which thought processes take (and therefore the form reality takes) may be said to be "the being than which nothing different can be conceived." Suggestions of the truth of this are provided in Lévi-Strauss's conviction that "elementary structures," and the source of their dynamism are transhistorical. However, he can never bring himself to clarify their "transcendent" nature. As a result, as we have pointed out above, the nature of the objective mind, the forms of collective representation, and the source of dynamism at work in "elementary structures," remain undefined. Their distinctive criteria are sealed in the mystery of the personal thought of the mythologician. In a curious paragraph evidently directed at unnamed theological critics, Lévi-Strauss himself underscores the fact that the nature of the transhistorical or transcendent objective mind remains his personal secret. He chides them for not asking him to make his thoughts known. "The believers who criticize us in the name of the sacred values of the human person, if they were consistent with themselves, would argue differently: they ought to be putting the question: if the finality postulated by your intellectual method is neither in the consciousness nor in the subject, since you attempt to locate it on the hither side of both, where can it be, except outside them? And they would call upon us to draw the logical consequences . . . the fact that they do not do so, shows that these timorous spirits attach more importance to their own selves than to their god" (Lévi-Strauss, *Naked Man*, p. 687-8; ellipsis is in original text).

81. Terence S. Turner, "Narrative structure and Mythopoesis," p. 124.

82. For instance, ". . . in his usage of Life and Death Lévi-Strauss seems persistently to assume the standpoint of an individual but of a very particular individual – what life and death may mean to *him* . . . is this not precisely that worst kind of psychologism against which Lévi-Strauss so inveighs? For most peoples, death is but a passage from one kind of being to another, and as a passage, death usually corresponds to birth and the movement from child to adult . . ." (K. Burridge, "Lévi-Strauss and Myth," p. 105). In the same way Terence Turner shows that nature/culture among Kayapó are not opposed in the formal relations Lévi-Strauss attributes to them. In the opinion of Turner, the shared meaning of Kayapó symbolic action establishes quite a different kind of relation between these terms. (Terence S. Turner, "The social structure of the Northern Kayapó," manuscript, n.d.).

83. Mircea Eliade, *The Quest: History and Meaning in Religion*, Chicago: The University of Chicago Press, 1969, p. 173.

84. As such these dichotomies and categories are not only unconscious and concrete in the cultures in which they are found, as Lévi-Strauss claims, but are abstractions self-consciously used in clear reflections and speculation. As we have instantiated above, this realization came home to Lévi-Strauss late in his studies in *Honey to Ashes*. Regrettably, he swept aside this insight and did not adjust his assessment of the nature of myth as, in the words of Kenelm Burridge, an "interminable dialogue between the mind and its object" (K. Burridge, "Lévi-Strauss and Myth," p. 96).

85. Mircea Eliade, *The Quest*, p. 173.

86. Cambridge, Mass.: MIT Press, 1970.

87. K. Burridge, "Lévi-Strauss and Myth," p. 113. "Like Freud, Marx, or Jung, Lévi-Strauss offers us a sweet-scented haven with many floral bowers in which to dally – or so it may seem. Yet perhaps it is an Erehwon" (ibid).

88. In Lévi-Strauss's view, says Burridge "all myths become much the same, dealing with the same things in the same ways. Yet it is evident – at least to the present writer – that this is just what myths do not do . . " (ibid).

89. Or, alternately, edifying and enriching. Cf. James W. Fernandez, "Edification by Puzzlement," in Ivan Karp and Charles S. Bird, eds., *Explorations in African Systems of Thought*, Bloomington: Indiana University Press, 1980, pp. 44-59.

90. The universal structures of the mind qualify for this kind of visibility because they are manifest in their rearrangements in specific symbolic forms, in the moving locations of images in variants of myth. As a science of the concrete, myth "makes visible" elemental thought processes.

91. It is interesting in this connection to review a criticism of Lévi-Strauss by K. Burridge. ". . . obsessed as he is with binary oppositions . . . Lévi-Strauss seems scarcely to notice that contemplation and accommodation of the idea of *the singular* which could be said to lie at the roots of civilized life" (K. Burridge, "Lévi-Strauss and Myth," p. 113). Ironically, without knowing it, Burridge has hit upon the very attractiveness of Lévi-Strauss who offers a singular science of the mind woven from very different intellectual threads. From this point of view what happens to myth is only a circumstantial by-product. Throughout this article we have attempted to show that Nature, conceived as systems of structural properties not unlike linguistic codes, becomes the basis of mental unity. ". . [S]tructuralism reintegrates man into nature . . ." (Lévi-Strauss, *Naked Man*, p. 687). Its ambition is "to link up the sensory with the intelligible" (ibid). Lévi-Strauss's outlook rings true to Karl Marx's vision: "history itself is a *real* part of *natural history* – of nature's coming to be man. Natural science will in time subsume under itself the science of man, just as the science of man will subsume under itself natural science: there will be *one* science" (Karl Marx, *Economic and Philosophic Manuscripts of 1844*, Moscow: Foreign Languages Publishing House, 1961 [1844], p. 111).

92. For example, Raffaele Pettazzoni, *Miti E Legende*, Volume 4, *America Centrale e Meridionale* (Torino: Unione Tipografico-Editrice Torinese, 1959). Paul Ehrenreich, *Die Mythen und Legenden der sudamerikanischen Urvölker und ihre Beziehungen zu denen Nordamerikas und der alten Welt*, Zeitschrift für Ethnologie, Volume 37, supplement (Berlin, 1905). Robert Lehmann-Nitsche, *Mitología Sudamericana. Revista del Museo de La Plata*, e.g., Volume 24: pp. 28-62 (1918) and Volume 1 (n.s.): pp. 27-33 (1937). See also Ehrenreich's *Studien zur sudamerikanischen Mythologie*. Hamburg: Friedericksen, de Gruyter, 1939.

93. Although we are recognizing that Lévi-Strauss makes this point with unusual effect, we

must also acknowledge that it is hardly original to him. Many fine investigators make the same point with more sensitivity to religious aspects of their data. One thinks of Johannes Wilbert, Egon Schaden, Curt Nimuendaju, Gerardo Reichel-Dolmatoff, Stefano Varese, Gerald Weiss, Franklin Pease, Otto Zerries, Hildegaard Matthäi, Ana Maria Mariscotti de Görlitz, Josef Haeckel, Joseph Bastien, Jacques Lizot, as especially notable examples.

94.   Stephen Hugh-Jones, *The Palm and the Pleiades: Initiation and Cosmology in Northwest Amazonia*, Cambridge: Cambridge University Press, 1979, p. xii.

95.   Christine Hugh-Jones, *From the Milk River: Spatial and Temporal Processes in Northwest Amazonia*, Cambridge: Cambridge University Press, 1979, p. 1.

96.   Stephen Hugh-Jones, *The Palm and the Pleiades*, pp. 251-252.

97.   Ibid.

98.   Ibid.

99.   Stephen Hugh-Jones, *The Palm*, p. 253.

100. Ibid, p. 254.

101. Stephen Hugh-Jones, *The Palm*, p. 255.

102. Stephen Hugh-Jones, *The Palm*, p. 255, 257.

103. Stephen Hugh-Jones, *The Palm*, p. 259.

104. Ibid. Hugh-Jones is quoting from Lévi-Strauss, *The Raw and the Cooked*, p. 12.

105. Lévi-Strauss has indeed proven to be a fruitful resource in the study of South American religions both in regard to content and method. See for example Reiner T. Zuidema, *The Ceque System of Cuzco*, Leiden: L. J. Brill, 1964, pp. 22ff.; Gary Urton, *At the Crossroads of the Earth and the Sky: An Andean Cosmogony*, Austin: University of Texas Press, 1981, pp. 85, 109, 191. An important development is taking place in the study of the conception of corporeality and constitution of the personality–a movement attributed, in part, to Lévi-Strauss; see Anthony Seeger, Roberto da Matta, E. B. Viveiros de Castro, "A Construção da Pessoa nas Sociedades Indígenas Brasileiras," *Boletim do Museu Nacional* (Rio de Janeiro) N.S. 32 (May, 1979) pp. 1-41. Manuela Carneiro da Cunha's work is a notable example of the fruitful use and correction of Lévi-Strauss insights. For example, see her two studies of eschatology: *Os Muertos e os Outros. Uma análise do sistema funerário e da noção de pessoa entre os indios Krahó*, São Paulo: Hucitec, 1978; and "Eschatology Among the Krahó: reflection upon society, free field of fabulation," in Sally Humphreys and H. King (eds.) *Mortality and Immortality. The Archaeology and Anthropology of Death*, New York: Academic Press, 1981, pp. 161-174. In this second study she is forced to conclude, "whatever my inclination for more detailed structuralist analysis, there appeared to be no footing for it in Krahó eschatology. The diversity of versions seemed to be irreducible, except for a limited core" (p. 161). Such an approach seems the typical and most useful application of Lévi-Strauss procedures and conclusions: a thoughtful and case-by-case examination of his conclusions with a necessary constriction of his exhaustive claims.

106. Lévi-Strauss, *Naked Man*, p. 627; emphasis is in the original text.

107. Ibid.

108. To such objections Lévi-Strauss responds: "The fallacious complaint that the myths have been impoverished hides a latent mysticism, nourished in the vain hope of the revelation of a meaning behind the meaning to justify or excuse all kinds of confused and nostalgic longings, which are afraid to express themselves openly" (Lévi-Strauss, 1981: 639). In this *argumentum ad hominem*, Lévi-Strauss does not deal with the accusation that he distorts the nature of the facts he chooses to investigate by selecting only some of the many aspects conjoined in myth.

109. Lévi-Strauss has been criticized for not giving due consideration to emotional experience. See his own discussion and rebuttal of Victor Turner's objections in Lévi-Strauss, *Naked Man*, pp. 668-670. For his rejection of what he terms "vague and general" statements about "religious feeling," see *Naked Man*, p. 688.

110. From the beginning Lévi-Strauss does not allow himself the possibility of dealing with important associations peculiar to myth. "I, too, of course, look upon the religious field as a stupendous storehouse of images that is far from having been exhausted by objective research; but these images are like any others, and the spirit in which I approach the study of religious data supposes that such data are not credited at the outset with any specific character." (Lévi-Strauss, 1981: 639). Of course, it is not something in the images *in se* which furnishes them a special character and which warrants scrutiny as a religious datum.

Rather, it is the attribution, an understanding universal among communities where myth is a living tradition, of a connection between the origin and meaning of these images and a sacred realm of being transcending them which sets myth apart as a special domain for interpretation. The religious attitude, perception, and experience accompanying myth form part of its unique character. These must be considered as part of the one complex reality of myth if one is to understand the meaning of its images and symbols. Whether or not in the end "we have to resign ourselves to the fact that the myths tell us nothing instructive about the order of the world, the nature of reality or the origin and destiny of mankind" (Lévi-Strauss, 1981: 639), in the beginning historians of religions take as a serious problem for research the fact that this is not the judgment of those who maintain mythic traditions. The goal, among others, is *to understand their* beliefs, acts, experiences, and the meanings they assign to them. How one proceeds carries consequences for an overall estimation of the nature and capacities of human being. That evaluation should not be prejudged by dwarfing the mythic complex one examines.

111. Jonathan Z. Smith, "I Am a Parrot (Red)," *History of Religions*, Vol. II, No. 4, pp. 391-402 presents the history of such a problem, its interpretations, and the inevitability of facing it.

112. Lévi-Strauss, *Naked Man*, p. 639.

113. ". . . Experience has taught me how impossible it is to grasp the spirit of a myth without steeping oneself in the complete versions, however diffuse they may be, and submitting to a slow process of incubation requiring hours, days, months—or sometimes even years—until one's thought, guided unconsciously by tiny details, succeeds in embracing the essential nature of myth" (Lévi-Strauss, *Naked Man*, p. 632).

CHAPTER VIII

The Text and Time:
Lévi-Strauss and
New Testament Studies[1]

Elizabeth Struthers Malbon

Contemporary French cultural anthropologist Claude Lévi-Strauss is generally regarded as the "father" of structuralism,[2] "the archetypal high priest of structuralism."[3] To Lévi-Strauss goes as well the dubious honor of being, in the words of biblical scholar Robert Polzin, "perhaps the best-known and [the] least understood structuralist."[4] His work is heralded as "the most extended and systematic application of structuralist methods and the structuralist vision to human phenomena,"[5] "a paradigm of the structuralist endeavor."[6] It will not be my purpose here to judge these statements, to evaluate the breadth of Lévi-Strauss's influence, but only to consider certain aspects of the impact of the work of Lévi-Strauss in New Testament studies. My focus will be on issues concerning the biblical text and time, an area in which the debate —not only between Lévi-Straussian thought and traditional biblical study but also between varieties of structural exegesis—has been dramatic.

Before exploring the topic of the text and time, however, we must briefly consider a prior question biblical studies addresses to structuralism in general and to Lévi-Strauss in particular: is structuralism a methodology or an ideology?[7] Lévi-Strauss's desire to understand the structure of the human mind from an examination of its cultural products, his discovery of "vast homologies,"[8] represents, of course, an ideological goal of structuralism. Yet the two items of Lévi-Strauss's published work that seem to have exercised the greatest influence in New Testament studies, "The Structural Study of Myth"[9] and "The Story of Asdiwal,"[10] present in some detail a methodology for the study of myth. It has been my experience that those who have found the work of Lévi-Strauss stimulating for New Testament studies have focused on his methodology for studying myth as the mediation of irreconcilable opposites,[11] whereas those who have found the work of Lévi-Strauss problematic for New Testament studies have focused on his ideological presuppositions and goals.[12] Unfortunately for the clarity of the scholarly debate, the distinction between methodology and ideology has not always—not even often—been clearly drawn by the various participants.

A second area in which clarity in the critical review of Lévi-Strauss's work could well be gained involves the distinction between *what* Lévi-Strauss has to say (whether in its ideological or methodological dimensions) and *how*

Lévi-Strauss says it. Numerous critics have found the latter simultaneously engaging and enraging. One finds many complaints, and not a few tirades, against the use of an incomprehensible jargon by structuralists in general[13] and by Lévi-Strauss in particular.[14] Many readers of Lévi-Strauss empathize perhaps with Edmund Leach ("Lévi-Strauss often manages to give me ideas even when I don't really know what he is saying"[15]) or Mary Douglas ("However, I do not think it is fair to such an ebullient writer to take him literally"[16]). Howard Gardner seems to uncover the reason for such responses in his analysis of the style of Lévi-Strauss's thinking and writing.

> Lévi-Strauss's thinking is characterized by a dialectical interplay between two dominant tendencies: a penchant toward logical analysis and systematic comparisons on the one hand; a flair for the suggestive metaphor, the unanticipated link, the synthesis of two apparently contradictory notions, on the other. And this curious amalgam of the precise and the poetic is reflected, naturally enough, in his writing, which consists in methodical, dry presentations, sporadically and dramatically interrupted by enthusiastic pronouncements, unlikely similes, sweeping generalizations.[17]

Yet Gardner refuses to let the way Lévi-Strauss communicates block perception of the content and scope of Lévi-Strauss's communications; indeed, Lévi-Strauss's manner enlivens that perception. In Gardner's view, too many of Lévi-Strauss's critics are "overly concerned with proving him wrong on one or another point, rather than accepting such errors as the unfortunate concomitant of a courageous attempt to take on issues of dizzying difficulty and to make some kind of tentative sense out of them."[18] Certainly Lévi-Strauss is more Dionysian than Apollonian in his approach,[19] but that does not judge the more important issue: "whether the problems studied . . . are significant and whether the solutions offered are meaningful and revealing."[20]

Surely structuralists and New Testament scholars have agreed that the problem of the relation of a text, whether a traditional mythic text or a biblical text, to time is significant. What New Testament critics have debated is whether the solution the thought of Lévi-Strauss offers to this problem is meaningful and revealing. Here we will consider Lévi-Strauss's own analysis of texts in relation to time and three New Testament examples of a Lévi-Straussian analysis of texts in relation to time. Our goal is to draw out the implications of structuralism, especially Lévi-Straussian structuralism, for the New Testament study of the text and time.

LEVI-STRAUSS AND TWO DIMENSIONS OF TIME

Traditional biblical exegetes often comment that structuralism, and especially Lévi-Straussian structuralism, ignores the dimension of time.[21] Structural exegetes themselves often suggest that, whereas traditional biblical criticism and structural criticism are complementary, the former is diachronic and the later synchronic. According to Daniel Patte, "traditional historical exegesis" or "diachronic exegesis" includes text criticism, philological study, literary [source] criticism, history of tradition, form criticism, and redaction criticism. "Synchronic exegesis" includes structural exegesis and "the reformulations of traditional historical methods (results of the research of the New Hermeneutic)."[22] Historical exegesis is chronological, linear, horizontal; structural exegesis is achronic, in-depth, vertical. Yet structural exegesis challenges not the existence of traditional historical exegesis but its centrality or exclusivity. "Any adoption and adaptation of structuralism by New Testament hermeneutic," Dan Via observes, "will entail, not a rejection of the historical method, but a relegating of it to a more marginal position than it has been enjoying."[23] According to Edgar McKnight, it is the "failure of historical study to accomplish the intention of the biblical text [which] opens the way for the structural approach, not to supplant the historical-critical approach but to supplement it, guide and modify it, and in turn to be guided and modified by the historical approach."[24] Traditional biblical criticism is primarily concerned with diachrony, movement *through time*; structural criticism is primarily concerned with synchrony, a moment in which all occurs as if at the *same time*; the text must be considered from both points of view.

The relation of the text and time has been of importance to Lévi-Strauss's critics beyond as well as within New Testament studies. According to Paul Ricoeur, "the kind of *intelligibility* expressed by structural semiotics is *antihistorical* by nature and it tends, in its most extreme and fanaticist use, to dismiss all historical inquiry concerning the redactional stages of the text and even, in a kind of provocative way, to emphasize the *last* text, the one we now read."[25] According to Mary Douglas, Lévi-Strauss's "structural analysis cannot but reveal myths as timeless, as synchronic structures outside time . . . [because his] method reduces all to synchrony"; furthermore, ". . . if myths have got an irreversible order and if this is significant, this part of their meaning will escape the analysis."[26]

A further temporal distinction needs to be made, however, between a time dimension external to the text and a time dimension internal to the text.[27] Lévi-Strauss's positions vis-à-vis these two time dimensions are somewhat different, but neither is as simply antagonistic as Ricoeur and Douglas seem to suggest.

Lévi-Strauss affirms the necessity of historical study for structural study in the way he carries out his analyses of myth. In "The Story of Asdiwal," for example, after a brief statement of goals and a list of the variants of the myth, Lévi-Strauss states: "We shall begin by calling attention to certain facts which must be known if the myth is to be understood."[28] These "facts" consist of an overview of the ethnography of the Tsimshian Indians, that is, the historical context of the myth of Asdiwal. Likewise, *The Raw and the Cooked* opens with this statement of procedure:

I shall take as my starting point *one* myth, originating from *one* community, and shall analyze it, referring first of all to the enthnogrphic context and then to other myths belonging to the same community. Gradually broadening the field of inquiry, I shall then move on to myths from neighboring societies, after previously placing them, too, in their particular ethnographic context. Step by step, I shall proceed to more remote communities but only after authentic links of a historical or a geographic nature have been established with them or can reasonably be assumed to exist.[29]

Thus, while the dimension of time external to myth is certainly not Lévi-Strauss's focus, neither does he ignore this temporal dimension, that is, history.[30]

If Lévi-Strauss distinguishes history and myth sharply it is because he is aware of the danger of reading myths as transcripts of historical reality. "[I]t is always rash," Lévi-Strauss notes, "to undertake, as Boas wanted to do in his monumental *Tsimshian Mythology*, 'a description of the life, social organization and religious ideas and practices of a people . . . as it appears from their mythology.' "[31] Lévi-Strauss continues:

The myth is certainly related to given (empirical) facts, but not as a *re-presentation* of them. The relationship is of a dialectic kind, and the institutions described in the myths can be the very opposite of the real institutions. This will always be the case when the myth is trying to express a negative truth.

This conception of the relation of the myth to reality no doubt limits the use of the former as a documentary source.[32]

Far from discrediting history, Lévi-Strauss's intention is to rescue myth from overly historicized interpretation.

Lévi-Strauss's perception of and attention to the dimension of time internal to myth, that is, the myth's own process of unfolding, is somewhat more problematic. On the one hand, Lévi-Strauss maintains that "the specific character of mythological time" is that it is "both revertible and non-revertible, synchronic and diachronic."[33] Yet, on the other hand, he concludes that the chronological order of the myth, its sequence, reveals only the "apparent content" of the myth, whereas its "latent content" is suggested by its schema. Thus, to "understand" the myth, the task that Lévi-Strauss takes up, one must concentrate on the paradigmatic schema.

Sequence and schema, syntagm and paradigm, however, are not entirely unrelated, as Lévi-Strauss himself admits. After explaining his procedure for charting a myth in rows (the syntagm) and columns (the paradigm), Lévi-Strauss concludes:

Were we to *tell* the myth, we would disregard the columns and read the rows from left to right and from top to bottom. But if we want to *understand* the myth, then we will have to disregard one half of the diachronic dimension (top to bottom) and read from left to right, column after column, each one being considered as a unit.[34]

Note that we do not disregard the diachronic dimension in its entirety, but only "one half of the diachronic dimension." The relationships between the columns (1 is to 2 as 3 is to 4) reflect the impact of the syntagmatic dimension upon the paradigmatic dimension. Furthermore, in analyzing a version of "The Story of Asdiwal" that relates the adventures of Waux, the son of Asdiwal's second marriage, Lévi-Strauss notes that the son

> seems to be a doublet of his father, although his adventures take place after those of Asdiwal. In chronological order, they form supplementary sequences of events. But these *later* sequences are organized in schemata which are at the same time *homologous* to those [of Asdiwal] which have been described and more *explicit* than them. Everything seems to suggest that, as it draws to its close, the obvious [apparent] narrative (the sequences) tends to approach the latent content of the myth (the schemata); a convergence which is not unlike that which the listener discovers in the final chords of a symphony.[35]

Narrative meaning emerges from the intersection of syntagm and paradigm,[36] although one does sense that, as a general rule in Lévi-Strauss's analyses, syntagm is sent out through the door and welcomed in through the window of the house that paradigm built.

The opposition diachrony vs. synchrony has to do with the dimension of time external to myth, the historical time in which the myth is embedded. The opposition syntagmatic vs. paradigmatic has to do with the dimension of time internal to myth, the narrative time that unfolds within the myth. Both oppositions derive from Saussure. The first, diachrony vs. synchrony, represents two ways of studying language; the second way is preferred by Saussure and, in regard to the "language" of myth, by Lévi-Strauss. The second opposition, syntagmatic vs. paradigmatic, represents the two dimensions of language (*langue*) as it is studied synchronically. While acknowledging the existence and illustrating the interdependence of both dimensions in the "language" of myth, Lévi-Strauss finds the paradigmatic dimension definitive for "understanding" myth.[37] Thus, critics who complain that Lévi-Strauss ignores both the diachronic dimension (the time dimension external to myth) and the syntagmatic dimension (the time dimension internal to myth) oversimplify both the problem and Lévi-Strauss's response. Neither syntagmatic vs. paradigmatic, nor diachronic vs. synchronic, are unmediated oppositions for Lévi-Strauss.

THREE NEW TESTAMENT EXAMPLES

Three brief examples from the Gospel of Mark must serve to suggest implications for New Testament studies of the relations of syntagm and paradigm, and diachrony and synchrony, as Lévi-Strauss conceives them. The first Markan example illustrates the relation of syntagm and paradigm in a Lévi-Straussian analysis; that is, it concerns the time dimension internal to the text. The Gospel of Mark, like a myth, is comprised of a number of "orders," each of which is a "transformation" of the others and "of an underlying logical structure common to all of them."[38] One of the "orders" of the Markan gospel, the spatial order, represents the geopolitical, topographical, and architectural framework of the narrative; it is concerned with the pattern of the locations of narrative events. The syntagm presents the chronological movement of each order, whereas the paradigm presents the logical or mythological movement from a fundamental opposition toward its mediation. Yet, as in the above mentioned Lévi-Straussian example of the version of "The Story of Asdiwal" that relates the adventures of Asdiwal's son, the Markan spatial order illustrates the convergence of syntagm and paradigm. The diagram below presents the overall schema of the Markan spatial order, its fundamental paradigm. The terms in parentheses represent the nonmanifest (unconscious or preconscious), fundamental opposition of the mythic text. The other pairs of terms represent the oppositions manifest in the narrative; their arrangement suggests the movement (logical or mythological movement, not chronological movement) from awareness of oppositions toward their progressive mediation which Lévi-Strauss considers one of the main processes of mythic thought. But oppositions indicated toward the left of the spatial schema, land vs. sea, Jewish homeland vs. foreign lands, are, in fact, manifest early in the Markan narrative; those toward the right, closer to mediation, environs of Jerusalem vs. Jerusalem proper, Mount of Olives vs. Temple, are manifest late in the gospel story. The "way" is the end of both the chronological sequence and the mythological schema. Thus it appears that the sequence itself may suggest movement toward mediation in the syntagmatic order of its relations. It is as if the paradigm were stretched out on the syntagm.[39]

(order)

    heaven

       land

          Jewish homeland

           Galilee

             isolated areas

               house

                 environs of Jerusalem

                  Mount of Olives

                    tomb

                      way

                    mountain

                 Temple

               Jerusalem proper

             synagogue

            inhabited areas

          Judea

        foreign lands

      sea

    earth

(chaos)

The second and third Markan examples illustrate the relation of synchrony and diachrony in a Lévi-Straussian analysis; that is, they concern the time dimension external to the text, history. Synnchronic and diachronic approaches to the spatial order of the Gospel of Mark result in different conclusions regarding the significance of (a) the narrative opposition of Galilee and Jerusalem, and (b) the Markan anti-temple theme. From the diachronic viewpoint, Werner Kelber understands "Jerusalem" as representative of the historical reality of the Jerusalem church which was the enemy of the Markan community[40] and "Galilee" as a symbol for the historical "Galilean Christians" who await the imminent parousia in Galilee after A.D. 70 and for whom Mark was the "spokesman."[41] From the synchronic viewpoint, the opposition of Galilee and Jerusalem represents the overturning of the progressive mediation of the fundamental opposition order vs. chaos.

The Markan narrative, which manifests the traditional Jewish associations of sea and foreign land with chaos and of land and Jewish homeland with order, reverses the expected associations of Galilee and Judea. Would not Judea, the region of Jerusalem—religious center of the Jewish people, home of the temple which ordered their worship and of the Tables of the Law which ordered their very lives—be expected to be the center of order? And would not Galilee, in contradistinction to the home of the religious establishment, Galilee "ringed" by foreign lands and their influence,[42] be anticipated as a manifestation of chaos? But, in the Markan gospel, Galilee, Jesus' homeland within the Jewish homeland, is the center of order. Wherever he journeys—to the Jordan to be baptized, to Tyre and Sidon to heal, to Jerusalem to be crucified—the Markan Jesus always returns to Galilee. Galilee forms a framework for the narrative action, ordering movements in space. In controversy with the leaders and representatives of the supposed religious order centralized in Jerusalem, Jesus calls the established religious order into question. A new and authentic order is both demanded and proclaimed by Jesus of Nazareth in Galilee;[43] to Jesus the old order is as chaos. Chaos breaks loose when Jesus arrives in Jerusalem in Judea. The chaos of the trial, in which the Markan chief priests and elders appear to ignore their own required order, leads to the chaos of the crucifixion, complete with darkness when there should be light and the rending of the temple curtain which makes chaos of the rigid demarcation of the sacred and profane within the religious structure. Thus Judea is linked with the chaos pole of the fundamental opposition, and Galilee with order.

At the level of the opposition Galilee vs. Judea, movement toward the mediation of chaos and order is implied in the Markan exchange of connotations between the two religions. When Galilee, supposedly chaotic, connotes a new order, and Judea, supposedly orderly, represents chaos, the fundamental opposition is severely weakened. Yet tension remains between Jerusalem and Galilee. At the close of the Gospel of Mark, Jesus' spatial location is neither Jerusalem nor Galilee, but somewhere in between; Jesus is in movement; he is "going before" (16:7); he is on the way. By understanding the system of relation-ships at the narrative level of the Gospel of Mark, including the relationship of Jerusalem and Galilee, we may be better able to understand the significance of Mark's gospel at the theological level, including the relationship of chaos and order.[44]

Thus my own synchronic study of the Gospel of Mark does not confirm Kelber's assertion that the imminent parousia in Galilee was the *terminus ad quem* of Mark's gospel. But my synchronic study, like Kelber's diachronic one, does suggest that the temple destruction in Jerusalem (A.D. 70) may well have been the *terminus a quo* of Mark's gospel. According to Kelber, the destruction of the temple was a "problem" for the Markan community because certain Christians had tied the parousia of Christ to the destruction of Jerusalem; Mark's solution was to rescue the parousia as an authentic future hope by detaching it from the historical event of the temple destruction.[45] That there is an anti-Jerusalem or anti-temple theme in Mark is clear from a number of exe-getical approaches.[46] The need to detach past loyalties (and possibly future ex-pectations) from the temple is also suggested by the narrative opposition of house and synagogue and house and temple in Mark. The house, not the synagogue or the temple, becomes the meeting place of Jesus and his disciples, just as the house became the meeting place of early Christians after the destruc-tion of the temple (see Mark 13:2, 14) and the antagonism against Christians in the synagogues (see Mark 13:9).[47] Thus, although the temple destruction is placed on the lips of the Markan Jesus as a "prediction" (13:2), it seems more a presupposition of the author and the reader (see 13:14). Our knowledge of the destruction of the temple comes not from the Gospel of Mark, but from more direct archaeological and literary sources. What we know of this historical world, however, may indeed be suggestive for understanding the text that exists in relation to it. The danger is in reading the text as a coded description of the historical world.[48]

My study of Markan space is, like Kelber's, concerned with theology and geography; but for Kelber geography itself is theological (Galilee is *the place* of the parousia) and theology itself is geographical (to await the parousia one must go to Galilee), whereas for me the *distinctions and interrelations* of the geographical (and, in a larger sense, spatial) system of the Markan narrative may signal theological *distinctions and interrelations* of the Markan gospel; rela-tionships are compared with relationships, not places with dogmas. Whereas Kelber's work considers Markan geography an indicator of the historical world of the text, my work investigates Markan geography in the context of the text as a literary world.[49] Thus my approach is *primarily* synchronic in orientation, whereas Kelber's approach is *primarily* diachronic—concerned with the relation of the text and the time dimension external to the text, that is, history. As im-portant as historical investigation may be, the investigation of the relation of the text to its historical world must proceed with appreciation of the text itself, the interrelations within the text, and the relation of the text to its literary world.[50] Such appreciation, it seems to me, is a gift and a demand that struc-turalism – including Lévi-Straussian structuralism – presents to New Testament studies.

STRUCTURALISM, THE TEXT, AND TIME

One might ask, however, whether the contribution of structuralism to New Testament studies becomes at some point a confrontation. There are those who judge that structuralism in general, and Lévi-Straussian structuralism in particular, does not represent the complementing of a diachronic approach with a synchronic one, or the complementing of an emphasis on the syn-tagmatic with an emphasis on the paradigmatic, but the ignoring – if not the at-tempted abolishment – of the dimension of time itself. The debate is best cap-sulized, perhaps, in an interview of Lévi-Strauss by a group of critics, led by Ricoeur, and entitled, in the English translation appearing in the *New Left Review*, "A Confrontation."[51]

Ricoeur suggests that Lévi-Strauss's structural approach is not as appropriate for the materials and cultures of Judaism and Christianity – which emphasize history – as for the materials and cultures of non-literate peoples – which em-phasize myth.[52] But the issue here is not the unmediated opposition of history and myth,[53] not whether there are purely diachronic cultures and purely syn-chronic cultures – a nonsensical assertion, although both Ricoeur and Lévi-Strauss agree that there are cultures in which one or the other dimension is more important to the culture's self-understanding and self-expression. The issue of diachrony vs. synchrony is an issue of the interpreter's *approach* to the complex materials of complex cultures, not of the materials or cultures themselves.

It is important, then, to appreciate Lévi-Strauss's chief reason for his ap-proach, and especially important in the present case because his reason is generally paralleled by New Testament scholars who choose to make a struc-tural approach to biblical texts.[54] Thus I quote substantially from Lévi-Strauss's response to a question from Jean Lautman concerning history:

I have nothing against history; I have the greatest respect for it; I read the works of historians with infinite interest, even passion, and I have always maintained that it is impossible to em-bark on any structural analysis without having first obtained from history all it is able to give us in illumination, which is unfortunately every little when we are dealing with non-literate societies. I merely sought to redress, or at least I rebelled against, what seems to me to be a very manifest tendency in contemporary philosophical France to regard historical knowledge as a kind of knowledge superior to all others. So I limited myself to the statement that history was one kind of knowledge among others, that there could be no knowledge of continuity, only of discontinuity, and that history was no exception in this respect. So I do not claim that history's code is any more meagre than any other: this would obviously be inaccurate; merely that it is a code and that therefore historical knowledge suffers from the same weaknesses as all of knowledge, which is not to say that it is not very important. . . . This raises a major problem which we have touched on several times . . . that is, the problem of diachronic structures. After all, the fact that events are situated in time is not sufficient to exclude them from structural analysis; it merely makes the latter more difficult. But the linguists' position on this point is quite clear: they accept that there is a diachronic linguistics as well as synchronic linguistics, but the former raises many problems, the principal one being the necessity to begin by revealing recurrent sequences in a development which does not always allow of an isolation of terms of comparison. Perhaps with the assistance of sociology, ethnography, and who knows what else, history will one day achieve this, but that day has not yet arrived. Consequently, it is better to leave the problem of diachronic structures aside for the moment, and devote ourselves to those aspects on which we have a firm grip.[55]

Lévi-Strauss chooses his approach because he judges it will help him make sense of the phenomena he finds interesting, the phenomena he wishes to understand, primarily mythic texts.[56] I too have sometimes chosen a structural approach because I have found it helps me make sense of the phenomena I find interesting, the phenomena I wish to understand, New Testament texts. As my dialogue with Kelber indicated above, I have found that a structural approach raises important questions and suggests intriguing interpretations that are not raised, are not suggested, by the more historically oriented approaches of source, form, and redaction criticism. As a methodology, structuralism rewards attention. As a "methodolatry," structuralism subverts investigation—but, as "methodolatries," so do source, form, and redaction criticism.

Thus structural exegesis has an important contribution to make to New Testament interpretation. Structuralism alone, however, can no more complete the task than form or redaction criticism alone. The biblical text came into existence in time, and our understanding of the text is quite rightly influenced by our understanding of that time. Yet, since much of what we know of that time must be gleaned from the text itself (as well as other texts), an initial appreciation of the text as text is essential to further understanding. Markan scholar John Donahue has suggested that a combination of critical approaches, one more historical and one more literary in orientation, has the advantage of being

true to the dual nature of Mark: (a) as a document which does build on previous traditions and does have contact with history even though the actual shape of the traditions and the exact historical referents are not immediately apparent and (b) as a narrative text which represents one of the most creative moments in the history of early Christian literature. General literary criticism [including structural criticism] does justice to Mark as text and narrative; composition criticism [or redaction criticism broadly conceived] respects the conditions under which the narrative emerged.[57]

Through such a combination of approaches, New Testament interpreters seek to do justice to the text and time. And Lévi-Straussian structuralism can be an important element in that combination.

Structural criticism approaches New Testament studies with the potential

(1) to deepen understanding of the biblical text in itself and (2) to broaden understanding of the biblical text in relation to other texts. Initially, the very newness, and often strangeness, of structural exegesis tends to slow down the process of interpretation; the result, however, is paradoxically advantageous, for a "slow motion" viewing of a familiar text can be a stimulus to new insights. Amos Wilder suggests this possibility via a metaphor: "Structural investigation can therefore also be compared to open-heart surgery. Going deep into the sacred text the procedure appears neutral and austere, not being concerned with meaning in the usual sense. But this attention to the laws and workings of language can alert us to the bearings and dynamics of a text otherwise overlooked."[58] Thus structural exegesis may deepen understanding of the text by providing a correction of and/or complement to the historical bias of traditional biblical exegesis, by supplementing a diachronic view with a synchronic view. And structural exegesis may deepen understanding of the text by bringing into focus not only the text's syntagmatic presentation but also its paradigmatic organization.

Secondly, it seems quite possible that structural criticism may broaden our understanding of the text in relation to other texts as it broadens our understanding of the types of texts with which the biblical text may be fruitfully compared. "The promise of structuralist activity lies," Robert Spivey has suggested,

in its possibilities for reopening the biblical and early Christian tradition in a way that avoids the oppressive rigidity of much modern scholarship. By recognizing that no texts are irrelevant, by viewing in such a way that relations rather than final meanings emerge, by providing a neutral way of comparing the biblical tradition with other religious traditions, by reversing a trend toward narrow concentration on the canonical tradition, structuralism affords the opportunity to modify and renew classical biblical scholarship.[59]

Thus structural exegesis may broaden understanding of the text by drawing attention to its linguistic context as well as its historical context.

In both cases—deepening and broadening understanding of the biblical text—structural exegesis has the possibility of renewing biblical exegesis by its concentration not upon isolated elements but upon relations: relations within texts (both syntagmatic and paradigmatic) and relations between texts (both diachronic and synchronic). It may well be that as the possibilities of structural exegesis are actualized, and its problems kept in perspective, structural exegesis will be, in effect, absorbed into a more refined literary critical approach to biblical texts. "Structuralism as a distinct and controversial school," Howard Gardner suggests, "may well disappear, of course, as succeeding generations come to assimilate its basic tenets." For structuralism is, as Gardner sees it,

simply the most imaginative and suggestive current statement of the professional code of any thoughtful and synthetically oriented scientist [or interpreter]: finding the relationship between disparate phenomena, formulating them in a communicable and testable way, discovering the overall organization between parts and wholes, moving from mastery of a particular area of inquiry toward interdisciplinary syntheses which converge upon the same underlying principles.[60]

One would not seek, of course, universal agreement to Gardner's broad description of structuralism. But it does seem to me that he has appropriately described the most significant gift and demand structuralism offers, the most important contribution and confrontation structuralism presents, to New Testament studies.

Notes and References

1. This work has been stimulated in various ways: for encouraging my initial efforts to apply Lévi-Straussian thought to the New Testament, I thank Robert Spivey; for inviting this essay I thank Frank Reynolds; and especially, for arguing with me about Lévi-Strauss and Ricoeur and myth and history and whatever, I thank Frank Burch Brown.

2. Francis Bovon ("French Structuralism and Biblical Exegesis," in *Structural Analysis and Biblical Exegesis: Interpretational Essays*, trans. Alfred M. Johnson, Jr. [Pittsburgh Theological Monograph Series, 3; Pittsburgh: Pickwick Press, 1974], p. 8) applies this label within the context of *French* structuralism. Philip Pettit (*The Concept of Structuralism: A Critical Analysis* [Berkeley and Los Angeles: University of California Press, 1975], p. 68) applies the term "father of structuralism" to Lévi-Strauss in a broader context.

3. Robert M. Polzin, *Biblical Structuralism: Method and Subjectivity in the Study of Ancient Texts* (Semeia Supplements; Philadelphia: Fortress Press, 1977; Missoula, Montana: Scholars Press, 1977), p. 41.

4. Ibid., p. 17.

5. Michael Lane, ed., *Introduction to Structuralism* (New York: Basic Books, 1970), p. 12. The possible exception to this generalization is, according to Lane, the work of Roman Jakobson.

6. Ibid., p. 30.

7. Although the labels vary, see Lane, pp. 11-19; and Robert Scholes, *Structuralism in Literature: An Introduction* (New Haven and London: Yale University Press, 1974), pp. 1-12. I raise this distinction between methodology and ideology as a descriptive one, not as an evaluative one, although "ideology" or its equivalent generally serves as the negatively valued pole among commentators on structuralism. I have suggested elsewhere that structuralism—especially as it relates to biblical studies—might be regarded as pursuing four distinct yet interrelated goals: ideology, theory, structural exegesis, narrative hermeneutics (" 'No Need to Have Any One Write'?: A Structural Exegesis of 1 Thessalonians," *Society of Biblical Literature 1980 Seminar Papers* [Missoula, Montana: Scholars Press for SBL, 1980], pp. 318-21 [forthcoming in *Semeia*]; "Structuralism, Hermeneutics, and Contextual Meaning," *Journal of the American Academy of Religion* 51 [June 1983]).

8. Bovon, p. 11.

9. *Journal of American Folklore* 68 (1955): 428-44. Reprinted in *Myth: A Symposium*, ed. T. A. Sebeok (Philadelphia: American Folklore Society, 1955), pp. 50-66. Reprinted with slight modifications in Claude Lévi-Strauss, *Structural Anthropology* (New York: Basic Books, 1963), pp. 206-231.

10. Trans. Nicholas Mann, in *The Structural Study of Myth and Totemism*, ed. Edmund Leach (London: Tavistock Publications, 1967), pp. 1-47. Reprinted in Claude Lévi-Strauss, *Structural Anthropology*, Vol. 2 (New York: Basic Books, 1976), pp. 146-97.

11. E.g., Daniel Patte, *What Is Structural Exegesis?* (Philadelphia: Fortress Press, 1976), pp. 53-83; Daniel Patte, "Structural Analysis of the Parable of the Prodigal Son: Toward a Method," in *Semiology and Parables*, ed. Daniel Patte (Pittsburgh Theological Monograph Series, 9; Pittsburgh: Pickwick Press, 1976), pp. 119-42; Elizabeth Struthers Malbon, "Mythic Structure and Meaning in Mark: Elements of a Lévi-Straussian Analysis," *Semeia* 16 (1979): 97-132; Elizabeth Struthers Malbon, " 'No Need to Have Any One Write'?."

12. E.g., Paul Ricoeur, *The Conflict of Interpretations: Essays in Hermeneutics*, ed. Don Ihde (Evanston: Northwestern University Press, 1974), pp. 27-61 ("Structure and Hermeneutics"), pp. 79-96 ("Structure, Word, Event"). See below.

13. .E.g., Polzin, pp. iv, 40-43 (and this may qualify as a "tirade"), 47; Brian W. Kovacs, "Philosophical Foundations for Structuralism," *Semeia* 10 (1978): 85; Robert C. Culley, "Structural Analysis: Is It Done With Mirrors?," *Interpretation* 28 (1974): 165.

14. E.g., Miriam Glucksmann, *Structuralist Analysis in Contemporary Social Thought: A Comparison of the Theories of Claude Lévi-Strauss and Louis Althusser* (International Library of Science; London and Boston: Routledge & Kegan Paul, 1974), pp. 31-32; K. O. L. Burridge, "Lévi-Strauss and Myth," in *The Structural Study of Myth and Totemism*, ed. Edmund Leach (London: Tavistock Publications, 1967), pp. 96-97 (Lévi-Strauss "is absolutely his contrary self"), 98, 111, 113.

15. Edmund Leach, Introduction to *The Structural Study of Myth and Totemism*, p. xvii.

16. Mary Douglas, "The Meaning of Myth, with special reference to 'La Geste d'Asdiwal,'" in *The Structural Study of Myth and Totemism*, p. 50. Pettit finds Douglas's statement "a useful word of policy" (p. 82).

17. Howard Gardner, *The Quest for Mind: Piaget, Lévi-Strauss and the Structuralist Movement* (New York: Alfred A. Knopf, 1972), p. 117.

18. Ibid., p. 158.

19. Ibid., pp. 244-45. It may perhaps be said that "The Structural Study of Myth" (with its charts and its "formula") and "The Story of Asdiwal" (with its schemata) represent the more Apollonian side of Lévi-Strauss's expression, whereas the four volumes of the *Mythologiques* (E.T.: *Introduction to a Science of Mythology*, trans. John Weightman and Doreen Weightman, vol. 1: *The Raw and the Cooked*; vol. 2: *From Honey to Ashes*; vol. 3: *The Origin of Table Manners*; vol. 4: *The Naked Man*; 4 vols. [New York: Harper & Row, 1969-81]) represent the more Dionysian side of Lévi-Strauss's thinking and writing. *Both* sides need to be taken into account by interpreters.

20. Gardner, p. 12.

21. See, e.g.: Robert A. Spivey, "Structuralism and Biblical Studies: The Uninvited Guest," *Interpretation* 28 (1974): 143-45; Anthony C. Thiselton, "Keeping Up With Recent Studies. II. Structuralism and Biblical Studies: Method or Ideology?," *Expository Times* 89 (1978): 329, 331, 334; Vern S. Poythress, "Structuralism and Biblical Studies," *Journal of the Evangelical Theological Society* 21 (1978): 232-33; D. A. Carson, "Hermeneutics: A Brief Assessment of Some Recent Trends," *Themelios* 5 (1980): 17.

22. Patte, *What Is Structural Exegesis?*, pp. 9-20, 14.

23. Dan O. Via, Jr., *Kerygma and Comedy in the New Testament: A Structuralist Approach to Hermeneutic* (Philadelphia: Fortress Press, 1975), p. 2.

24. Edgar V. McKnight, *Meaning in Texts: The Historical Shaping of a Narrative Hermeneutics* (Philadelphia: Fortress Press, 1978), p. 242. Cf. Polzin, p. 201.

25. "Biblical Hermeneutics," *Semeia* 4 (1975): 29.

26. "The Meaning of Myth," pp. 67-68.

27. Via also perceives the necessity of such a distinction, commenting, for example, that "Marxsen denies internal temporality but is concerned about Mark's diachronic relation to its own time" (p. 116).

28. "The Story of Asdiwal," p. 1.

29. *Introduction to a Science of Mythology*, Vol. 1 (New York: Harper & Row, Harper Colophon Books, 1969, 1975), p. 1.

30. McKnight notes that "Not only is historical investigation necessary for structural analysis in the view of Lévi-Strauss, but structural analysis may validate historical interpretation" (p. 137). McKnight presents a Lévi-Straussian example of such "validation" on pp. 137-38, but see also the caution presented below.

31. "The Story of Asdiwal," p. 29.

32. Ibid., pp. 29-30. This does not mean, however, that the myth is to be read as a transcript of sociological/psychological reality. Lévi-Strauss criticizes "psychoanalysts and many anthropologists" with whom "the interpretation becomes too easy: if a given mythology confers prominence to a certain character, let us say an evil grandmother, it will be claimed that in such a society grandmothers are actually evil and that mythology reflects the social structure and social relations; but should the actual data be conflicting, it would be readily claimed that the purpose of mythology is to provide an outlet for repressed feelings" ("The Structural Study of Myth," p. 429).

33. "The Structural Study of Myth," p. 431.

34. Ibid., p. 433.
35. "The Story of Asdiwal," p. 21. Compare this description of the process of "global integration": "the myth is finally reduced to its two extreme propositions [paradigm], the initial state of affairs and the final [syntagm], which together summarize its operational function" (Ibid.).
36. Compare the discussion of syntagm and paradigm by Via (pp. 155-63; see also pp. 30-31) and see especially his conclusion (p. 162).
37. As Lévi-Strauss may be said to "correct" Vladimir Propp's over emphasis of the syntagmatic by an emphasis on the paradigmatic (see Susan Wittig, "The Historical Development of Structuralism," *Soundings* 58 [1975]: 153-58), so Daniel Patte and Aline Patte may be said to "correct" Lévi-Strauss's over emphasis of the paradigmatic by combining it with an emphasis on the syntagmatic based on a reading of Greimas (Patte and Patte, *Structural Exegesis: From Theory to Practice* [Philadelphia: Fortress Press, 1978]). Although I agree with Patte and Patte that the interrelation of the syntagmatic and the paradigmatic is sometimes overlooked in the work of Lévi-Strauss, I find their "correction" problematic.
38. Lévi-Strauss, "The Story of Asdiwal," p. 1.
39. Compare Polzin's observations about the Book of Job: ". . . the story is a paradigm. What is on the surface a diachronic linear treatment of a problem reveals itself as containing an underlying or latent synchronic structure" (p. 74).
40. Werner H. Kelber, *The Kingdom in Mark: A New Place and a New Time* (Philadelphia: Fortress Press, 1974). The influence of Weeden is, of course, obvious at this point (see Kelber, p. xi). See Theodore J. Weeden, "The Heresy that Necessitated Mark's Gospel," *Zeitschrift für die neutestamentliche Wissenschaft* 59 (1968): 145-58; and *Mark — Traditions in Conflict* (Philadelphia: Fortress Press, 1971). However, whereas Weeden views the Markan disciples as representatives of a false *theios anēr* (divine man) christology, Kelber links them with a false eschatology.
41. Kelber, *Kingdom*, p. 130: "So much in sympathy with Galilee is the author, and so tangibly does he argue from the perspective of its Jewish-Christian community that it seems plausible to see in him the spokesman of Galilean Christians. Galilee in its broadest sense, including the Decapolis and the area of Tyre and Sidon as outlined by Mark, furnishes the setting in life for Mark the evangelist."
42. The name "Galilee," which means "ring, circle," was, according to K. W. Clark, probably given to the district "in recognition of the circle of Gentile nations which had infiltrated the region" ("Galilee, Sea of," *Interpreter's Dictionary of the Bible*, vol. 2, p. 348).
43. Commentators who seek in Mark's gospel the "history of Jesus" suggest that Jesus "manifested a freshness and independence of mind as to the meaning and application of the Law, consonant with the religious spirit of the *galil*," that is, consonant with "the modified orthodoxy of Jews in the *galil* of the Gentiles" (K. W. Clark, "Galilee," *Interpreter's Dictionary of the Bible*, vol. 2, p. 347). Whatever the history, the Markan meaning remains: the traditional order (associated with Judea) is challenged by a new order (associated with Jesus of Nazareth in Galilee).
44. The above two paragraphs are taken from my "Galilee and Jerusalem: History and Literature in Marcan Interpretation" (*Catholic Biblical Quarterly* 44 [1982]: 252-53), which develops more fully this Markan example of diachronic (historical) and synchronic (literary) approaches.
45. It seems to me ironic that Kelber's "Mark" devotes all his energy to rescuing the parousia hope from its literal and dogmatic attachment to Jerusalem only to attach it just as literally and dogmatically to Galilee. The gospel of such a Mark would not be "good news" for long, and this is, in fact, Kelber's evaluation (p. 141).
46. Kelber, *Kingdom*, especially chapters V and VI. John R. Donahue, S.J., *Are You the Christ? The Trial Narrative in the Gospel of Mark* (Society of Biblical Literature Dissertation Series, 10; Missoula, Montana: Society of Biblical Literature, 1973), especially pp. 113-35. Donald Juel, *Messiah and Temple: The Trial of Jesus in the Gospel of Mark* (Society of Biblical Literature Dissertation Series, 31; Missoula, Montana: Scholars Press for Society of Biblical Literature, 1977), especially chapter 6, "The Temple Theme in Mark."
47. See my "*Tē Oikia Autou*: Mark 2:15 in Context," *New Testament Studies*, forthcoming.
48. See, e.g., Kelber's reading of the "here" and "there" of Mark 13:21 as a reference to Jerusalem (p. 116) and "the mountains" of Mark 13:14 as a reference to Galilee (p. 121).
49. Malbon, "Galilee and Jerusalem," p. 247.
50. Via, pp. 93-94: "To suppose that the historical phenomena somehow caused the text of Mark is to assume that language is an icon, that the text is primarily a reflection of the historical reality outside of itself. This view fails to recognize that both texts and history as meaningful are generated by 'grammars' or systems of meaning, linguistic competences which are sub-

structures of a fundamental matrix of possibilities of meaning. It has never been proved that the grammar of history is ontologically or epistemologically prior to the grammar (genre) of texts." Cf. the comments of Kovacs on the epistemological priority of structural criticism.

51. Claude Lévi-Strauss, "A Confrontation," *New Left Review* 62 (1970): 57-74 [ET of "Responses a quelques questions," *Esprit* 31 (1963): 628-53].

52. Ibid., p. 63.

53. On myth vs. history and myth and history in the larger sense, see especially: Claude Lévi-Strauss, *Myth and Meaning* (New York: Schocken Books, 1979), pp. 34-43 ("When Myth Becomes History"); and *Myth and the Crisis of Historical Consciousness*, ed. Lee W. Gibbs and W. Taylor Stevenson (Missoula, Montana: Scholars Press for The American Academy of Religion, 1975).

54. See, e.g., the comments of McKnight and Via cited above (p. 5; n. 50). Even New Testament scholars who are far from choosing a structuralist approach have raised questions (from a variety of theological orientations) concerning the adequacy of the historical-critical method as currently practiced in biblical studies; see, e.g. Reginald H. Fuller, "What Is Happening in New Testament Studies?," *Saint Luke's Journal of Theology* 23 (1980): 90-100.

55. Lévi-Strauss, "A Confrontation," pp. 71-72.

56. On the approach not chosen by Lévi-Strauss, Gardner comments: "In the dazzlingly obscure closing chapter of *The Savage Mind*, a lengthy and sharp attack on the dialectical materialism of his polemical rival Jean-Paul Sartre, Lévi-Strauss tries to show that the genetic approach to history is not free of myth-making" (p. 189).

57. John R. Donahue, S. J., "Two Decades of Markan Research," Address given at the Catholic Biblical Association General Meeting, University of Detroit, 17 August 1977, in memory of Norman Perrin (text supplied by the author).

58. Amos N. Wilder, "Semeia: An Experimental Journal for Biblical Criticism—An Introduction," *Semeia* 1 (1974): 10-11.

59. Spivey, p. 143.

60. Gardner, p. 11.

CHAPTER IX

Lévi-Strauss and the Structural Analysis of the Hebrew Bible

David Jobling

Direct applications of the work of Claude Lévi-Strauss to the Hebrew Bible by specialists in Hebrew Bible have not been numerous.[1] There have indeed been a good many such applications by others, including scholars in the general area of religious studies, to which reference will here be made; on the other hand, Hebrew Bible specialists have offered structural analyses along other than Lévi-Straussian lines.[2] I write as a specialist in Hebrew Bible, who for about a decade has worked intensively in structuralist exegesis, and whose own field has been opened up to him by Lévi-Strauss as by no other single figure. I am a partisan, therefore, but not an uncritical one; for certainly there are limitations to the applicability of Lévi-Straussian method within my field. Lévi-Strauss has, indeed, expressed his own misgivings, and these will form the basis of my discussion in Section I. Section II will deal in a general way with the effect Lévi-Strauss has had upon study of the Hebrew Bible, while in Section III I shall offer practical examples from my own exegetical work.

I. "RÉ PONSES À QUELQUES QUESTIONS": A RESPONSE

Lévi-Strauss expressed his misgivings about the application of his methods to the Hebrew Bible in 1963, in the context of a forum at which Paul Ricoeur, particularly, raised critical issues about Lévi-Strauss's neglect of western mythologies.[3] I believe that the problems raised can be answered in such a way as to make the use of Lévi-Strauss's approach legitimate. But they cannot be brushed aside cavalierly; in fact, they can be dealt with only by exploring a broad intellectual context. His misgivings seem to crystallize into three (with, perhaps, a rider to the first of them), all of them related to his concept of "pure" myth (my term). When myth is functioning in an unspoiled way, its "constraints are of a purely internal order",[4] that is, the elements of perception are freely combinable and recombinable for the carrying out of any intellectual task, without the constraint of conformity to any prior intellectual scheme. Leach puts it in terms of "a random distribution of the more superficially meaningful elements in the system".[5] The obvious analogy, which I shall repeatedly invoke, is to dream-discourse, as it is related to rational waking discourse.

The mythic materials of the Hebrew Bible have first, Lévi-Strauss suggests, been "deformed" by the "intellectual operation" to which the redactors have submitted them.[6] Conscious effort to make myth "make sense", that is, conform to a rational scheme, stifles the free recombination. Reflection on mythic oppositions weakens them, and eventually renders them unrecognizable. To this one may reply—and surely Lévi-Strauss would agree—that *any* human discourse will have mythic and reflective dimensions. "Pure" myth is a limiting case which is never actually found; while reflection, never able to resolve the basic oppositions with which myth works, can only suppress mythic operations, not abolish them. What we need is methods powerful enough to discern the deep-structural oppositions; given such methods, mythic analysis of any discourse is in principle possible. Daniel and Aline Patte, for instance, formulate a method of great power.[7] In terms of the psychological analogy, the analyst would dearly love to work with the "raw" dream-discourse, but it is never available—it must be recovered from an always more or less reflective waking discourse. I find it difficult, in fact, to see why one who counts Freud and Marx as key to his intellectual ancestry should be so cautious on this point.[8] Edmund Leach and Robert C. Marshall, for instance, seem to me thoroughly Lévi-Straussian when they suggest that large amounts of biblical narrative function to mediate, in post-exilic Judaism, contradictions whose existence could not be overtly admitted.[9]

The rider to this first misgiving is another issue which arose in the debate with Ricoeur, but which seems to me not to be clearly worked out there—whether there is an intrinsic limit to one's ability to analyze the myths of *one's own* culture, because of one's interiorization of them. Lévi-Strauss suggests, if I understand him, that this is *not* one of the reasons for his avoidance of western mythologies.[10] But the point remains an interesting one, and suggests again the psychological analogy—analysis implies self-analysis.[11] Again, we are looking at something requiring special and powerful methods, not at something intrinsically impossible.

Lévi-Strauss's second misgiving is that we possess very little of the ethnographic description of ancient Israel necessary if we are to understand what it is that the "random" mythic elements are conceptually organizing, so that we must fall into a *petitio principii* or vicious circle.[12] Leach's rebuttal is well taken, that Lévi-Strauss has tackled the myths of peoples of whom we certainly have no better knowledge than of the ancient Israelites,[13] but there is more to be said. Even in the absence of *external* ethnographic evidence, the text of the Hebrew Bible provides us with many ethnographic data—the same text that we analyze for mythic structure. The psychological analogy holds yet again. Lévi-Strauss's point might be expressed by saying that we can no more analyze the myth without knowing the myth-makers than we can analyze the dream without knowing the dreamer. But we may reply that the *one* discourse of the patient that is analyzed for deep psychic structures also provides referential information about the "reality" to which those structures are related. Even so mythic a text as Genesis 2-3 posits a social structure (the relationships between the sexes) in connection with which the myth is to be read. A fuller discussion of this point would include also the literary critical canon that a text should *first* be read as a system of intrinsic meanings and only then as a system of references—it is not that the text does not refer outside itself, but rather that the referential meanings have become part of the meaning-system of the text, and need to be accounted for *first* at this level.[14] Such a method of reading is certainly fraught with difficulty, and may have to proceed by successive approximations, but to call it impossible would be a total negation of recent trends in literary criticism.

Lévi-Strauss's final misgiving has to do with the effect of "historical" thinking on myth. In his "Réponses", this point is not clearly separated from the general "deforming" effect of intellectual operation (cf. above),[15] but it is worth dealing with separately, particularly so far as the Hebrew Bible is concerned. It is a severe constraint on mythic discourse to have to conform to events remembered (perhaps one ought to formulate this more generally as events whose factuality is felt in the society to be testable). But, we may reply, the reversion of such events into myth appears to be a normal and rather rapid process. Leach aptly points out how, among the English, the facts of Tudor history have already "come to be remembered as systems of patterned contradiction".[16] Relevant to this process is the work of Hayden White, not to mention that of Sellar and Yeatman![17] For Hebrew Bible, an important methodological issue is involved. It is interesting that scholars who do not view it with the specialist's eye, such as Leach and Marshall, automatically regard it *as a whole*, as the *canon* of post-exilic Judaism.[18] From this perspective, they are fully justified in working with the ancient traditions as "mythology", as "remythologization". The freedom with which, according to Leach, Judaism could work out its concerns through recombination of Solomon traditions (or, according to Marshall, Moses traditions) is scarcely affected by the value the historian finds in them for reconstructing the 10th century (or the 13th)—and one can make this point without in any way sharing Leach's "absurd historical scepticism".[19] Pre-exilic "history" becomes the stuff of post-exilic mythology. This is an issue that biblical specialists ought to ponder deeply, especially before doing structural analyses. It may be that Lévi-Strauss's methods are much more appropriately applied to the (late) total canon than to some group of passages considered to be "primitive".[20] Though such a "canonical" approach coincides with a recent trend in mainstream biblical scholarship,[21] it is not yet the approach we historically trained specialists are used to. I would affirm that structural analysis needs to begin at the canonical level, but would question whether it needs to end there. Is it possible to relate Lévi-Straussian analysis, performed on the final form of the text, to the text's historical development, to analyze it, that is, at the level of its hypothetical stages? I have explored in a very preliminary way the notion of the text's literary history being "inscribed" in the text itself, and Marshall makes some intriguing comments that point in the same direction; no one, so far as I am aware, has proposed a convincing method.[22] However, the matter needs to be considered since there is otherwise no obvious justification for applying Lévi-Strauss's methods to this or that piece of ancient Israelite tradition.

So much, then, for the issues Lévi-Strauss himself has raised. My own major problem lies in a different direction—it has to do not with the legitimacy of applying his methods, but with their inadequacy in one enormously important respect. The Hebrew Bible, at least the mostly prose material constituting roughly its first half (where most of my own work has been done) is overwhelmingly *sequential*. Genesis through II Kings (excluding Ruth), to which the term Primary Narrative has been aptly applied,[23] is a single narrative sequence marked not only by its immense extent, but by the great effort that has gone into supplying narrative links between highly disparate kinds of literature. The mythic material that Lévi-Strauss has worked with consists mostly of discrete pieces without narrative connection, and he himself regards narrative as a debasement of myth.[24] Thus, not only must any application of his work to the Hebrew Bible be complemented by the theory of structural analysis of narrative,[25] but Lévi-Straussian structuralism must be related *theoretically* to other approaches. Some such theoretical work exists, but the application of it to Hebrew Bible remains daunting.[26] In fact, work on Hebrew Bible inspired by Lévi-Strauss has normally consisted of setting discrete units in paradigmatic relationships, without regard to their narrative sequence.[27] In "The Legitimacy of Solomon", Leach shows an awareness of the issue; upon completion of his paradigmatic analysis, he presents I Samuel 4-II Kings 2 as a three-act play, and concludes that "the chronological sequence is itself of structural significance".[28] The attempt is admirable, though it rests on no theoretical base in narratology.

II. LÉVI-STRAUSS AND THE HEBREW BIBLE: A CRITICAL SURVEY

It is my intention here to look at ways in which Lévi-Strauss has been applied to the Hebrew Bible and, in doing so, to suggest some criteria for effective application of his approach. I may mention first a number of technical studies based on his kinship theory.[29] While I have been instructed by these, I am not equipped to assess them. To pursue such a line, one needs to be or to make oneself a competent anthropologist, and the number of biblical specialists doing so will probably remain small. Of course, kinship study can contribute to broader interpretive issues—it lies at the basis of Leach's far-reaching essay on "The Legitimacy of Solomon", and Andriolo has proposed a quite direct relationship between kinship patterns and theological mindset in the Hebrew Bible.[30]

It was no doubt natural that some of the first applications of Lévi-Strauss should be to the most overtly "mythic" sections of the Bible, and particularly to the first chapters of Genesis. It is doubtful whether Leach's two essays on these chapters are to be taken as more than a trial balloon, though they are a bit more than "a game".[31] Certainly they are not very successful—Carroll in particular has shown that, though soundly locating binary oppositions, Leach has been much less than plausible in finding their mediations.[32] A much more substantial effort on these chapters is Matthieu Casalis's "The Dry and the Wet", in which he makes use of much Lévi-Straussian theory (e.g., the idea of "codes"), and extends the analysis to other Near Eastern mythologies than the Hebraic.[33] But the "Genesis as Myth" seam is likely to be rapidly exhausted since little of the Hebrew Bible is so overtly mythic. Ongoing significance of Lévi-Strauss as a methodological impulse to biblical exegesis seems to me, therefore, to depend upon the productivity of his insights in relationship to our text as a whole. But before looking at the studies, a more general methodological comment is necessary.

There is a widespread impression that structuralists posit a few deductive models for analysis of great precision and immense (claimed) generality; and this has often been the view taken of Lévi-Strauss even by some of those attempting to apply his work to the Hebrew Bible. This view, at best limited—I would be prepared to say, down-right wrong—is the result of overemphasis on the essay "The Structural Study of Myth".[34] I have not done a survey, but I would be surprised if, of the references to Lévi-Strauss in works on the Hebrew Bible, less than three-quarters were to this one essay. Some techniques of analysis are sketched there, and it is not surprising that these should have dominated early "applications"—compare, among a number of instances, the use of columnar presentation of myths by Casalis, of the converging diagram for "mediations" by Roth, of the formula for mythic transformation by Polzin.[35] But any suggestion that "The Structural Study of Myth" provides adequate insight into what Lévi-Strauss actually *does* with myths is absurd; it applies the methods only to a few odds and ends of Amerindian mythology and to the Oedipus myth, the latter application being little more than a *bagatelle* which, despite Lévi-Strauss's unambiguous disclaimers, still is regarded by some as his great word on mythology. His real work on myth, aside from the classic "Asdiwal"[36] and a rather small number of other essays, is in the massive *Introduction to a Science of Mythology*,[37] and it is there we should go for true insight into his reading of myths and for a proper perspective on the matters briefly introduced in "The Structural Study of Myth".

Lévi-Strauss seems to me stimulating in two main ways. First, he provides a whole range of critical concepts clearly enough defined to be useful, and yet of sufficient comprehensiveness and openness to be related to a wide variety of textual phenomena.[38] The main ones are *binary thinking* and *mediation*; myth as generated by *contradictions* in experience; the substitution of *paradigm* for *syntagm*; the notion of *code*, with its value for preliminary semantic organization; that of *residue*, leading into an iterative process whereby what is bracketed at one stage of analysis becomes the material for the next stage; myths as *transformations* of each other. These are powerful concepts which suggest powerful methods without precisely defining them. Secondly, Lévi-Strauss fascinates as well as instructs by his ability to *make good moves* in myth analysis; to create constantly, that is, methods that are *ad hoc* to the immediate texts, yet comprehensibly related to larger methodological principles such as the ones I have just listed. To the *bricolage* of myth-making there must answer a *bricolage* of myth-interpretation! A quotation from Greimas well describes Lévi-Strauss's practical myth-analysis—one attempts "whenever one is confronted by a phenomenon which has not been analyzed, (to construct) a representation of it in such a way that the model is more general than the case under examination requires, so that the observed phenomenon registers itself (*s'y inscrive*) as one of (the model's) variables."[39]

For me, therefore, the best applications of Lévi-Strauss are those which are not straightly constrained methodologically, but those which are methodologically fecund without being promiscuous. Thus approaches like those of Carroll, and even of Casalis, are still too constrained—Carroll makes a bold attempt to make sense of Lévi-Strauss's formula for mythic transformation and applies his revised version to some biblical texts, but the exercise retains a sense of artificiality;[40] Casalis, though freer, aims to follow specific techniques of Lévi-Strauss as far as possible.[41] It is above all to Edmund Leach, in "the Legitimacy of Solomon", that we should be grateful, for reinterpreting Lévi-Straussian concepts in biblical terms, for attempting to apply them to "historical" materials, as well as for operating with them with notable freedom and creativity. Our debt at this point seems to me entirely to transcend the many technical errors he has been convicted of making.[42] His thesis that a great deal of the narrative prose in the Hebrew Bible has been generated by the need to prove Solomon legitimate is of the same kind as that of Robert C. Marshall in another application of Lévi-Strauss that is admirably free and original. Marshall studies "the Moses myth" as it has been deposited in the canonical text, and identifies "the major contradiction at the base of the myth as that between the notions of Law and Land as they develop in Israelite politico-religious thought."[43] That this contradiction was utterly basic to the development of post-exilic Judaism is clear, and this is why Marshall's approach to the Moses material seems a valuable one, even before detailed exegesis tests the results he achieves.

III. AN EXEGETICAL EXAMPLE: "THE JORDAN A BOUNDARY"

The following example is a fairly complex one, and deliberately so. It possesses something of the complexity of Lévi-Strauss's analyses of Amerindian mythology—he does not set artificial limits to his investigation, but follows the mythic connections where they seem to lead. My analysis will be far from complete, but I hope to show the sort of question in biblical studies to which Lévi-Straussian methods are applicable, and the scope and intricacy such application will sometimes have. I shall employ techniques derived directly from Lévi-Strauss: the analysis by codes, for which I prefer the term *isotopy*[44], and the reading of data paradigmatically. At the same time I shall stress what I have defined already as the major limitation of his method, namely its inability to

The two stories share a basic structure:

(a) A Transjordanian initiative sets the story in motion (Numbers 32:1-5, Joshua 22:10).

(b) Moses/the Cisjordanians express anger at the initiative, putting the worst possible construction upon it at first. They make use of allusions to the past to establish their case (Numbers 32:6-15, Joshua 22:11-20).

(c) The Transjordanians make a suggestion/response which is satisfactory, and provides the substance of a bargain (Numbers 32:16-19, Joshua 22:22-29).

(d) The bargain is accepted by Moses/the Cisjordanians (Numbers 32:20-24, Joshua 22:30-31).

The parties have basic aims, or "narrative programs", [48] which persist through both stories. The Transjordanians, who take the initiative, seek to be a geographically separate part of Israel, but to maintain their identity as adherents of Yahweh. Story II fills out these aims; they intend to carry out their duty to attend the western sanctuary; also, fearing eventual excommunication, they desire a guarantee of their status. Moses/the Cisjordanians, who are largely in a reactive situation, have aims of their own. They wish Israel to be/remain settled in the west; but this future they see as depending upon Israel's status before Yahweh, a status which may be threatened by Transjordanian actions. In what seems a paranoid way, they accuse the Transjordanians of deliberately making Yahweh angry, to the peril of the whole people. And, though they eventually acquiesce in the Transjordanian aims, in each story we find hints of a desire that the Transjordanians will *eventually* resettle with their fellows in the west (Numbers 32:30 – a most curious sanction should the Transjordanians break their promise! – and Joshua 22:19). Thus one may surmise that Moses/the Cisjordanians most basically see the Transjordanians as disunifiers of Israel, and cherish the hope of reunification.

To conclude this stage of analysis, we note the views the narration takes of the two parties. Moses/the Cisjordanians are quick to anger and ungenerous in their interpretations, though eventually open to compromise. The attitude towards the Transjordanians is harder to pin down. In Story I, they are so accommodating as to win the reader's sympathy away from Moses. They would do so again in Story II were it not for their deviousness. If their intentions in building the altar were so honorable, why did they not make them known? Their pious invocations of Yahweh in Joshua 22:22 look like "protesting too much"! Their readiness for compromise and avoidance of conflict is perhaps more like glibness in talking themselves out of a corner.

C. Syntagmatic reading of the two stories

A good deal might be said under this heading – in various ways the forming of the two stories into a sequence makes one read each in the light of the other.

But there is only one really significant point to be made, for it quite escapes the Lévi-Straussian paradigmatic reading. Story I is complete at Joshua 22:6; grammatically, as well as thematically, "and they went to their homes" marks a closure. No room is left for anything that happened on the way. But something did happen on the way, and this is made possible by the skillful *reopening* of Story I in vs. 7b (note the repetition of the verbs of vs. 6, "bless", "send away"). The harshness of the reopening is softened by vs. 8, which belongs to Story I, and looks like an afterthought. But the reopening, once achieved, is confirmed by the wording of vs. 9, "(they) left . . . *in order to go* to their own land," leaving room for new action *en route*. What is the effect of all this? A story of a conflict fully and happily resolved becomes the story of a conflict which issued only in further conflict. Is there not significance in this? Despite the resolution of the second conflict later in the chapter, conflict between Cis-/and Transjordanians has acquired a quality of recurrence, which makes the narrative redoubling much more than a factor of two.

D. Isotopic analysis of the two stories

One of Lévi-Strauss's major contributions to analysis is the definition of *codes*, pre-existing semantic fields associated with a dimension of experience or perception, and in relation to which semantic features of a text may be organized (for example, "alimentary" or "topographic" codes). Following Greimas (see note 44), I prefer the term "isotopy", which is less open to confusion – by it I mean a semantic category broadly enough defined to subsume a large number of meaning-elements (sememes) in the text, but precisely enough for useful organization of these elements. In the following analysis I shall draw, as part of the two stories, on the allusions which each makes to past incidents (Numbers 13-14 in Story I, Numbers 25 and Joshua 7 in Story II). For the effect of these allusions is to invite a paradigmatic comparison of our main stories with the stories alluded to.

(i) THE UNITY OF ISRAEL (POLITICAL ISOTOPY)

By their initial request in Numbers 32:1-5, the Transjordanians break the *integrity* of Israel. One people about to enter one land becomes two groups with different territorial intentions. The Cisjordanians interpret non-integrity as *division*, which means danger from Yahweh (since it tends to turn into religious division). The Transjordanians are quick to negate all thought of such division, and equilibrium is attained – but the Cisjordanians are still prone to ask, "If Israel is indeed undivided, why not demonstrate this by geographical integrity?" The concepts of the nature of Israel's unity held by the two sides are profoundly different; for the Cisjordanians, unity means integrity, and non-integrity is division. For the Transjordanians, unity need not depend upon integrity.[49]

It is instructive to consider the terminology used for the two parties, by the parties themselves, and by the narrator. There are two basic options:

(a) $\dfrac{\text{Transjordanians}}{\text{Cisjordanians}}$ $=$ $\dfrac{\text{“you”}}{\text{“your brethren”}}$

(b) $\dfrac{\text{Transjordanians}}{\text{Cisjordanians}}$ $=$ $\dfrac{?}{\text{“the people of Israel”}}$

Option (a), which occurs in Numbers 32:6 (Moses' first remark), and exclusively in Joshua's speech (Joshua 22:1-8), tends to include the Transjordanians as part of Israel. Option (b), which occurs in one form or another almost everywhere else, excludes the Transjordanians (the ? ought to be "non-Israelites", though this conclusion is not drawn). The occurences of (a) frame Story I, giving to it an inclusive cast, and the occurences of (b) in Story I do not give the impression of being deliberately "loaded". The occurences of (b) in Story II *do* give this impression; even at the point of conciliation (Joshua 22:31), the "we" and the "people of Israel" in Phinehas's speech are hard to interpret inclusively since the narrative reverts to option (b) in vs. 32-33. The two stories give different impressions; Story I varies its rhetoric to give a movement of unity lost and regained, while Story II subsumes this movement under a rhetoric which implies non-unity throughout.

The allusions to previous incidents have a contribution to make. If Israel's unity on which its position before Yahweh depends is so fragile, even a single individual, let alone two tribes and a half, can threaten it. This is the message of both the Peor (cf. Numbers 25:6-18) and the Achan stories, the latter being indeed *locus classicus* for this affirmation, a point not missed in the retelling – "wrath fell upon all the congregation of Israel though he (Achan) was but one man" (Joshua 22:20). An *a fortiori* argument is implied – the Transjordanians' offense is worse than the earlier ones. Rather different is the point implied by the exemplary punishment of the offenders as individuals (as opposed to the general punishment on Israel), which occurs not only in Numbers 14:36-38, but also in both the Peor and the Achan stories: Though you Transjordanians will bring trouble on all Israel, this seems to say, be sure you will bring special trouble on yourselves.

(ii) Israel's land (geographical isotopy)

Story I casts no doubt on the status of Transjordan as Israelite territory – it is indeed described as "the land which Yahweh smote before the congregation of Israel." (Numbers 32:4). But Story II explicitly contrasts Transjordan with "Yahweh's Land" and raises the possibility of its being "unclean". It is significant in this connection that in both stories the Transjordanians undertake *to cross the Jordan for the service of Yahweh*. Since this obligation means that they are on Cisjordanian soil only temporarily, it is a renewable obligation, as the redoubling of Story I by Story II underlines. Is it the point that those whose status as Israelites is rendered dubious by their Transjordanian residence acquire sanctity by crossing the Jordan for the service of Yahweh? This question will be of special importance for the next section.

Of the enclosed stories the following may be said: Numbers 13-14, though concerned with a different boundary, has the element of entering the land and returning for the service of Yahweh. But only those of the spies acquire grace thereby who make the proper response to the land. Numbers 25 shows Israel, or some element of it, tempted *to remain in Transjordan for the service of another god*. And the Achan story, in the form in which we have it in Joshua 7, shows remarkable similarity in its structural elements to Numbers 13-14:

> Sending of spies (vs. 2)
> Their favourable report (vs. 3)
> Premature, unsuccessful attack (vs. 4-5)
> Complaint (by *Joshua*) (vs. 6-9)
> Revelation of sin (vs. 10-21)
> Exemplary punishment (vs. 22-26)

All the implications cannot be pursued, but the point of major interest is the wish expressed by Joshua in vs. 7, "Would that we had been content to dwell beyond the Jordan!", a wish for which he is not rebuked. If not crossing the Jordan is sin, then sin is in a sense equivalent to not crossing the Jordan. The presence of uncleanness makes the attempt upon the land *premature*, and its removal will allow a successful occupation (Joshua 8).

(ii) Children and Women (Temporal/Generational Isotopy)

In Story I, in the Numbers 13-14 story to which it makes allusion, and in Story II there is a concern for the coming generation which amounts to an *idée fixe*. In Story I, the Transjordanians reiterate the need to provide for their "little ones" (Numbers 32:16, 17, 26, cf. 24), while showing almost no comparable concern for their wives (in vs. 26 they do appear, *after* the little ones). Adult males are to risk themselves, children are to be safeguarded, and women are scarcely an issue. In Story II, the great concern of the Transjordanians is that their *children* may be disinherited, and it is to safeguard the interests of coming generations that they take, at least as the story stands, the risk of internecine warfare. In this light, the dynamic of Numbers 13-14 stands out very clear, and it is in this connection that Moses' allusion has its appositeness. The wilderness generation which refused to enter the land did so on the grounds that they would be risking their wives and little ones (Numbers 14:3). But in Yahweh's response, it is the little ones who become significant (vs. 31). It is they, for whom such false concern has been shown, who will be the object of Yahweh's concern. Yahweh will uphold *their* interest in the land, while the present generation will not see that land.

In one sense, the message is everywhere the same. Authentic provision for coming generations consists in faithfully entering the land for the service of Yahweh, even at risk to the present generation. This accounts at one level for the greater prominence of children than of women, where the safety of both is at issue (women being in any case, no doubt, semantically akin to the coming generation). Nor is the syntagmatic point to be overlooked that the "little ones" of Numbers 13-14 become the adult generation of Numbers 32 and Joshua 22, again underlining the element of *recurrence* generation by generation.

But none of this says anything specific about the Transjordanians. They are (at best) Israelites *outside the land*, or at least in a dubious part of it. Their situation is regularized by crossing the Jordan for the service of Yahweh. This logically means that each new generation is born in irregularity, and must *renew* its connection with Yahweh's land. But, whether it be for war or for the service of the sanctuary, it is only the males who are under this obligation. Thus while each new (male) generation of Transjordanians create a problem which can be solved, Transjordanian women are a potentially dangerous anomaly, dealt with in these texts at least, largely by silence. But we note that the Peor story of Numbers 25, to which Story II alludes, raises the issue of Transjordanian women to paramount importance—it was women who tempted Israel to remain on the wrong side of the Jordan.[50]

(i) Text and context; some examples and problems

The remaining part of my analysis, which will be extremely incomplete, is made up of a few examples of how the interpretation of Numbers 32 and Joshua 22 depends on the larger narrative context of which these chapters form a part. My chief aim is to show the relative significance of paradigmatic and syntagmatic readings. Example (i) is purely paradigmatic, (ii) largely syntagmatic — concerned with the specifics of narrative sequence — while in (iii) paradigmatic and syntagmatic dimensions are particularly hard to separate.

PARADIGMATIC RELATIONS AMONG REUBEN, GAD, AND MANASSEH

Other parts of the biblical narrative make reference to the Transjordanian tribes (including Manasseh, half of which settled in Transjordan), or to their eponymous ancestors as they appear in the legends of Genesis. In this section I analyze these references, to see if the three tribes share any semantic features.

In the tradition of Genesis 29:31-30:24, Reuben is Jacob's firstborn, and in other places where the tribes are listed he almost always heads the list.[51] But Reuben lost his precedence by sleeping with his father's concubine, Bilhah; Genesis 35:22 records the act, and 49:3-4 the consequence (though Reuben appears here still at the head of the list of brothers). Reuben then is one who (a) *loses precedence*, (b) *on account of a concubine*.

Loss of precedence is no less clear in the case of Manasseh, who in Genesis 48:8-20 is Joseph's elder son, but gets ranked below the younger, Ephraim. In Joshua 17:1, Machir (eponym of a tribal subgroup) is specified as the Transjordanian half of Manasseh, and is said to be Manasseh's firstborn, evoking an issue of precedence between the Cis- and Transjordanian halves of the tribe (cf. iii below). But the Manasseh tradition knows also of a concubine connection, involving Machir. In the genealogy of I Chronicles 7:14-19, Machir is said to be Manasseh's son by "his Aramean concubine" (Aram indicating Transjordan). Machir, Transjordanian Manasseh, thus combines *loss of precedence* (in his father) with *concubine* (his mother).

The traditions concerning Gad are scant and featureless compared with Reuben or Manasseh. He is a concubine-son of Jacob's by Zilpah, and is his mother's first-born. It may not be insignificant that he occupies the important *seventh* place in the traditions of the birth of Jacob's sons (Genesis 29:31-30:24). But one would scarcely think in Gad's case of precedence, were it not for the extraordinary passage Deuteronomy 33:20-21, within Moses' blessings on the twelve tribes. Of Gad it is said, "He sought out the precedence (possibly 'the best of the land[52]) for himself", and acquired "*a mḥqq's* share". The word *mḥqq* is controverted, but means something like "leader" or "commander". It is used elsewhere in a similar way not only of Judah, which was to become the leading tribe (Genesis 49:10), but also of Machir (Judges 5:14)!

Thus a link is forged between Reuben, Gad, and Manasseh (especially Machir, the Transjordanian half of Manasseh) under the headings "lost precedence" and "concubine" (though the latter element is weak in the case of Gad, since Jacob had several concubine-sons). In relation to our analysis of Numbers 32 and Joshua 22, the element "concubine" may link up with the "problematic" Transjordanian women, though more evidence is needed. More securely, "loss of precedence" was a semantic feature of those chapters. The Transjordanians grasped for precedence in the allotment of land. In a sense they got it, but in another sense they were the *last* to enjoy their land, doing so only after the Cisjordanians were settled.

(ii) NUMBERS 32 IN ITS NARRATIVE CONTEXT: TRANSJORDAN AS AMBIGUOUS LAND

In Numbers 32:4, Gad and Reuben refer to the land they desire as "the land which Yahweh smote before the congregation of Israel", inferring, presumably, that it is therefore fair game for their settlement. But there is much in the context that suggests that Israel is at this time in *foreign* territory, and subject to the attendant dangers (cf. below, iii); specifically that they are in territory legitimately belonging to Israel's kindred people, Moab.[53] For instance, the tradition that Moses may not enter the Promised Land is repeated in Numbers 27:12-14, implying that Israel is not yet in territory it may properly call its own.[54]

In Numbers 26:52-56, Moses instructs Israel about the division of the land which they will shortly be occupying. Its extent is not defined, but the division is to be by tribal size, and by lot. But neither tribal size nor the lot is mentioned in the allocation of Transjordanian territory in 32:33-42. In 33:54, Moses repeats his earlier instructions almost verbatim, reiterating the issues of tribal size and the lot—but now in connection with the division of *Cisjordanian* land to the remaining nine tribes and a half. This looks like an attempt to suppress the problem of the irregularity of the allocation of the Transjordanian land, and hence, perhaps, of the irregularity of that land itself.[55] Moreover, 33:54 occurs within a section (vs. 51-56) whose chief concern is the future persistence of non-Israelites in Cisjordan (a very basic problem in all the traditions of the occupation of Canaan[56]). The Canaanites are to be exterminated with all trace of their influence, for any who remain will cause great trouble. Is there an undercurrent here that the continued existence of *non-Israelites in Cisjordan* has something to do with the existence of *Israelites in Transjordan* (as a result of ch. 32)? This would be an excellent example of mythic logic and would explain the Cisjordanians' continuing hope (Numbers 32:30, Joshua 22:19) that the Transjordanians may come west after all. It is room which the Transjordanians ought to be filling which is filled with Canaanite troublers of Cisjordanian Israel!

Thus although Numbers 32 and parallel traditions assert an Israelite claim on Transjordanian land, the context in several ways reveals suspicion that this land is not truly Israel's, in Yahweh's intention. The total effect is that Israel's Transjordanian holdings appear as *ambiguous* land.

(iii) Transjordanian women: The Daughters of Zelophehad

The narrative context of Numbers 32 provides further data on the theme of Transjordanian women. Numbers 25 has already been referred to, since our Story II alluded to it—in it Transjordanian women, Moabite or Midianite, seduced Israel (both sexually and religiously) at Peor, and tempted Israel not to cross the Jordan. This chapter has a sequel in Numbers 31. After defeating the Midianites in battle, the Israelite force takes booty including "the women of Midian and their little ones" (31:9). When he sees these women, Moses points out that it was precisely they—specifically the non-virgin among them—who seduced Israel at Peor (vs. 15-16). The male children and non-virgin women are thereupon killed, while the virgin women are kept alive (vs. 17-18). I suggested earlier that Transjordanian women are a problem because they are permanently out of contact with "Yahweh's land" (since no obligation takes them there, cf. above, D iii). The present passage may then suggest that it is virtuous to bring a Transjordanian virgin into Yahweh's land, by marriage, while a married woman has taken the Transjordanian contagion irredeemably, and is therefore a danger.

The case of the daughters of Zelophehad, with which I conclude, is a complex one, but certain features of it support points I have already made, and it provides a powerful example of the semantic significance of narrative sequence. The case itself is covered in Numbers 27:1-11 and ch. 36, and there is an aftermath in Joshua 17:1-6. The characters belong to the tribe of Manasseh, according to the following genealogy (stated in Numbers 26:29-33 and assumed in ch. 27 and 36):

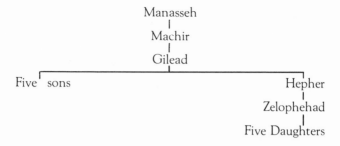

The names of Hepher and of some of the sons and daughters point us to *Cisjordan*, where they appear as place-names in Manasseh.[57] But the top of the genealogy, Machir and Gilead, points us to Transjordanian Manasseh, suggesting some sort of precedence for the Transjordanian half of the tribe.[58]

In Numbers 27:1-11, the daughters of Zelophehad come to Moses with the request that, since their father died without sons, his name should be preserved by them, the daughters, through their receiving a possession along with their male relatives. This is granted. The entire issue of land-inheritance seems premature at this point, since Israel has no land. But the next part of the "case", ch. 36, stands in a quite different light because of the intervention of ch. 32. Not merely is settlement now a reality, but the parties to the case belong to the stock of *Machir*, who has already received land in Transjordan (32:39-40). In this new situation, the male members of the tribe raise a problem about the earlier ruling. Should the daughters of Zelophehad marry out of their tribe, it will lose the inheritances which they have been granted. The force of this is allowed, and propertied women are bound by law to marry within their tribe, which Zelophehad's daughters in fact do.

This completes the "case", but the application of it in Joshua 17:1-6 is remarkable. First, there is an adjustment of the genealogy:

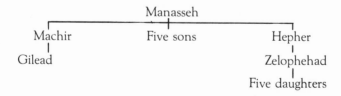

This allows for Machir (who, uniquely here, is called Manasseh's "firstborn") to represent the Transjordanian, and the rest of the family the Cisjordanian, part of Manasseh. And in fact the inheritances of the five daughters, along with those of the five sons (their "great uncles"!) make up the *totality* of Cisjordanian Manasseh (cf. "ten portions" in vs. 5). Between Numbers and Joshua, the daughters of Zelophehad have shifted, with their inheritances, from Transjordan to Cisjordan. Did they "marry west"—a virtuous thing to do, as I have surmised? Because of Manasseh's unique division into halves, they could do this, and remain in the tribe. The message is not easy to pin down, but there is again some sense of Transjordanian women as problematic, and of the problem being solved by their moving west.

CONCLUDING SUMMARY AND A DEEP-STRUCTURAL HYPOTHESIS

Our attempt to answer the initial question about Cisjordanian attitudes to Transjordan has led us into a constellation of narrative meanings which to some extent has taken convincing form and which may be considered with some confidence as a symbolization of real attitudes. Transjordan is ambiguous Israelite territory; along with the claim to it goes a sense of danger from it, along with the desire for a formalized relationship, the wish that it would just go away. The unity of Israel is felt to be deeply called in question by Transjordan. There is a sense that Transjordan possesses some sort of precedence, in face of which Cisjordanian precedence needs to be the more strongly affirmed; reversal of precedence relationships is found everywhere. The issues have something to do with women and children. Transjordanian women present a logical problem and a danger, but marrying them is a means of overcoming this. Definitions of the relationship with Transjordan lack continuity from generation to generation.

Malamat[59] puts forward a literary-sociological model for the reading of biblical genealogies, including particular reference to female terms. "Daughters . . . generally represent either clans or, rather, settlements—dependent on and subject to the principal tribal group or urban centre." "The merging of a tribe, settling in a new area, with an earlier or indigenous population may be formulated as the marriage of tribal eponym with one of the local women. Union with a concubine may personify a fusion with a foreign or inferior ethnic element." ". . . in attributing lineage through a concubine or maidservant, the Bible intends to convey the idea of migration . . . from (the) ancestral home to peripheral regions." The anthropological status of such a model would need to be established, but, taking it at face value, it relates "females", particularly "concubines", to the meaning-elements of (socio-political) *dependency, peripherality, foreignness, inferiority,* and *indigeneity.* These are elements which could be traced, with considerable precision, in the foregoing analysis of the views taken of Transjordan. Such metaphors as these female ones, however much they turn into technical terms, do not become innocent of their basic semantic content, and I suggest that, at a deep level, Cisjordan and Transjordan are coded simply as male and female. Nothing so bald as this ever appears on the surface, for many other semantic organizations overlay it; nonetheless, the hypothesis is worth framing that this is the semantic force most deeply charging the manifest texts.

Notes and References

1. In English, we may note Robert M. Polzin, *Biblical Structuralism: Method and Subjectivity in the Study of Ancient Texts* (Philadelphia: Fortress Press, 1977), pp. 74-83; J. W. Rogerson, *Myth in Old Testament Interpretation,* BZAW 134 (Berlin: De Gruyter, 1974), pp. 124-26 (hereafter

Myth); Wolfgang Roth, "Structural Interpretations of 'Jacob at the Jabbok' (Genesis 32:22-32)," *Biblical Research* 22 (1977), pp. 51-62 (hereafter "Jacob"). Cf. further the bibliographical remarks of Polzin, pp. 124-25.

2. E.g. James Crenshaw, "Journey into Oblivion: A Structural Analysis of Genesis 22:1-19", *Soundings* 58 (1975), pp. 243-56; Robert C. Culley, *Studies in the Structure of Hebrew Narrative* (Philadelphia: Fortress Press, 1976); Robert Polzin, " 'The Ancestress of Israel in Danger' in Danger", *Semeia* 3 (1975), pp. 81-98. Cf. also *Semeia* 18, *passim*.

3. Claude Lévi-Strauss, "Réponses a quelques questions", *Esprit* 31 (1963), pp. 628-53 (hereafter "Réponses"). Cf. also Mary Douglas, "The Meaning of Myth: With special reference to 'La Geste d'Asdiwal' ", in Edmund Leach, ed., *The Structural Study of Myth and Totemism*, A.S.A. Monographs 5 (London: Tavistock, 1967), pp. 66-68.

4. Lévi-Strauss, "Réponses", p. 630.

5. Edmund Leach, "The Legitimacy of Solomon", in Michael Lane, ed., *Introduction to Structuralism* (New York: Basic Books, 1970), p. 251 (hereafter "Legitimacy"; original publication in *European Journal of Sociology* 7 [1966].)

6. Lévi-Strauss, "Réponses", p. 631.

7. Daniel and Aline Patte, *Structural Exegesis: From Theory to Practice* (Philadelphia: Fortress Press, 1978). Cf. my critique of their model in "Structuralism, Hermeneutics, and Exegesis: Three Recent Contributions to the Debate", *Union Seminary Quarterly Review* 34 (1978/79), pp. 135-47.

8. Claude Lévi-Strauss, *Tristes tropiques*, trans. J. and D. Weightman (New York: Atheneum, 1975), pp. 55-59. The best discussion of his relationships to Freud and Marx is in F. Jameson, *The Prison-House of Language: A Critical Account of Structuralism and Russian Formalism* (Princeton: Princeton U.P., 1972), pp. 111-44. I have discussed these issues more fully in "Structuralism, Hermeneutics, and Exegesis", pp. 142-45.

9. Leach, "Legitimacy"; Robert C. Marshall, "Heroes and Hebrews: The Priest in the Promised Land", *American Ethnologist* 6 (1979), pp. 772-90.

10. Lévi-Strauss, "Réponses", pp. 633-35.

11. I became aware of this particularly in analyzing Genesis 2 and 3; see "The Myth-Semantics of Genesis 2:4b-3:24", *Semeia* 18 (1980), pp. 41-49. This issue leads into an area of discussion which recently had grown in importance – structural analysis of the communication event between text and reader. Cf., e.g., the essays in Part III of *Semeia* 18, and E. McKnight, *Meaning in Texts: The Historical Shaping of a Narrative Hermeneutics* (Philadelphia: Fortress, 1978).

12. Lévi-Strauss, "Réponses", p. 632.

13. Leach, "Legitimacy", p. 252. So also Douglas, "The Meaning of Myth", p. 68.

14. Cf. particularly the method of Roland Barthes in *S/Z*, trans. R. Miller (New York: Hill and Wang, 1974). Lévi-Strauss himself adopts a related procedure in his collaborative essay with Roman Jakobson: "Charles Baudelaire's 'Les Chats' ", in Lane, *Introduction to Structuralism*, pp. 202-21 (original French publication in *L'homme* II [January - April, 1962]).

15. Lévi-Strauss, "Réponses", p. 629, where Ricoeur alludes to Lévi-Strauss's well-known debate with Sartre, for which see Claude Lévi-Strauss, *The Savage Mind* (Chicago: University of Chicago Press, 1966), pp. 245-69.

16. Leach, "Legitimacy", pp. 291-92.

17. Hayden V. White, *Metahistory: The historical imagination in nineteenth-century Europe* (Baltimore: John Hopkins U.P., 1973); W. C. Sellar and R. J. Yeatman, *1066 and All That* (New York: Dutton, 1958).

18. Leach, "Legitimacy"; Marshall, "Heroes and Hebrews". The latter's remarks on pp. 772-74, 787-88 are of particular methodological importance.

19. Rogerson, *Myth*, p. 111.

20. This is exactly the opposite of Lévi-Strauss's own point that, for his methods to apply, biblical specialists would need to do a "preliminary work" of isolating pristine mythological material! See "Réponses", pp. 631-32.

21. I refer to the "canonical criticism" of James A. Sanders, *Torah and Canon* (Philadelphia: Fortress, 1972), comprehensively developed by Brevard S. Childs, *Introduction to the Old Testament as Scripture* (Philadelphia: Fortress, 1979).

22. David Jobling, " 'The Jordan a Boundary': A Reading of Numbers 32 and Joshua 22," *SBL Seminar Papers* (Chico, CA: Scholars Press, 1980), pp. 186, 205-06; Marshall, "Heroes and Hebrews", pp. 773-74.

23.   D. N. Freedman, "Deuteronomic History, The," in *The Interpreter's Dictionary of the Bible, Supplementary Volume*, ed. K. Crim and others (Nashville: Abingdon, 1976), p. 226.

24.   Claude Lévi-Strauss, *The Origin of Table Manners: Introduction to a Science of Mythology*, 3, trans. J. and D. Weightman (New York: Harper, 1979), pp. 128-31. Cf. the remarks of Lawrence E. Sullivan in this volume, pp. xxx-xxx.

25.   Cf. the following, representative of a very large literature on this subject: Roland Barthes, "Introduction à l'analyse structurale des récits", *Communications* 8 (1966), pp. 1-27; A. J. Greimas, *Sémantique structurale* (Paris: Larousse, 1966), *Du sens* (Paris: Seuil, 1970), Maupassant (Paris: Seuil, 1976); Robert Scholes, *Structuralism in Literature: An Introduction* (New Haven: Yale U.P., 1974); Jonathan Culler, *Structuralist Poetics: Structuralism, Linguistics, and the Study of Literature* (London: Routledge and Kegan Paul, 1975).

26.   Cf. particularly Daniel Patte, *What is Structural Exegesis?* (Philadelphia: Fortress, 1976), pp. 53-83, and the developed theory of narratives in Patte and Patte, *Structural Exegesis*, pp. 33-36. Cf. also the works of William O. Hendricks, such as "Methodology of Narrative Structural Analysis", *Semiotica* 7 (1973), pp. 163-84, "Folklore and the Structural Analysis of Literary Texts", *Language and Style* 3 (1970), pp. 83-121.

27.   E.g. Michael P. Carroll, "Leach, Genesis, and Structural Analysis: A Critical Evaluation", *American Ethnologist* 4 (1977), pp. 671-77; Marshall, "Heroes and Hebrews"; Rogerson, *Myth*, pp. 124-26. Terry J. Prewitt, in a generally excellent article, chooses to regard "the stories of Genesis . . . as a concatenation rather than a narrative": see "Kinship Structures and the Genesis Genealogies", *JNES* 40 (1981), p. 87 (hereafter "Kinship Structures"). This seems to me not legitimate at any level.

28.   Leach, "Legitimacy", pp. 277-90 (quotation from p. 290).

29.   Karin R. Andriolo, "A Structural Analysis of Genealogy and Worldview in the Old Testament", *American Anthropologist* 75 (1973), pp. 1657-69 (hereafter "Genealogy and Worldview"); Mara E. Donaldson, "Kinship Theory in the Patriarchal Narratives: The Case of the Barren Wife", *JAAR* 49 (1981), pp. 77-87; Prewitt, "Kinship Structures". Two articles forthcoming in *Proceedings of the Semiotic Society of America* (Nashville meeting, 1981), ed. John Deely, may be added: Prewitt, "Story Structures and Social Structures in Genesis: Circles and Cycles"; Dorothy Gaston, "The Matrilineal Background of Kinship in Genesis."

30.   Leach, "Legitimacy"; Andriolo, "Genealogy and Worldview", pp. 1663-66. The two essays by Prewitt in the previous note, though they proceed at a highly theoretical level, also serve wider exegetical aims.

31.   Edmund Leach, "Lévi-Strauss in the Garden of Eden: An Examination of Some Recent Developments in the Analysis of Myth", *Transactions of the New York Academy of Science*, Series II, 23 (1961), pp. 386-96; "Genesis as Myth", in *Genesis as Myth and Other Essays* (London: Jonathan Cape, 1969), pp. 7-23 (original publication in *Discovery* 23 (1962).) Lévi-Strauss referred to the former as "en partie seulement, un jeu" ("Réponses", p. 631).

32.   Carroll, "Leach", pp. 664-68. Cf. his own constructive attempts in the remainder of the article.

33.   Matthieu Casalis, "The Dry and the Wet: A semiological Analysis of Creation and Flood Myths", *Semiotica* 17 (1976), pp. 35-67.

34.   Claude Lévi-Strauss, "The Structural Study of Myth", in *Structural Anthropology*, trans. C. Jacobson and B. G. Schoepf (New York: Basic Books, 1963), pp. 206-31.

35.   The columnar technique appears on pp. 213-14, 219-20 of the essay mentioned in the previous note, the converging diagram on p. 224, and the formula on p. 228. My references are to Casalis, "The Dry and the Wet", e.g. p. 43; Roth, "Jacob", p. 60; Polzin, *Biblical Structuralism*, pp. 74-83.

36.   Claude Lévi-Strauss, "The Story of Asdiwal", in E. R. Leach, ed., *The Structural Study of Myth and Totemism* (London: Tavistock, 1967), pp. 1-48.

37.   In four volumes, three of which have appeared in the English translations of J. and D. Weightman: *The Raw and the Cooked; From Honey to Ashes; The Origin of Table Manners* (New York: Harper, 1970, 1973, 1978). Volume 4 is *L'homme nu* (Paris: Plon, 1971).

38.   I do not provide specific references for the following, precisely because it is Lévi-Strauss's entire work which defines them for me, rather than some formal definitions he may somewhere have given.

39.   Greimas, *Maupassant*, p. 263.

40.   Carroll, "Leach", pp. 671-73, cf. 673-75. For the formula, see note 35 above.

41. As well as the parallel he himself notes ("The Dry and the Wet", pp. 62-63), cf. his basic diagram on p. 52 with Lévi-Strauss, *The Raw and the Cooked*, p. 98.
42. See J. A. Emerton, "An Examination of a Recent Structuralist Interpretation of Genesis XXXVIII", *Vetus Testamentum* 26 (1976), pp. 79-98, and the other critics of Leach mentioned by Emerton on p. 82.
43. Marshall, "Heroes and Hebrews", pp. 773-74.
44. Cf. Greimas, *Sémantique structurale*, pp. 69-70; *Du sens*, pp. 189-97; Lévi-Strauss, *The Raw and the Cooked*, p. 199.
45. The following is a condensed version of my article, " 'The Jordan a Boundary' " (see above, note 22). I have tried, in making the condensation, to keep all the logical connections clear, but the reader may find points of unclarity resolved in the longer version.
46. There are parallels in each case: cf. Deuteronomy 2:26-3:22; Joshua 13:8-32; Judges 11:12-28.
47. I do not include here the recapitulations of Numbers 32 in Deuteronomy 3:12-22 and Joshua 13:8-32.
48. Cf. Jobling, *The Sense of Biblical Narrative*, pp. 33-35.
49. For a fuller theoretical discussion of this isotopy, cf. Jobling, " 'The Jordan a Boundary' ", pp. 194-95 (§2.511).
50. Numbers 25 is not a unity; the different accounts in vs. 1-5 and vs. 6-18 are awkwardly juxtaposed. But the theme of temptation by women is common to both accounts.
51. The cases in Numbers 2, 7, and 10, where Judah leads, are not really lists. In the genealogies of I Chronicles 2-8, Reuben's demotion is accounted for (5:1-2), and in Joshua 21 it can be explained by geography. Particularly interesting are Deuteronomy 27:12-13 and Judges 5:14-18, where Reuben heads not the whole list, but the list of tribes presented negatively.
52. So the *Revised Standard Version*.
53. On this very complex issue, cf. David Jobling, "Judges 11:12-28: Constructive and Deconstructive Analysis", forthcoming in *Proceedings of the Semiotic Society of America* (see note 29 above).
54. Cf. Jobling, " 'The Jordan a Boundary' ", pp. 201-02 (§§3.211-3.213).
55. More generally, the function of the entire section 33:50-34:29 is to integrate ch. 32 convincingly into the larger narrative.
56. Cf. above all Judges 1; also Joshua 9, 15:63, 16:10, etc.
57. Hepher, Abiezer, Shechem, Tirzah.
58. The less stylized Manasseh genealogy in I Chronicles 7:14-19 gives the same general picture.
59. Abraham Malamat, "Tribal Societies: Biblical Genealogies and African Lineage Systems," *Archives européennes de sociologie* 14 (1974), p. 132.

CHAPTER X

The Language of Ascent: Lévi-Strauss, Silverstein and Maaseh Merkabah*

Naomi Janowitz

As a historian of religions I approach with caution most attempts to apply linguistic models to religious texts. Too often linguistic theories are raided for random insights, or tracks of intellectual indebtedness are covered over, making it difficult to assess the application of linguistic models. Lévi-Strauss, however, carefully recounts in his short introduction to Roman Jakobson's influential book *Six Lectures on Sound and Meaning*[1] his early encounters with linguistic theories. In this introduction Lévi-Strauss reminisces about Jakobson's lectures at the Free School of Advanced Studies in New York in 1942, which he says provided him with conceptual and methodological tools needed to refine his work on incest taboos, kinship, etc. It was at those lectures that Lévi-Strauss heard the phrases which became the foundation of much structural analysis. He cites in particular Jakobson's statement about phonemes, the distinctive sound units from which words are constructed.

> The important thing . . . is not at all each phoneme's individual phonic quality considered in isolation and existing in its own right. What matters is their reciprocal opposition within a . . . system.[2]

In other words, Lévi-Strauss learned that "p" and "b" in and of themselves do not mean anything; instead what matters "is their reciprocal oppositions within a *phonological* system."[3] The sounds "p" and "b" help us distinguish between the words "pill" and "bill." Or, as Jakobson explained,

> The linguistic value of the nasal *a* phoneme in French, and in general of any phoneme in any language whatever, is only its power to distinguish the word containing this phoneme from any words which, similar in all other respects, contain some other phoneme.[4]

If we turn to the lecture from which Lévi-Strauss quotes this statement, we discover that he has quoted very selectively from Jakobson's work. Jakobson develops a subtle and important argument about phonology, and the difference between phonemes and all other levels of linguistic structure. He first traces

213

his observations about phonemes to the work of Saussure, agreeing with Saussure that phonemes are oppositional, relative and negative. "Negative" means that each phoneme does not have its own positive content, but rather its usefulness derives from the fact that it is not one of the other phonemes. While he clearly agrees with Saussure on this point he continues and writes,

> Saussure understood the purely differential and negative character of phonemes perfectly well, but instead of drawing out the implications of this for the analysis of the phoneme he overhastily generalized this characterization and sought to apply it to all linguistic entities.[5]

According to Jakobson, Saussure made a "serious mistake"[6] by stressing that the most significant aspect of all linguistic categories is that they are oppositional, contrasting categories. He uses the example of the category "plural" to develop his objection to Saussure.

> The grammatical category of the plural presupposes and implies the existence of an opposite category, that of the singular. But what is crucial is its own positive value, i.e., the designation of plurality . . . All opposition of grammatical categories necessarily has a positive-content, whereas the opposition of two phonemes never has.[7]

If we then return to Lévi-Strauss and his introduction, we find that he does not follow Jakobson's lead, but instead argues that *all* levels of language are oppositional and negative, that all units of language have meaning only in terms of their placement within a system of oppositions. He even moves beyond a simple category like plural to create cultural categories such as the "mytheme," a piece of myth which is to be studied in a fashion parallel to the phoneme. Unfortunately, as we have just seen, the very person who developed the model that Lévi-Strauss draws on, rejects this application of the study of phonemes to meaning levels of culture. If Lévi-Strauss wishes to use this linguistic model in a manner rejected by Jakobson, he must first make an argument as to its applicability and not simply cite Jakobson. As far as I have been able to find, he does not make that argument.

Lévi-Strauss has not simply cited Jakobson out of context, he has also dropped the word "phonological" in his citation from Jakobson. In taking one particular observation about a distinct linguistic level and generalizing it, he has lost the theoretical underpinnings provided by Jakobson's careful work. Yet he has failed to supply his own justification for his method of analysis. If any linguistic level is found to be even in part motivated, as opposed to arbitrary, or having positive content as opposed to being negative, Lévi-Strauss has no guidelines by which to proceed. The growing number of scholars who study the non-arbitrary (motivated) and non-negative (having positive content) aspects of language challenge Lévi-Strauss's methodological assumptions. Indeed

Jakobson himself has studied the contributions of sounds to meanings, a notion which would make no sense in a purely oppositional system. As Paul Friedrich writes in his important article "The Symbol and Its Relative Non-Arbitrariness,"

> Many probabilistic determinisms also inhere in various parts of the linguistic system itself, ranging from pervasive synaesthetic correlations, to the implicational rules of grammar, to iconic relations between syntax and logic and the 'real world.' Third, if so many components in language are entirely determined at some level, it follows that every entity and relation is at least *partly* determined: the realistic and interesting question is not whether lexical symbols are arbitrary or not, but rather *the manner and degree to which they are non-arbitrary.*[8]

In order to better understand the limitations of a structural approach as articulated by Lévi-Strauss, I will contrast it with another, quite different structural approach also highly influenced by the work of Jakobson. This approach, broadly called pragmatic or functional, concerns language as effective social action and is exemplified particularly in the work of Michael Silverstein.[9] It encompasses the now-popular theory of speech acts made famous by Austin and exploited by many students of ritual language.[10] Silverstein, however, strives to study linguistic ideologies, what native speakers think they are doing with language, and relates this ideology to the linguistic forms and categories used. His work begins with an issue entirely left out of Lévi-Strauss's work and impossible in the Saussurean system, the relation between language and context.

Silverstein examines the extent to which meaning is determined by placement within a system, and also addresses the general question of the relation of language structure to contexts of use. This approach enables him not only to extract general patterns from texts, but also to articulate the motivation for uses of language and language forms as goal-directed strategies within particular situations. Silverstein is concerned with the specific cultural understandings of language functions, including those usages in which language effects socially recognized goals.

> A pragmatic or functional view of speech as a social activity is in principle to be sharply differentiated from a semantic or logical view of language as a coding mechanism of the rational faculty. Pragmatics is the study of the way indexical features of speaking presuppose and create the parameters of the event of speaking, as a socially shared system of meaning.[11]

Silverstein begins with Jakobson's influential studies on parallelism. Parallelism is not limited to biblical poetry; it is a basic artifice of verse. Jakobson states in his famous article on parallelism

> We must consistently draw all inferences from the obvious fact that on every level of language the essence of poetic artifice consists in recurrent returns.[12]

As such an omnipresent device, parallelism extends to all linguistic levels and forms. Recurrent returns include all the repetitive patterning from phonetics to grammar.

> Pervasive parallelism, inevitably activates all the levels of language, – the distinctive features, inherent and prosodic, the morphological and syntactical categories and forms, the lexical units and their semantic classes in both their convergencies and divergencies acquire an autonomous poetic value.[13]

The basic unit of analysis is the entire composition, for the pattern extends throughout the text. Parallelism is not merely a device to extend the meaning of one line in the next line, nor to highlight delimited rhetorical effects of paired lines.

> This focusing upon phonological, grammatical and semantic structures in their uniform interplay does not remain confined to the limits of parallel lines but extends throughout their distribution within the entire context: therefore the grammar of parallelistic pieces becomes particularly significant.[14]

Parallelism is the heart of poetics because the repetition of words and phrases creates the comparisons and contrasts, the creative aspects of poetry. These comparisons extend to all functions of words within the composition. Words which occur in the same relative place in several layers of the parallel structure are literally to that extent juxtaposed. Analysis of the effects of these juxtapositions is as complex as the study of metaphor.

> Phonetic features and sequences, both morphological and lexical, syntactical and phraseological units, when occurring in metrically or strophically corresponding positions, are necessarily subject to the conscious or sub-conscious questions whether, how far, and in what respect the positionally corresponding entities are mutually similar.[15]

Here Jakobson reflects the Russian Formalists' concern to develop more dynamic means of describing poetic language and the relation between form and content. His conclusions about the defining and glossing aspects of parallelism (verse structures) mirror Tynianov's analysis of the specific alterations of the meanings of words dependent upon the verse constructions.[16]

The poetic function, as defined by Jakobson, "projects the principle of equivalence from the axis of selection into the axis of combination."[17] In other words, instead of choosing between the variant ways of saying the same thing, in poetics linguistic units are arranged in equivalent positions in order to facilitate comparison. Thus even rhyme becomes part of the study of parallelism, as it creates patterns of sound arrangement.

Briefly, equivalence in sound, projected into the sequence as its constitutive principle, inevitably involves semantic equivalence and on any linguistic level any constituent of such a sequence prompts one of the two correlative experiences which Hopkins neatly defines as "comparison for likeness' sake" and "comparison for unlikeness' sake."[18]

According to Jakobson, parallelism or "the use of the equivalence relations as
the constructive device of the sequence,"[19] establishes the levels of meaning in a
poetic composition, from individual words to the overall directionality of the
work. Poetic arrangement of language enables patterns of words to be considered at the same time. Parallelism, now defined as the juxtaposition of any
linguistic unit in comparable position (equivalent location) is a guide to interpreting the overall message of the text. Patterning of linguistic units results in
multiple comparisons which are an intrinsic part of the message. For example,
the juxtaposing of words imputes meaning-equivalence glossing or patterns
(metaphors) between those words, which contributes to the meaning of those
words in the context of that composition. Structural equivalence (similar placement within the larger structure) does not create meaning based on *opposition*.
To review, Silverstein sums up the poetic function of language as follows:

Construct utterances with unit lengths measured out, in as many layers as you want, so that
units in relatively similar (or regularly computable) positions in some higher structural layer
have some special metaphorical pseudo-definitional (or antidefinitional) relationship, which in
effect suggests categorical identity (or oppositeness).[20]

According to Silverstein, diagrams can be extracted from these "higher structural layers," diagrams which are guides to the manipulation of ritual. These
structures provide icons (images) of the context of the rite and invoke that context for the rite. He introduces the notion of maximally-creative language;
language that is not highly context-dependent but which instead is context-
creating.[21] His distinction between presupposition-of-context as opposed to
entailment-of-context is reflected in a growing number of articles on language
and social context.[22] For Silverstein, the transformative power of a rite is the
transformation of the diagrams and thereby of the context. The diagrammatic
icons are reshaped and manipulated by the inherent asymmetry of the flow of
discourse, the movement from the beginning of the text to the end. These
diagrams thus create and then re-create the contexts of use, thereby "effecting"
the rite.

Ritual language can thus both index (indicate) the transformation that is occurring and at the same time provide an icon (image or formal resemblance) of
that transformation.

That is to say, it is the diagrammatic pragmatic application (in actual discourse sequence defined by the poetic structural chunks) of the principle of pseudo-equivalence set up by the

poetic structure that enacts the transformation-by-(re)-definition of the situation.[23]

The possibilities created by the poetic function of language enable the text to have this efficacy. Therefore, analysis of a text begins with locating the specific devices employed in the text, and by aligning them with the goals of the rite.

In order to better understand Silverstein's approach we will give an example of a pragmatic analysis. First, a brief introduction to the text. *Maaseh Merkabah* (The Working of the Chariot) is a Hebrew text first edited and printed by Gershom Scholem in his book *Jewish Gnosticism, Merkabah Mysticism and Talmudic Tradition*.[24] The text is a rich portrayal of the techniques of ascent, i.e., traveling through the heavens. The central issue of the text is the form and context of hymns which an individual recites when traversing the heavens.

The text consists of two dialogues which are intertwined in the text as it presently stands. In both of them Ishmael is the student, receiving instruction from a variety of experts. His first teacher, Akiba, reports successful ascents and the formulas said during them.

Section 1
R. Ishmael said: I asked R. Akiba for a prayer that a man does when ascending to the chariot and requested from him praise of RWZYY Adonai, God of Israel, who knows who he is, and he said to me: Purity and holiness are in his heart and he prays a prayer: You will be blessed forever on the throne of glory . . .

His second teacher, Nehunya, teaches Ishmael the language of the heavenly realm, telling his student to recite the letters and names the heavenly chorus recites. The formulas he reveals also enable Ishmael to have a vision of the highest heaven. Nehunya teaches Ishmael to summon angelic figures, who descend and give Ishmael wisdom.

Large sections of the text describe the heavenly chorus which surrounds the throne of the deity. These choruses are constantly praising the deity, and their actions provide a model for the one who wishes to ascend. By copying the behavior of those who inhabit the upper reaches, an individual can become part of the chorus. Also by describing the activities of that heavenly group, an individual can prove he has ascended and has seen the upper world.

As to the form of the text, it consists entirely of reported speech: speech of individual rabbis, angels and heavenly choruses. The cast of characters talk, and each speech act is introduced by one of a small selection of verbs (say, pray, recite, call out). Not only is the entire text "talk," but the subject of their dialogue, what they talk about, is again modes of speech. They outline and discuss the proper way of speaking so as to be successful in ascent. The text is brimming with examples of the author's ideology of language use. In outlining the ascent process, the characters report not deeds, but various verbal actions,

THE LANGUAGE OF ASCENT: 219

such as "Akiba said, he prays a prayer" and "Nehunya said to me: When you pray, recite the three names that the angels of glory recite." Thus ascent is based on special modes of language use, uses which have a ritual efficacy. These characters present to the reader the types of talk which cause ascent. And, in order to ascend, each individual talks about ascent. The text thus constantly reflects back on itself, explicitly talking about the very process toward which it is directed.

The text contains two main types of material, verbal formulas and dialogic frames which introduce these formulas. The formulas are introduced as "prayers" or "praise," and include descriptions of praising activity and praises. Some sections consist of dense praise phrases, repeated and slightly altered.

> Blessed in heaven and on earth
> Glorified in heaven and on earth
> Compassionate in heaven and on earth
> Holy in heaven and on earth (Section 4)

One cluster of prayers includes long strings of "nonsense words," introduced by dense phrases with numerous uses of "Name."

> He is his Name and his Name is him
> He is in him and his Name is in his Name
> Song is his Name and his Name is song
> Z'WPH Z'P ZW''WHSY HWHSYN DMYY . . . (Section 28)

These formulas are constructed using a variety of devices, including strings of words (shouting, gladness, friendship, faithfulness, humility), extended noun constructs (king of kings of kings), reversible phrases (Y is X and X is Y), equations with "Name" (Name is X), repeating a word or phrases in the subsequent line, or after several lines, and repeating syntactic patterns exactly, or with variations. All of these devices are deviations from standard usage. Our problem is to account for the specific selection of devices, and to relate them to the goals of the text, in this case ascent.

The formulas are introduced in the Akiban source by enumerations, highly parallelistic listing, for example, of the number of fiery chariots in each heaven, or some aspect of each heaven's spatial layout. In one particularly interesting case, the listing occurs twice, once in a static form and once dynamic.

> In the first palace stand 40,000 of chariots of fire and 40,000 of flames are interspersed between them.
> In the second palace stand . . . (through seven palaces)
>
> In the first palace chariots of fire say:

Holy, holy, holy is Adonai of hosts
He fills the whole world with his glory.
And their flames of fire scatter and gather together towards the second palace and say:
Holy, holy, holy is Adonai of hosts
He fills the whole earth with his glory,
In the second palace chariots of fire say . . . (through seven palaces)

Each of these enumerations contains a brief, but complete ascent through the heavens. Here the highly repetitive patterns create an icon of the heavenly world. By moving through the levels, the reader literally travels from layer to layer. When the entire structure is repeated a second time, the mapping of the heavens becomes a dynamic negotiation. The "fuel" for this ascent is provided by the verbal formulas the chariots say. The recitation of praise causes them to re-form on the next higher level. This enumeration, as with many other sections, can stand by itself as a summation of the textual process—providing a guide for how to ascend by illustrating an ascent.

The formulas and enumeration are introduced in each section by elaborate reported-speech frames such as "R. Akiba said . . ." The frames vary in complexity, embedding the reported formulas anywhere from one to four layers.

Section 1
R. Ishmael said   (Outer narrative)
I asked R. Akiba for a prayer a man does when ascending to the chariot . . .
     He said to me: (Reported Dialogue)
Purity and holiness are in his heart . . . (when) he prays a prayer:
                                                         (Reported Content of Dialogue)
You will be blessed   (Reported Formula)

Section 2
R. Akiba said   (Outer narrative)
When I ascended . . .   (Reported Content)

The frames describe the situations in which the dialogues took place, and in which the formulas are to be used. They are extensions of the terse "X said," articulating how and why the speaker spoke. As reported speech, the text contains interpretations of the role of the formulas; each section introduces and creates situations in which the use of the formula is described.

Having been introduced to the text, we must pause to ask whether a pragmatic analysis is possible for a text which lacks a clear context of use. We hope to correlate details of language use with the specific contexts in which those forms are used. As Silverstein writes,

to understand how speaking . . . is effective social action, accomplishing such various social ends as warning, insulting, marrying, condemning, christening, growing yams, making sores heal, creating light in the world, etc., we must systematize the description of relationships of coexistence (understood copresence) that hold between elements of speech and elements comprising the context in which speech elements are uttered.[25]

It is the reported speech frames which enable us to see the formula "in action." *Maaseh Merkabah* depicts every single formula in action by creating the contexts for the verbal compositions in the dialogic frames. The necessary contextual elements are outlined in the dialogic frames, creating a commentary or meta-text for their use. These frames make the text a "performative" verb writ large; they describe or define the verbal process, and then immediately carry out or instantiate that process.

We begin the next step of analysis by looking for ideas included in the text about the efficacy of words. The most important theory of language is that found in the summations of the creation story. The text states, for example,

You created the heights and the depths by your word . . .

You spoke and the world existed/By the breath of your lips you established the firmament . . .

Creator of this world by his one Name/Fashioner of all by one word.

These phrases present a specific view of divine language in which the words of the deity have a special efficacy. Here we do not mean the out-of-date theories of biblical semantics according to which the Israelites could not distinguish between thought and action. These phrases do, however, encode a pragmatics of divine language which, unlike human language, is immediately effective. In the Genesis model, God does not have to speak in a subset of performative verbs. All of his words are efficacious; they entail deeds.

If divine speech is the basic model of effective language, how then do the users tap into or make use of this mode of speech? If we return to the text, we find that one detail of the Genesis creation story is changed; that the word spoken by God in creating was his Name ("Creator of the world by his one Name"). Genesis reports that God said "Let there be light . . ." Not only does this encode a proposition, but the specific deed was determined by the reference and predication of the proposition. (There will be light). Uttering the word "Light" led to the creation of light. To state now that God spoke his Name is completely to alter the story, and the theory of language on which it is based.

The entire theory of language has shifted because the new theory contains a different explanation than the Biblical texts for God's effective word. By stating that the creative word was God's Name, the pragmatics of divine speech has now been located in a specific semantic unit, the divine Name. The relation between the utterance of "light" and the creation of light is gone. The primordial act of creation is no longer the primordial reference.

God's Name, as with all proper names, has no fixed sense, but only reference, the self-reference that all names have. God's speech, when he speaks his Name, does not refer to the deeds it effects. Now it refers back to the creator himself. This constitutes the new basis for divine language. God's words are deeds because they refer to him and hence to his power. The pragmatics of divine speech has been "semanticized," as it were, located in the reference potential of a semantic unit. That power can now be utilized by anyone who gains the knowledge of the Name. Now by speaking that Name, the pragmatics of that speech can be acquired; speaking God's Name is speaking like God. It is now possible to appropriate and to teach the powerful, goal-oriented use of language in a way which was not possible before God's pragmatics were objectified. This has created the very possibility of ritual language.

Genesis

"Let there be light"   light

   refers to

word   deed

  effects

Merkebah

"Name"   light

effects

word   deed

refers to

     deity

Realizing the importance of the "name" we return to the text and the literary devices. These devices now take on an additional importance. The non-standard usages manipulate each linguistic level so that the level can be integrated into and made use of according to their theory of efficacious language. They all, in more and less explicit ways, establish new semantic equivalents for God's Name. When the word "Name" is introduced in the equation and in the dense webs of repeated words and phrases, entire chunks of texts become substitutes for "Name".

For example, the reversible phrases (Name is X, X is Name) highlight the same equations (Name#word) which are made less explicitly in the other forms of parallelism, and thus are aids in interpreting the formulas. The special dimension of these forms is that the reversal of the phrase literally effects the transformation. The place of "his song" is now taken by "his Name," and that of "his Name" by "his song." The transformation of language, or word, into his Name has been carried out on the plane of language.

To again use the vocabulary of speech acts theories, all of the words of the text have become performative because they are all the "Name." The pragmatic content of the most performative word has been conveyed to all the other words, supplementing their semantic context with a new pragmatic force.

In the rabbinic tradition, God's Name is not to be written or spoken. The name is shrouded in mystery and utterance is forbidden. How then does one make use of the name of the deity in a tradition which forbids its recitation?

In *Maaseh Merkabah* the problem of blasphemy is solved since all these versions of God's name are permutations and derivations of the true divine Name. The multiple levels of the text present hundreds of ways of speaking God's Name without speaking THE NAME which cannot be spoken. These versions are as powerful as the spoken Name, for the text explicitly equates them with the Name. The phrases, attributes, clusters of phonemes are all derived from the divine Name.

Just as severe is the problem that such speech belongs only to the deity. Surely using substitutes for the Name, if used in the manner of the Name, is also forbidden. Some traditions solve that problem by advocating silence. If efficacious speech is restricted to the deity, adherents will not speak in that manner. Here, however, the problem is solved in a different manner. In not one single case in this text does any individual directly speak a formula. All the prayers are reported speech, with a dialogic introduction constructed in such a way that the prayers are reports of prayers.

The frame is thus a means of distancing the participants from the direct uttering of prayers. The speakers in the frames set up elaborate systems of presentation, telling the reader that the speaker is merely reporting something from another occasion. The speaker introduces the formulas as stemming from past events, from earlier ascents. The frame is a device which enables the speakers to set up a long past situation as the origin of the formula, "When I was thirteen . . ." or "When I ascended . . ." The frame repeats again and again that the content conveyed is merely the recounting of, or remembering of, past events. Yet, and here is the core of the problem, once each verbal formula is begun, it is repeated in its entirety and the difference between the earlier recitation and the present "report" disappears. Once the first word is stated, the rest functions equivalently to direct speech, negating the effect of the frame. According to *Maaseh Merkabah*, an ascent is a true ascent to the extent that it mirrors a successful ascent, down to the very syllables. The past events are reported in order to establish a paradigm for the present ascent. The efficacy of the rite is based on replication of the previous speech event, which was a successful ascent. Any break in the correspondence breaks the relation between the previous successful ascent and the present attempt, and the efficacy of the prayer is negated. The prayers must be diagrammatic icons, exact replicas, of previous ones to achieve their goal. *Maaseh Merkabah* is a striking text in that it is able to establish and use the paradigm at the same time, collapsing each ascent into such a close approximation of the first ascent that it is that first ascent.

The frame acts as a guarantee of the prayers, for the frame repeatedly reasserts the efficacy of these compositions (I prayed—I was delivered). The prayers were learned in the very process of successful ascent. The most basic guarantee of the text is none other than the existence of the text itself, for if the rabbis had not ascended, they would not have been able to report and repeat the prayers.

If the entire ritual is contained in the text, how is it conveyed to the reader?

How do we know that it does not work only for Akiba? First, we have already explained that the ascent prayers are exact replicas of the successful ones and therefore carry the same power. The components necessary for the successful completion of the rite are listed in the very first section: purity and holiness of the heart, and the proper verbal formula. Second, the frame operates in several ways to include the reader in the text. To whom after all, is Ishmael speaking? He is not talking to Akiba, for he reports things that Akiba told him. The reader becomes the other half of the dialogue, for it is to the reader that Ishmael speaks. The elaboration of the frame (section 1: R. Ishmael said . . . I asked Akiba . . . he said to me . . .) and its manipulation (section 2 reads only: Akiba said) draw the reader deeper into the text. This is similar to the device of a play within a play in *Midsummer's Night Dream*, which draws the audience into the play as it becomes part of the new audience which includes the audience on the stage.

There is one more dimension to this investigation which will also help highlight the ability of the pragmatic analysis to account for the details of the text's construction. Here we return to the issue with which we began – sounds. Jakobson also stresses the role of sounds in poetic texts. The set of lectures introduced by Lévi-Strauss discuss the multiple ways in which sounds contribute to meaning. In Lévi-Strauss's adaptation of Jakobson there is no role for sounds, the very units from which he created his approach. For sounds to be meaningful, their use and meaning must be motivated by other linguistic levels. Sounds simply placed in opposition continue to be meaningless.

However, guided by Silverstein and pragmatic considerations, we now find that in *Maaseh Merkabah* even the sounds are efficacious. This is most explicit in the "nonsense" words. These words consist entirely of sound, having no recognizable semantic value. Instead of having semantic meaning, narrowly defined, these words highlight the "letterness" of words. Words, including the divine names, consist of clusters of sounds. In order to make us maximally aware of these sounds, the most effective device is semantically-depleted words where we hear each letter, or sound. The link between letters and words is, again, the name, for all these letters are manipulations of the divine Name. God's Name is presented over and over again in terms of the letters and their sounds. Since the nonsense words are made out of letters of the name, they have the force, or, in a performative view, the meaning of the name as the creative word par excellence. The status of these letters is the same as words, that is, they are efficacious in and of themselves. This means that even the sounds can create and effect. These sound-clusters are the logical extension of the theories of language present throughout the text.

To review, in *Maaseh Merkabah*, all of the deviations from standard usage are developed in order to create new meanings for words, phrases, and even sounds. The parallelistic structures enact glossing relations which equate words and phrases. The parallelistic structures, the equations, and the reversible phrases create glossing relations between the words and other units. As we saw, when, "Name" is introduced into these webs, other words are compared to "Name." Many of these deviations parade more or less explicitly as semantic definitions. As such, they extend the semantic content to the new words.

The rabbinic use of the divine Name in this text is presupposed in other rabbinic stories and discussion. The Name is used as a concrete substitute or manifestation of the divine presence.[26] Because the Name was used in creating the world, the proper manipulation of the letters might enable an individual to perform acts of creation. Trachtenberg mentions one specific brand of magic centered on the laws of creation, interpreted by the rabbis to mean the Names of God and the angels.[27] The authors of this text were working with the biblical concepts but in an altered and transposed form. Their theory of language, especially of the role of the Name, was quite distinct from the biblical ideas. Gods no longer spoke like they used to and humans strove to talk like the gods. The name of a deity had itself become an instrument of ritual efficacy, as seen, for example, in the Talmudic stories about rabbis who manipulated the letters of the divine Name and created a calf (b. Sanhedrin 67b). As the power of the deity became concretely connected with his Name, the Name became shrouded by secrecy and religious injunctions. These issues were not unique to the rabbis, and the next step of investigation is to relate these notions to similar developments in other religious groups.

The transformation carried out in the ritual context reflects transformations which are not limited to language. The ritual transformation can be achieved in terms of language because the distinction between gods and people is conceived in terms of language. Here the transformation is the creation of a "magical" speaker, with a repertoire of divine words. Knowing the words and their usages reflects the heightened status of the speaker.

Perhaps the most interesting passages in the text are those that reject the entire didactic process. In section 6 Akiba chides Ishmael that if he were pure, he would know the answer to his question. This is the most extreme "spiritualization" possible, whereby inner purity fills the place of instruction. Yet the framers of this text knows no spiritual/cultic dichotomy. For them the question is the encoding of the divine/human status in the modes of human language use. Speaking is the real action. Ascending is learning and then instantiating the mode of speech of the divine realm.

At this point it is significant to contrast our findings with a Lévi-Straussian investigation into ascent. Alan Segal, in his insightful article "Heavenly Ascent in Hellenistic Judaism, Early Christianity and their Environment," extracts two main propositions from the work of Lévi-Strauss.[28] First, both language and myth are generated by a "general property of the human mind,"[29] and second, "mythic structures are reducible to binary contrasts."[30] The study of language thus provides a model for the study of myth.

> The structural study of myth may be analogous to the structural study of language to the extent that both are analyses of the formal aspects of a complex symbolic system—analyses

of the system itself rather than the individual components of the system, "holistic" analyses rather than exegeses of the parts of the system.[31]

According to Segal, however, there are important differences between language and myth. One difference he mentions in particular is that myth is more affected by external stimuli than language. In order to take these external stimuli into account, Segal develops a distinction between the "meaning" and the "understanding" of a myth. Myths have the same "meaning" from community to community because they have the same underlying pattern. This pattern is, therefore, not historical, as it transcends any particular context. However, in addition to the seemingly universal "meaning," the "different social structures, histories and theologies will work towards unique cultural understandings."[32]

Linguistic analysis, as Segal notes, is not concerned only with the individual words, but instead with the entire system of language. By analogy Segal argues that myths should be studied in their entirety, instead of selecting out one theme or motif and basing arguments on that specific "unit." His concern about narrowly conceived mythic investigations is well placed. The problem, however, is that Segal fails to provide specific linguistic arguments on which to base his acceptance and modification of Lévi-Strauss. He rejects the idea that myths are necessarily created in their binary forms due to the structure of the mind.

To see this pattern as the inevitable result of the structure of the mind is perhaps too grandiose . . .[33]

He also recognizes the differences between language and myth. Yet his approach is still one of using linguistic terms metaphorically, freely applying terminology to disparate constructs and units. Thus myths, like sentences, have deep and surface structures. Yet myths are not sentences, as Segal himself states. He wishes to modify Lévi-Strauss and in doing so loses his analytic foundation without supplying a substitute. The question of how to locate meaning remains unanswered; if meaning is not arbitrary and oppositional on all levels, then the motivation of meaning must be directly discussed. Segal attempts to supplement the ahistorical aspect of Lévi-Strauss's schema by instituting the meaning/understanding distinction. It is not clear, however, exactly how to distinguish these levels, which presumably are both part of "meaning" generally conceived.

Silverstein differs from this approach in several ways. He defines meaning as including both the semantic and pragmatic components of linguistic units. Pragmatic analysis is not limited to ritual texts, for "narrative is to a large extent a description of verbal interaction."[34] Because Silverstein links language forms to their contexts of use, his approach is "historical." Meaning is related to situations of use, and is not based only on internal opposition. The native ideologies of language use are compared and related to the linguistic forms employed in the text.

The application of these linguistic ideas to ritual and mythic texts is especially rich for historians of religion. *Maaseh Merkabah* can now be viewed as a strategy for dealing with the particular problems of teaching about ascent and ritual language which confronted the authors. It is now possible to ask questions about the sources of these linguistic ideas, especially those concerning God's Names, and to compare them to similar ideas from that time period.

This approach also permits us to focus on the transformative ability of language, a particularly rich area for students of religion. Ritual texts are interesting, according to Silverstein, because they provide models (icons) of the very transformations they create, or enact. This enables them to be both didactic (teaching about transformation) and "performative" (bringing the rite to a successful conclusion). Structure (the patterns and their alterations) is still at the center of the endeavor, but the process of Lévi-Strauss has been reversed. He begins with the phonemes, and proceeds to derive meaning of other linguistic levels from the model of opposition and arbitrary "meaning" of the phonemes. A pragmatic approach begins with the motivated units of the text, in this case Name and its multiple manifestations, and proceeds to find the particular "meaning" of phonemes as sounds from the divine Name.

Notes and References

* I would like to thank Richard Parmentier and Margaret Wenig-Rubenstein for their comments and suggestions.
1. Roman Jakobson, *Six Lectures on Sound and Meaning*, (Cambridge, Mass.: MIT Press, 1978).
2. *Ibid.*, p. xiii.
3. *Ibid.*, p. 76.
4. *Ibid.*, pp. 61-2.
5. *Ibid.*, p. 64.
6. *Ibid.*, op. cit.
7. *Ibid.*, pp. 64-5.
8. Paul Friedrich, "The Symbol and Its Relative Non-arbitrariness," in *Language, Context and the Imagination: Essays by Paul Friedrich* (Stanford: Stanford University Press, 1979), 42.
9. See in particular "Metaforces of Power" and "The Culture of Language in Chinookan Narrative Texts," both unpublished lectures. Also, "Language Structure and Linguistic Ideology," in *The Elements* (Chicago Linguistics Society, Paris Section, 1979), 193-247.
10. J. L. Austin, *How to Do Things with Words* (Cambridge, Mass.: Harvard, 1979). For partial bibliographies of ritual studies using Austin, see Wade Wheelock, "The Problem of Ritual Language," *Journal of the American Academy of Religion* 50:1, (1982), 49-69, and S. J. Tambiah, "A Performative Approach to Ritual," *Proceedings of the British Academy*, 65 (1979), 113-169.
11. Michael Silverstein, "The Culture of Language," p. 2.
12. Roman Jakobson, "Grammatical Parallelism and Its Russian Facet," *Language*, 42 (1966), 339.
13. *Ibid.*, p. 423.
14. *Ibid.*, op. cit.
15. *Ibid.*, p. 399.
16. Yuri Tynianov, *The Problem of Verse Language* (Ann Arbor: Ardis, 1981).
17. Roman Jakobson, "Linguistics and Poetics," in *Style in Language*, edited by T. Sebeok (Cambridge: MIT Press, 1966).
18. *Ibid.*, pp. 368-369.
19. *Ibid.*, p. 358.
20. Silverstein, "Metaforces," p. 5.

21. "Briefly put, these relationships are as follows: pragmatic presupposition means that we know something (we must presuppose some feature or features) about the context of use of a speech signal in order to interpret it as an instance of a particular type; pragmatic entailment means that once we know that a speech signal of a certain type has occurred, we automatically know certain entailed features of the speech situation." Silverstein, "The Culture of Language," p. 1.

22. See for example *Language and Social Context*, edited by P. Giglioli (Harmondsworth: Penguin, 1972).

23. Silverstein, "Metaforces," p. 9.

24. Gershom Scholem, *Jewish Gnosticism, Merkabah Mysticism and Talmudic Tradition*, (New York: Jewish Theological Seminary, 1965), Appendix C, pp. 101-117. The manuscripts that Scholem used as the basis for his edition date from the 14th century. The main thrust of Scholem's work however has been to argue for a much earlier date for many of the texts concerned with visions of the heavenly world and aspects of ascent. Scholem was able to show the extent to which other texts from the early centuries A.D. illuminate the chariot texts, as well as finding references throughout rabbinic texts to esoteric traditions related to heavenly visions. As there is no standard English translation of this specific text, I cite it according to the paragraph numbers of Scholem's edition. Translations are my own.

25. Silverstein, "Language Structure and Linguistic Ideology," p. 205.

26. For example, Moses killed the Egyptian by pronouncing the divine Name (Leviticus Rabba 32, Exodus Rabba 2). Midrash Hallel answers the question "What did the sea behold?" by stating "It beheld the Shem Ha-Meforash (the explicated Name) graven on Aaron's staff and fled." (Pesk 140a in Jellinek).

27. J. Trachtenberg, *Jewish Magic and Superstition* (New York: Atheneum, 1970), p. 84.

28. Alan Segal, "Heavenly Ascent in Hellenistic Judaism, Early Christianity and their Environment," in *Aufstieg und Niedergang der römischen Welt*, ed. by W. Haase (Berlin: de Gruyter, 1981), 23:2,1, pp. 1334-1394.

29. *Ibid.*, p. 1337.

30. *Ibid.*, op. cit.

31. *Ibid.*, p. 1338.

32. *Ibid.*, op. cit.

33. *Ibid.*, p. 1388.

Notes About the Contributors

Caroline Walker Bynum is Professor of History at the University of Washington. She is the author of *Docere Verbo et Exemplo: An Aspect of Twelfth-Century Spirituality* (1979), and *Jesus as Mother: Studies in the Spirituality of the High Middle Ages* (1982). Her most recent papers include "Did the Twelfth-Century Discover the Individual?" in the *Journal of Ecclesiastical History* (1980), and "Women Mystics and Eucharistic Devotion in the Thirteenth Century," in *Women's Studies*, forthcoming.

Naomi Janowitz is an Instructor in the Department of Theology at Notre Dame. Her article, "Parallelism and Framing Devices in a Rabbinic Ascent Text," will appear in *Psycho-Social and Symbolic Mediation* (1984).

David Jobling is Professor of Old Testament Language and Literature, St. Andrew's College, Saskatoon. He is the author of *The Sense of Biblical Narrative* (1978). Recent papers include "The Myth Semantics of Genesis 2:4b-3:24" in *Semeia 18* (1980), and "Judges 11: 12-28: Constructive and Deconstructive Analysis" in *Semiotics 1981* (1983).

Judith Van Herik is Assistant Professor of Religious Studies at the Pennsylvania State University. Her *Freud on Femininity and Faith* (1982) examines relationships between Freud's theories of religion and gender.

Elizabeth Struthers Malbon is Assistant Professor of Religion at Virginia Polytechnic Institute and State University. Her most recent essays include "Galilee and Jerusalem: History and Literature in Marcan Interpretation," *Catholic Biblical Quarterly* (1982), "Structuralism, Hermeneutics, and Contextual Meaning," *Journal of the American Academy of Religion* (1983), "Fallible Followers: Women and Men in the Gospel of Mark," *Semeia* (1983), and "Tē Oikia Autou: Mark 2:15 in Context," forthcoming in *New Testament Studies*.

Richard C. Martin is Associate Professor and chair of the Department of Religious Studies at Arizona State University. He is the author of *Islam: A Cultural Perspective* (1982), and guest editor of *Islam in Local Contexts* in *Contributions to Asian Studies 17* (1982). His recent research articles include "Structural Analysis and the Qur'ān: Newer Approaches to the Study of Islamic Texts," *Journal of the American Academy of Religion* (1979), and "Understanding the Qur'ān in Text and Context," *History of Religions* (1982). He is a contributor to the forthcoming *Encyclopedia of Religion*, ed. Mircea Eliade, and a member of the editorial board of the *Journal of the American Academy of Religion*.

Robert L. Moore is Professor of Psychology and Religion at the Chicago Theological Seminary. He is the author of *John Wesley and Authority: A Psychological Perspective* (1979), and co-author of *The Cult Experience: Responding to the New Religious Pluralism* (1982). Recent articles include "Contemporary Psychotherapy as Ritual Process: An Initial Reconnaissance" in *Zygon: Journal of Religion and Science* (1983). Since 1978 he has served as the Chairman of the Religion and Social Sciences Section of the American Academy of Religion. A diplomate analyst in private practice, he has studied at both the Alfred Adler Institute of Chicago and the C. G. Jung Institute of Chicago.

Frank E. Reynolds teaches at the University of Chicago where he serves as Professor of History of Religions in the Divinity School, Professor of Buddhist Studies in the Department of South Asian Languages and Civilizations, and Chairman of the Committee on Southern Asian Studies. He is co-author of *Two Wheels of Dhamma* (1972), *Guide to Buddhist Religion* (1981), and *Religions of the World* (1983). He is the co-editor and translator of *Three Worlds According to King Ruang: A Thai Buddhist Cosmology* (1982). He has also co-edited three books: *The Biographical Process* (1976); *Religious Encounters with Death* (1977); and *Transitions and Transformations in the History of Religions* (1980).

Lawrence E. Sullivan is Associate Professor of the History of Religions at the University of Missouri-Columbia and Associate Editor of the 16-volume *Encyclopedia of Religion* being produced by Macmillan Publishing. His research includes field experience in Latin America and Central Africa. His most recent essays include "Multiple Levels of Religious Meaning in Culture: A New Look at Winnebago Sacred Texts," *Canadian Journal of Native Studies* (1983), "Astral Myths Rise Again: Interpreting Religious Astronomy," *Criterion* (1983), "The Irony of Incarnation: The Comedy of *Kenosis*," *Journal of Religion* (1982), and "Mircea Eliade," in *Religious Studies Review* (1983). He received the Ph.D. from the University of Chicago in 1981 and wrote the essay in this volume while a Fellow at the Institute for the Advanced Study of Religion.

Joanne Punzo Waghorne teaches in the Department of Religion, Bowdoin College. Her recent publications include "A Body for God: An Interpretation of Myth Beyond Structuralism," *History of Religions* (1981), and "The Case of the Missing Autobiography," in the *Journal of the American Academy of Religion* (1981). She is presently completing a book on sacral kingship in Pudukkottai, India and co-editing a volume, *God of Flesh/God of Stone: The Embodiment of Divinity in India*, forthcoming.

Dario Zadra is Professor of Anthropology of Religion at the Gregorian University, Rome. General Editor of the series, 'Human Sciences' (Morcelliana Press), he is author of *Sociologia della Religione* (1969). His most recent essays include "Symbol und Sakrament," *Christlicher Glaube in moderner Gesellschaft. Enzykolpädische Bibliothek* (1982); "Symbolic Time: The Christian Liturgical Year," University of Rome Lectures 1981-1982, *Sociologia* (1983); and "Sacramenti e Tempo," in *Problemi e Prospettive di Teologia Dogmatica* (1983).